Sarah C...

Roger Wilkes is a fre...
the BBC in Manchest...

By the same author

Wallace: the final verdict

ROGER WILKES

An Infamous Address

GRAFTON BOOKS

A Division of the Collins Publishing Group

LONDON GLASGOW
TORONTO SYDNEY AUCKLAND

Grafton Books
A Division of the Collins Publishing Group
8 Grafton Street, London W1X 3LA

A Grafton Paperback Original 1989
Copyright © Roger Wilkes 1989

ISBN 0-586-20350-8

Printed and bound in Great Britain by
Collins, Glasgow

Set in Garamond

All rights reserved. No part of this publication may
be reproduced, stored in a retrieval system, or
transmitted, in any form, or by any means, electronic,
mechanical, photocopying, recording or otherwise,
without the prior permission of the publishers.

This book is sold subject to the condition that it
shall not, by way of trade or otherwise, be lent,
re-sold, hired out or otherwise circulated
without the publisher's prior consent in any
form of binding or cover other than that in
which it is published and without a similar
condition including this condition being imposed
on the subsequent purchaser.

Contents

For my mother and father

Introduction

Welcome to my infamous addresses!

The classic address to have explored would have been 10 Rillington Place, but it no longer exists. Shortly after the execution of John Reginald Halliday Christie in 1953, the dingy little cul-de-sac in Notting Hill was renamed Ruston Close. This conveniently masked its notoriety, but the stain and stigma of six necrophiliac murders remained. A state of grace was only achieved some years later when the demolition gangs moved in and flattened the entire street. A similar fate awaited a gaunt semi-detached council house in the Manchester suburb of Hattersley. On a winter's day in 1987, in response to a prolonged campaign by the neighbours, who complained of ghoulish sightseers and a disturbing, sinister feel to the place, bulldozers moved in and razed 16 Wardle Brook Avenue to rubble. This was the setting appointed by Ian Brady and Myra Hindley in the 1960s for a depraved series of pornographic killings that, over the years, resulted in the bodies of several children being uncovered on Saddleworth Moor above Oldham. I am not sorry that both these infamous addresses have disappeared; I would not have relished recounting their stories. In this collection of true cases, I have confined myself to homes and houses that are still standing and whose walls and windows once witnessed a deed of darkness that the years have never quite managed to efface.

An Infamous Address is the result of a series of eleven short programmes under that title which I made for BBC Radio Four in 1985 and 1986. They were produced in Manchester by Diana Stenson, who devised the format and the title. To Diana, and to the distinguished crime historian Jonathan Goodman, who encouraged the writing of this book, I express my warmest thanks.

The radio series concerned itself with assorted brands of infamy: murder, scandal, treachery, and intrigue. We visited the addresses concerned, and told their stories with the help of writers, historians, present occupiers and (where possible) people who were there at the time. There is a special magic in the words of these witnesses as they reach back in their memories to events so distant that they seem quite beyond recall. The uncannily vivid first-hand accounts of Dora Pepper, Billy Roe and Reggie Friend at Peasenhall, and those of Mabel Goldsworthy and William Lloyd at Hay-on-Wye, were especially remarkable in this regard, and I thank them also.

This book concerns itself exclusively with murder. It is a singular, sharply focused act that changes the nature of a place, be it a Victorian gentleman's town house in a fashionable Glasgow square or a pretty seaside bungalow on the North Shore at Blackpool. This is not to say that these infamous addresses are necessarily sinister, brooding places; on the contrary, most are now happy homes, filled with light and laughter. But to climb the stairs to the dim lit landing where Charles Bravo screamed for water in his death throes, or to pace the bedroom where poor, poisoned Katharine Armstrong sank at the hands of her philandering husband, is to brush against a particular shade of melancholy. I owe a large debt to the present occupiers of these infamous addresses for allowing me over the threshold to invoke these long-departed spirits.

1

7 Blythswood Square, Glasgow

Glasgow smells stale in the gathering fog. It is dusk on a November afternoon, and Miss Madeleine Smith is waiting impatiently for the cabman. Lamps are flaring behind the blinds in Blythswood Square. Miss Smith, with her younger sister and a hint of musk, is going to meet her secret lover. The year is 1856, and Madeleine Smith is twenty-one.

The Smiths have only recently moved in to the corner house at number seven from a smaller place in India Street. It is the fashion in Glasgow to move west, and Madeleine's father is a fashionable and successful architect. But James Smith knows nothing of his daughter's twilight assignation, and this is just as well. He has already forbidden his daughter to marry this man.

And the scene freezes. The two bonneted figures, their hands thrust deep into fur muffs, stiffen on the step beneath the great granite portico and then dissolve. Soot flakes from the walls to reveal the original stone the colour of honey. The wisps of yellow fog and the gloom of approaching winter have lifted. It is a summer's morning in 1986, and Mrs Ruby Burgess is on the step at 7 Blythswood Square on behalf of Scottish and Universal Investments. 'It's an extremely fine building, as you can see. Three floors and a basement, Georgian-style. It's a highly prestigious address, now being used for a commercial office. We've been here for two years,' she tells me.

We brush past the ghosts and into the reception hall. It is a beautiful building. The ceilings are the original Georgian. Mrs Burgess leads me through a door on the right.

'This is Mr and Mrs Smith's drawing room where the family lived. It overlooks the garden square, and there's a beautiful view of the trees and flowers. Very colourful.'

The room is huge and empty. The ground floor and basement of 7 Blythswood Square are to let for office space. The headquarters of Scottish and Universal Investments occupy only the top two floors. Traffic squeals up the hill in Blythswood Street. Men are drilling in the road.

The geography of the house is important. This huge downstairs room was originally two: the drawing room at the front overlooking Blythswood Square, and the dining room further down the hall, looking out at what, in the 1850s, was known as Mains Street (now Blythswood Street). But more crucially, the ground floor also contained the sleeping quarters of Madeleine's parents and those of her younger sister, Bessie, and brother Jack. Mr and Mrs Smith themselves slept in a small room at the back of the house; Madeleine's bedroom was towards the front, but below, on the basement level. This configuration, presumably laid down by Mrs Smith, was to serve her eldest daughter well; it put the maximum distance between them, and whatever Madeleine got up to at night, her parents would be unlikely to hear or see anything suspicious. The fact that Madeleine shared her bedroom with her twelve-year-old sister, Janet, might have been a problem. It wasn't.

James Smith would have liked everyone to think, as they gazed approvingly at his new home, that he possessed the entire building. He didn't. Even in those far-off days the property was split. The Smiths only occupied the ground floor and basement. The two upper floors were divided into separate flats, or chambers. One was let to a Mr Douglas. The second was occupied by a young merchant named William Minnoch. These two gentlemen came and went through a side-door on Mains Street, which has now been bricked up and replaced by a window. So to all intents and purposes their chambers were self-contained. The Smiths, of course, used the imposing front door beneath the pillared portico facing Blythswood Square.

So much for the house. What of the inhabitants? James Smith was the typical Victorian father, pompous and self-important, middle-aged and losing his hair. He was an architect and a successful one, so successful that he had designed and built his own country house a few miles west of Glasgow, on the Gareloch at Row (now Rhu). The house was called Rowaleyn, and this was where James Smith took his growing family at weekends and for holidays. Blythswood Square was his town house, and used normally only during the week. (Again, this arrangement was to suit Madeleine's purpose.) James's wife, Elizabeth, a morose-looking, mousey woman, had borne him seven children in all, two of whom had died in childhood. This left three daughters and two sons: Madeleine, the eldest girl, Jack, Bessie, Janet and finally James junior. A family photograph taken in 1851 shows Madeleine (a gawky sixteen) to be a slender, rather shapeless young lady, with dark hair, pointy nose and dark, flashing eyes. In later adolescence, we are told in contemporary accounts, her figure blossomed, and by the time of her trial, when she was twenty-two, she was considered beautiful. 'She wore a dress of rich, brown silk with a large brooch set low on the neck so that it lay on the rounded contour of her bosom. On her head was a white straw bonnet, trimmed with white ribbon, and beneath it a black veil which she raised to display her whole face but which yet lent a touch of mystery to the eyes.' Her appearance in the dock prompted 'a muffled gasp, almost a sigh'.[1]

The Glasgow journalist and crime historian, Jack House, agrees that Madeleine must have been good-looking. 'She's been described as the belle of the ball. She wasn't very tall, she was slightly plump, but attractive nonetheless.' But more important was her personality. Jack House is convinced that Madeleine was years ahead of her time. 'She would have fitted into today's society very well. Today, Madeleine would have been regarded as a very normal person, but she was regarded as completely *ab*normal by Victorian standards. But of course Victorian standards were all built up on hypocrisy. I think she was very much her own woman.'[2]

Madeleine was a self-assured, almost wilful nineteen-year-old in early 1855 when she first met Pierre Emile L'Angelier. He was thirty-two, an impoverished clerk with a seed firm, earning ten shillings (50p) a week. His parents were French, but they had moved to the island of Jersey, off the Normandy coast, to set up a small market-garden business, and Emile was born in St Helier. At the age of nineteen he had been sent to Scotland to acquire experience as a seedsman. He became engaged to a young woman in Edinburgh, but after a period serving in the Paris National Guard he returned to Scotland, only to find that the woman he planned to marry had grown tired of waiting. In 1852 he finally settled in Glasgow and took a job as a packing clerk with Huggins and Co. in Bothwell Street. Putty-faced and weedy, Emile nevertheless exercised a certain charm with women. They admired his undoubted worldliness, his dandified appearance, his fashionably twirled moustache, his ambition to break out of his humdrum world as a humble clerk in search of something better. Madeleine, in particular, admired his Frenchness, having learned at finishing school that Frenchmen were creatures of passion; the thought of romancing a Frenchman filled her with shiveringly delicious anticipation.

One of Emile's few pleasures in life was to promenade along Sauchiehall Street in his latest fashionable clothes. He liked to be fancied as the gentleman about town, and it was on one of these excursions that he first set eyes on

Miss Madeleine Smith, also walking in Sauchiehall Street, unchaperoned except for the company of her younger sister, Bessie. He was smitten. But he knew that the social gap between him and Madeleine was too wide for him to expect a formal introduction at a dance, for example. So on St Valentine's Day 1855 he sent her a single red rose. A few days later, by a subterfuge, he persuaded a mutual friend to introduce him to her in the street. The match was made. A further meeting was arranged, at which Emile evidently proceeded to lecture Madeleine on the need for propriety in their new relationship. It was a smart move. He also impressed on her the benefits of cultivating her mind. A few days later, writing from her father's country house, Rowaleyn at Row, Madeleine set down her first impressions:

My dear Emile – I do not feel as if I were writing you for the first time. Though our intercourse has been very short, yet we have become as familiar friends. May we long continue so. And ere lang may you be a friend of Papas is my most ernest desire. We feel it rather dull here after the excitement of a Towns Life. But then we have much more time to devote to study and improvement. I often wish you were near us, we could take such charming walks. One enjoys walking with a pleasant companion, and where could we find one equal to yourself?

I am trying to break myself off all my *very* bad habits it is you I have to thank for this, which I do sincerely from my heart – Your flower is fading.

> I never cast a flower away,
> The gift of one who cared for me
> A little flower a faded flower,
> But it was done reluctantly.

I wish I understood Botany for your sake, as I might send you some specimens of moss. But alas! I know nothing of that study. We shall be in Town next week. We are going to the Ball on the 20th of this month, so we will be several times in Glasgow before

that. Papa and Mama are not going to Town next Sunday. So of
course you do *not* come to Row. We shall not expect you. Bessie
desires me to remember her to you. Write on Wednesday or
Thursday. I must now say adieu. With kind love, believe me,
your very sincerely,

Madeleine³

Reading and re-reading this remarkably frank first letter,
Emile had no doubt that Madeleine was signalling her
willingness to begin an affair. He wrote back. At this point,
at least two other members of the Smith family – Madeleine's father, James, and her younger sister, Bessie – got
wind of Emile. Both disapproved, James Smith because
this grubby little clerk was not a suitable candidate for the
hand of his eldest daughter, and Bessie because, like so
many younger sisters, she was jealous. Madeleine, unde-
terred, wrote again to Emile:

My dear Emile,
Many thanks for your kind epistle. We are to be in town
tomorrow (Wednesday). Bessie said I was not to let you know.
But I must tell you why! Well, some friend was *kind* enough to
tell papa that you were in the habit of walking with us. Papa was
very angry with me for walking with a Gentleman unknown to
him. I told him he had been introduced, and I saw no harm in it.
Bessie joins with Papa and blames me for the whole affair. She
does not know I am writing you, so dont mention it. We are to
call at our old quarters in the Square on Wednesday about quarter
past 12 o'c. So if you be in Mr McCall's Lodgings – see us come
out of Mrs Ramsay's – come after us – say you are astonished to
see us in Town without letter you know – and we shall see how
Bessie acts. She says she is not going to write you. We are to be
in Town all night. We are to be with Mrs Anderson. Rest assured
I shall not mention to anyone that you have written me. I know
from experience that the world is not lenient in its observations.
But I don't care for the world's remarks so long as my own heart
tells me I am doing nothing wrong. Only if the day is fine expect
us tomorrow. Not a word of this letter. Adieu until we meet.
Believe me, yours most sincerely.

Madeleine

A few days later, under growing pressure from two disapproving parents and a jealous sister, Madeleine wrote a third letter to Emile, proposing that the exchange of letters should stop. For a time it did. But the couple continued to meet secretly. Emile confided his feelings for Madeleine to an old lady called Miss Mary Perry, with whom he often took tea. Miss Perry was evidently touched, and suggested that he bring Madeleine for tea as well. The old lady also hinted that she would keep discreetly out of the way if Emile wished to hold his assignations with Madeleine at her house. Emile seems to have taken Miss Perry up on her offer, but once again Madeleine's father intervened and forbade his daughter from seeing Emile. Madeleine, vexed, sat and did some hard thinking. She could scarcely disobey her father and continue to live under his roof; and maybe, she thought, Emile might make a new start in South America, where he had spoken of making his fortune. It was a tough decision, but Madeleine realized she had no alternative. Heavy-hearted, she took up her pen again and wrote both to Emile and then to Miss Perry. She signed both letters with the pet name bestowed by Emile: Mimi.

Dearest Miss Perry,
Many thanks for all your kindness to me. Emile will tell you I have bid him adieu. My Papa would not give his consent, so I am in duty bound to obey him. Comfort dear Emile. It is a heavy blow to us both. I had hoped some day to have been happy with him, but alas it was not intended. We were doomed to be disappointed. You have been a kind friend to him. Oh! Continue so. I hope and trust he may prosper in the step he is about to take. I am glad now that he is leaving this country, for it would have caused me great pain to have met him. Think my conduct not unkind. I have a father to please, and a kind father too. Farewell, dear Miss Perry, and with much love believe me, yours most sincerely.

Mimi

When Emile received Madeleine's letter telling him the affair was off he was angry and indignant. He sat down at his desk and wrote:

Glasgow, 10 Bothwell Street
19th July, '55

In the first place, I did not deserve to be treated as you have done. How you astonish me by writing such a note without condescending to explain the reasons why your father refuses his consent. He must have reasons, and I am not allowed to clare myself of accusations.

I should have written you before, but I preferred waiting until I got over surprise your last letter caused me, and also to be able to write you in a calm and a collected manner, free from any animosity whatever.

Never, dear Madeleine, could I have believed you were capable of such conduct. I thought and believed you unfit for such a step. I believe you true to your word and to your *honour*. I will put questions to you which answer to yourself. What would you think if even one of your servants had played with any one's affections as you have done, or what would you say to hear that any lady friends had done what you have – or what am I to – of you now? What is your opinion of your own self after those solemn vows you uttered and wrote to me. Shew my letters to anyone, Madeleine, I don't care who, and if any find that I mislead you I will free you from all blame. I warned you repeatedly not to be rash in your engagement and vows to me, but you persisted in that false and deceitful flirtation, playing with affections which you knew to be pure and undivided, and knowing at the same time that a word from your father you would break all your engagement.

You have deceived your father as you have deceived me. You never told him how solemnly you bound yourself to me, or if you had, for the honour of his daughter he could not have asked to break off an engagement as ours. Madeleine, you have truly acted wrong. May this be a lesson to you never to trifle with any again. I wish you every happiness. I shall be truly happy to hear you are happy with another. You desire and now you are at liberty to recognise me or cut me just as you wish – but I give you my word of honour I shall act always as a Gentleman towards you. We may meet yet, as my intentions of going to

Lima are now at an end. I would have gone for your sake. Yes, I would have sacrificed all to have you with me, and to leave Glasgow and your friends you detested so very much. Think what your father would say if I sent him your letters for a persual. Do you think he could sanction your breaking your promises. No, Madeleine, I leave your conscience to speak for itself.

I flatter myself he can only accuse me of a want of fortune. But he must remember he too had to begin the world with dark clouds around him.

I cannot put it into my mind that yet you are at the bottom of all this.[3]

We cannot be sure that Emile ever sent this letter, since either the original or a copy was found in his possessions after his death. At any rate, it seems clear that he managed to talk Madeleine out of ending the affair. At about this point Emile appears to have convinced himself that he was seriously in love with the architect's daughter. He and Madeleine met frequently during the late summer and autumn of 1855, sometimes in the extensive grounds of Rowaleyn, sometimes at the Smiths' town house in India Street. These furtive encounters were becoming more and more passionate, as Madeleine's letter of 3 December suggests:

Tuesday, 2 o'c
My own darling husband,
I am afraid I may be too late to write you this eveng., so as all are out I shall do it now, my sweet one. I did not expect the pleasure of seeing you last evng., of being *fondeled* by you, dear, dear Emile. Our Cook was ill, and went to bed at 10 – that was the reason I could see you – but I trust ere long to have a long, long interview with you, sweet one of my soul, my love, my all, my own best beloved. I hope you slept well last evng., and find yourself better today. I was at St Vincent Street today. B/ and M/ are gone to call for the Houldsworths and some others. Never fear me, I love you well, my own sweet darling Emile. Do go to Edr. and visit the Lanes – also, my sweet love, go to the Ball given to the Officers. I think you should consult Dr McFarlan – that is,

go and see him, get him to sound you, tell you what is wrong
with you. Ask for him to prescribe for you – and if you have any
love for your Mimi follow his advice, and oh! sweet love, follow
the Md. advice – be good for once, and I am sure you will be
well. Is it not horrid cold weather? I did, my love, so pity you
standing in the cold last night, but I could not get Janet to sleep –
little stupid thing. This is a horrid scroll, as I have been stoped
twice with that bore – visiter. My own sweet beloved, I can say
nothing as to our marriage, as it is not certain when they may go
from home, or when I may go to Edr. it is uncertain. My beloved,
will we require to be married (if it is in Edr.) in Edr. or will it do
here. You know I know nothing of these things. I fear the Banns
in Glasgow, there are so many people know me. If I had any
other name but Madeleine it might pass – but it is not a very
common one. But we must manage in some way to be united ere
we leave Town . . . Much much love kisses tender long embraces
kisses love. I am thy own they ever fond they own dear loving
wife thy

Mimi L'Angelier

   In the spring of 1856, the Smiths were staying at Row,
and Madeleine was receiving Emile's letters care of the
village post office, where they had been addressed to a
'Miss Bruce'. (The letters were collected by her maid,
Christina Haggart, in whom Madeleine had confided her
secret affair.) Emile continued to make frequent, furtive
visits to Rowaleyn, meeting Madeleine in the part of the
grounds furthest from the house. Here, under the cloak of
darkness, they could talk, walk and embrace. Finally, in
the month of June, Madeleine and Emile made love in the
gardens of Rowaleyn. Madeleine wrote to him the next
morning:

My own, my beloved husband,
I trust to God you got home safe, and were not much the worse
of being out. Thank you, my love for coming so far to see your
Mimi. It is truly a pleasure to see you, my Emile. Beloved, if we
did wrong last night, it was in the excitement of our love. Yes,
beloved, I did truly love you with my soul. I was happy, it was a

pleasure to be with you. Oh, if we could have remained, never more to have parted. But we must hope that the time shall come. I must have been very stupid to you last night. But everything goes out of my head when I see you, my darling, my love. I often think I must be very, very stupid in your eyes. You must be disappointed with me. I wonder you like me in the least. But I trust and pray the day may come when you shall like me better. Beloved, we shall wait till you are quite ready. I shall see and speak to Jack on Sunday. I shall consider about telling Mama. But I don't see any hope from her – I know her mind. You, of course, cannot judge of my parents. You know them not ... Darling Emile, did I seem cold to you last night. Darling I love you. Yes, my own Emile, love you with my heart and soul. Am I not your wife. Yes I am. And you may rest assured after what has passed I cannot be the wife of any other but dear, dear Emile. No, now it would be a sin ...

I did not bleed in the least last night – but I had a good deal of pain during the night. Tell me, pet, were you angry at me for allowing you to do what you did – was it very bad of me. We should, I suppose, have waited till we were married. I shall always remember last night. Will we not often talk of our evening meetings after we are married. Why do you say in your letter – 'If we are NOT married' I would not regret knowing you. Beloved, have you a doubt but that we shall be married some day. I shall write dear Mary soon. What would she say if she knew we were so intimate – lose all her good opinion of us both – would she not.

Adieu again, my husband. God bless you and make you well. And may you yet be very, very happy with your Mimi as your little wife. Kindest love, fond embrace, and kisses from thy own true and ever devoted Mimi. Thy faithful

Wife

Once again, whether Emile actually sent his reply is unclear. But a draft letter, in his handwriting, brims over with guilt and self-reproach:

My dearest and beloved Wife Mimi,
Since I saw you I have been wretchedly sad. Would to God we had not met that night. – I would have been happier. I am sad at what we did, I regret it very much. Why, Mimi, did you give way

after your promises? My pet, it is a pity. Think of the consequences if I were never to marry you. What reproaches I should have, Mimi. I never shall be happy again. If I ever meet you again, love, it must be as at first. I will never again repeat what I did until we are regularly married. Try your friends once more – tell your determination – say nothing will change you, that you have thought seriously of it – and on that I shall firmly fix speaking to Huggins for Sepr. Unless you do something of that sort, Heaven only knows when I shall marry you. Unless you do, dearest, I shall have to leave the country; truly dearest, I am in such a state of mind I do not care if I were dead. We did wrong. God forgive us for it. Mimi, we have loved blindly. It is your parents' fault if shame is the result; they are to blame for it all.

I got home quite safe after leaving you but I think I did my cold no good. I was fearfully excited the whole night. I was truly happy with you, my pet; too much so, for I am now too sad. I wish from the bottom of my heart we had never parted. Though we have sined, ask earnestly God's forgiveness and blessings that all the obstacles in our way may be removed from us. I was disappointed, my love, at the little you had to say but I can understand why. You are not stupid, Mimi, and if you disappoint me in information, and I have cause to reproach you of it, you will have no one to blame but yourself, as I have given you warning long enough to improve yourself. Sometimes I do think you take no notice of my wishes and my desires, but say yes for a mere matter of form.

Mimi, unless Huggins helps me I cannot see how I shall be able to marry you for years. What misery to have such a future in one's mind. Do speak to your brother, open your heart to him, and try and win his friendship. Tell him if he loves you to take your part. And besides, my dear, if once you can trust, how pleasant it would be for you and me to meet. I could come over to Helensburgh when you would be riding or driving, or of a Sunday (though I stoped with the Whites) I could join you in a walk of a Sunday afternoon. Mimi, dearest, you must take a bold step to be my wife. I entreat you, pet, by the love you have for me, Mimi do speak to your mother – tell her it is the last time you shall ever speak of me to her. You are right, Mimi, you cannot be the wife of anyone else than me. I shall ever blame myself for what has taken place. I never never can be happy until you are my own, my dear fond wife. Oh! Mimi, be bold for once, do not fear them – tell them you are my wife before God. Do not let them leave you without being married, for I cannot answer what would happen. My conscience reproaches me of a sin that marriage can only efface . . .

We must not be separated at all next winter, for I know, Mimi, that you will be as giddy as last. You will be going to public balls, and that I cannot endure. On my honour, dearest, sooner than see you or hear you running about as you did last, I would leave Glasgow myself. Though I have truly forgiven you, I do not forget the misery I endured for your sake. You know yourself how ill it made me – if not, Mary can tell you, my pet.

Dearest Mimi, let us meet again soon, but not as last time. See if you can plan anything for the Queen's birthday. I intend to be in Helensburgh some night to cross over with Miss White to Greenock. I could refuse stoping with them, and come up to see you, but I cannot fix the day, and as I do not know how to let you know except by sending a newspaper to B/, and the evening after the date of the newspaper would be the evening I would come, or tell me a better arrangement. Do you not think it would be best to meet you at the top of the Garden, same as last Summer? Remember, if the newspaper answers be sure and repeat the arrangement, that I may see we agree.

My dear wife, I could not take you to Lima. No European woman could live there. Besides, I would live 3 or 4 thousand miles from it, far from any white people, and no Drs. if you were ill or getting a baby. No if we marry I must stay in Glasgow until I get enough to live elsewhere. Besides, it would cost £300 alone for our bare passage money. I do not understand, my pet, your not bleeding for every woman having her virginity must bleed. You must have done so some other time. Try to remember if you never hurt yourself in washing, &c. I am sorry you felt pain. I hope you are better. I trust, dearest, you will not be – Be sure and tell me immediately you are ill next time, and if at your regular period. I was not angry at your allowing me, Mimi, but I am sad it happened. You had no resolution. We should indeed have waited till we were married, Mimi. It was very bad indeed. I shall look with regret on that night. No, nothing except our Marriage will efface it from my memory. Mimi, only fancy it was know. My dear, my pet, you would be dishonoured, and that by me! Oh! Why was I born, my pet? I dread lest some great obstacle prevents our marriage. If Mary did know it, what should you be in her eyes?

My sisters' names are Anastie and Elmire. I cannot help

doubting your words about flirting. You promised me the same thing before you left for Edin., and you did nothing else during your stay there. You cared more for your friends than for me. I do trust you will give me no cause to find fault again with you on that score, but I doubt very much the sincerity of your promise. Mimi, the least thing I hear of you doing, that day shall be the last of our *tie*, that I swear. You are my wife, and I have the right to expect from you the behaviour of a married woman – or else you have no honour in you; and more, you have no right to go anywhere but where a woman could go with her husband. Oh! Mimi, let your conduct make me happy. Remember when you are good how truly happy it makes Emile – but remember this, and if you love me you will do nothing wrong. Dearest, your letter to Mary was very pretty and good. I thought a great deal of it, and I liked its seriousness. Fancy how happy I was when Mary told me the other day how Mimi was improving fast; she could tell it by her letters.

At the foot of this extraordinary letter, Emile had written:

For God's sake burn this, Mimi, for fear of any thing happening to you, do dearest.

Emile had set out his emotional stall, and no mistake. He makes it clear that Madeleine had seduced *him*, rather than the other way round, and makes self-righteous noises about them not making love again until they are married. On the other hand, he suggests that unless his employer, Huggins, raises his salary, marriage could be years away. He then puts Madeleine on her honour to behave herself during the approaching season of balls and dances; he is aware that she is an inveterate flirt, and he goes as far as to threaten to end the affair if he hears that she is up to her old tricks again. The closing pompous thought about Madeleine's self-improvement is typical. One wonders what Madeleine must have made of it all, assuming she ever read the letter. We do know that the romance continued as before, and that the exchange of letters continued. Emile was soon able to tell Madeleine that Mr Huggins had doubled his salary to £1 a week, but this change in his fortunes came too late; by now Madeleine was becoming disenchanted with the Frenchman, and paying more and more attention to another, more eligible, prospect. At first, she contrived to brush this man aside in her letters to Emile:

I am longing to see you, sweet pet – to kiss and pet you. Oh! for the day when I could do so at any time. I fear we shall spoil each other when we are married, we shall be so loving and kind. We shall be so happy, happy in our own little room – no one to annoy us, to disturb us ... If it were not for these thoughts I should be sad, miserable and weary of this cold, unfeeling thoughtless world. Wealth is the ruling passion. Love is a second consideration, when it should be the first, the most important ... True and constant shall I prove. Dont fear me. I shall be thine. Dont give ear to any reports you may hear. There are several I hear going about regarding me going to get married – regard them not. A kiss dear love from they devoted and loving, much attached wife, thine own

Mimi

Emile should have smelt a rat. Perhaps he did. These 'reports' concerned Mr William Minnoch, the wealthy merchant who lived in one of the flats on an upper floor of 7 Blythswood Square. He was a familiar figure in Glasgow society and earned £3,000 a year, sixty times Emile's miserable pittance. Minnoch and Madeleine met frequently at fashionable balls and dances. James Smith approved hugely of Mr Minnoch, and encouraged him to visit Rowaleyn as often as he liked. In the summer of 1856, Madeleine was writing to Emile:

Minnoch was here again today. *Only* left on Saturday and back today again. He was here for four hours. He brought a fellow Weymiss with him. I think he might have a little better feeling than come so soon knowing that everyone down here has heard the report regarding myself and him – even for the people on our own place. P/ and M/ were much displeased at him – they said nothing, but M/ said it was enough to make people think there was something in the report. Say nothing to him in passing – it will only make him rude if you say anything.

By late summer, the treacherous Madeleine was entertaining William Minnoch openly at Rowaleyn, meeting Emile in the garden late at night for heavy petting sessions which evidently stopped short of full sex. Emile was now distinctly uneasy. Again he was threatening to throw up his job and leave Glasgow altogether; on one occasion he told Madeleine he was thinking of emigrating to Australia. 'Would you leave me to end my days in misery?' asked Madeleine in her next letter:

For I can never be the wife of another after our intimacy. But, sweet love, I do not regret that – never did, and never shall. Emile, you were not pleased because I would not let you *love* me last night. Your last visit you said 'You would not do it again till we were married.' I said to myself at the time well, I shall not let Emile do this again. It was a punishment to myself to be deprived of your *loving* me, for it is a pleasure, no one can deny that. It is but human nature. Is not every one that *loves* of the same mind? Yes, I did feel so ashamed after you left of having allowed you to see (any name you please to insert). But as you said at the time, I was your wife.

In November 1856, James Smith moved his family out of India Street and into 7 Blythswood Square. It was a tight fit for a family of seven and their three servants, so Madeleine was allocated a basement bedroom where she doubled up with her little sister, Janet. Emile, too, was on the move; he left his lodgings in the Botanic Gardens and took a room with a Mrs Jenkins in Franklin Place, part of Great Western Road and much closer to Blythswood

Square. Shortly before her family moved house, Madeleine
wrote to Emile:

I promised to marry you knowing I would never have my father's
consent. I would be obliged to marry you in a clandestine way. I
knew you were poor. All these I did not mind. I trust we have
days of happiness before us – but God knows we have days of
misery too. Emile, my own, my ever dear husband, I have
suffered much on your account from my family. They have
laughed at my love for you – they taunted me regarding you. I
was watched all last winter. I was not allowed out by myself for
fear I should meet you – but if I can I shall cheat them to allow
me out myself. I shall write to you as often as I can – but it
cannot be three times a week as it has been . . .

I have come to the conclusion that you do not know me. If
you were with me long you would know me better – it is only
those I love that I am indifferent to – even my Dog – which I
love – sometimes I hate it, and for no reason – it is only a fancy
which I cannot help.

Once ensconced at Blythswood Square, with Mr Minnoch already in residence in the upstairs flat, Madeleine
pondered her predicament. Probably at this moment, she
was unsure of her true feelings; she had experienced
physical love for the first time with an older, skilful lover,
and she had tasted ecstasy. However, her father was
obdurate. Emile L'Angelier was marrying no daughter of
his. As for William Minnoch, he was dull by comparison
but a safe financial prospect. Madeleine decided to carry
on with her duplicity, keeping Minnoch interested, and
playing Emile along until an opportunity arose when she
might finally ditch him. But there was a small problem. At
Row, Emile's letters had been delivered using a false name.
But how was he to send letters to Blythswood Square
without the family noticing the contents of the post? She
hit on an idea. She saw that the windows of the basement
bedroom she now shared with young Janet faced out on to

Mains Street at the side of the house. They were set very low on street level, indeed, they were partly below the pavement. They were fitted with stanchions, but if Emile were to drop his letters between the bars, Madeleine worked out that she could then raise the window and pull the letters inside.

'Sweet love,' she wrote to Emile:

You should get those brown envelopes – they would not be so much seen as white ones put down into my window. You should just stoop down to tie your shoe, and then slip it in . . .

Well, dearest love of a husband, I am going to bid you goodnight. Would you were beside me, and I would fall asleep on your bosom, dearest love. What would I not give to place my head on your breast, kiss and fondel you – and then I am sure you would kindly love me – but some night I hope soon we may enjoy each other – what delightful happiness to be loved by a dear, sweet husband – our love then shall be more than we shall be able to express. I can fancy the first night we spend in each other's arms. Emile, my love, my all, my husband, if you were here now I am sure I would allow you to love me – I could not resist you, my love, my own beloved Emile. I have been ordered by the Dr since I came to town to take a fearful thing called 'Peice Meal', such a nasty thing, I am to take at Luncheon. I don't think I have tasted breakfast for two months. But I dont think I can take this Meal. I shall rather take Cocoa. But dearest love, fond embraces much love and kisses from your devoted wife. Your loving and affet. wife,

Mini L'Angelier

Cocoa! Madeleine had hit on a way out. It was only a few short steps from her bedroom to the kitchen, so it was easy for her to prepare poisoned cocoa in her room. She could then hand the drink through the barred window to Emile, shivering in the murky street above. Most nights he was to be found hanging about the corner of Blythswood Square and Mains Street, hoping to snatch a few words with Madeleine through her bedroom window

while little sister Janet slept soundly on. The patrolling
constable was persuaded to turn a blind eye to this curious
scene, Emile having bribed him with a few cigars. In any
case, the officer assumed that the pot-bellied foreigner
was courting one of the servants rather than the daughter
of the house, who would scarcely be sleeping in the
basement.

The winter social scene was well under way, and Madeleine spent several evenings every week at the theatre, at
dinners, concerts or dances. Emile, meanwhile, probably
spent many lonely hours listening to the hiss of the gas fire
at his room in Franklin Place before tramping through the
late-night streets, glistening in winter rain, for his wretched
tryst crouched on the pavement in Mains Street. To make
matters worse, Emile was hearing more and more about
Mr Minnoch, and becoming increasingly irritated by
Madeleine's behaviour. Some of the letters Emile dropped
on to Madeleine's window ledge were thickly peppered
with indignation, so much so that the shameless Madeleine
was having to resort to lies and sophistry in her replies:

I wept for hours after I received your letter, and this day I have
been sad, yes very sad. My Emile, I love you, and only you. I
have tried to assure you no other has a place in my heart. It was
Minnoch that [I] was at the concert with. You see I would not
hide that from you. Emile he is P's friend, and I know he will
have him at the house. But need you mind that when I have told
you I have no regard for him. It is only you, my Emile, that I
love – you should not mind public report.

But Emile did mind. Christmas 1856 must have been a
miserable time for him. He was convinced that Madeleine
was seeing Minnoch, and that there was something in it.
She, meanwhile, continued to speak of her hopes for an
elopement and a secret marriage with Emile. To keep him
on the boil, Madeleine started taking risks, allowing Emile

into the house at Blythswood Square when her parents were out and, on at least one reckless occasion, entertaining him alone in the drawing room. Something seems to have happened at Hogmanay 1857 to force Madeleine's hand. Minnoch was moving in for the kill. Her letters to Emile became noticeably briefer and cool. In mid-January she was tightening the screws:

Mr M/ dined with us tonight – do you know I think if you knew him you would like him, he is most kind. I like him very much better than I used to.

And then, unforgivably, only a week later:

Emile, my own beloved, you have just left me. Oh, sweet darling, at this moment my heart and soul burns with love for thee, my husband, my own sweet one. Emile, what would I not give at this moment to be your fond wife. My night dress was on when you saw me. Would to God you had been in the same attire . . . I never felt so restless and so unhappy as I have done for some time past. I would do anything to keep sad thoughts from my mind. But in whatever place some things make me feel sad. A dark spot is in the future. What can it be. Oh God keep it from us. Oh may we be happy – dear darling, pray for our happiness. I weep, now, Emile, to think of our fate. If we could only get married, and all would be well. But alas, alas, I see no chance, no chance of happiness for me.

Five days later, Madeleine Smith announced her engagement to Mr William Minnoch.

She could not summon up the courage to tell Emile L'Angelier. Instead, she kept him wriggling on the hook, injecting more and more coolness into her letters until, in the first week in February, Emile could take no more. He sent one of Madeleine's letters back. Here was her chance to make the break. Accordingly she wrote this petulant reply:

I felt truly astonished to have my last letter returned to me. But it will be the last you shall have the opportunity of returning to me. When you are not pleased with the letters I send you, then our correspondence shall be at an end, and as there is coolness on both sides our engagement had better be broken. This may astonish you, but you have more than once returned me my letters, and my mind was made up that I should not stand the same thing again. And you also annoyed me much on Saturday by your conduct in coming so near me. Although I think owing to coolness and indifference (nothing else) that we had better for the future consider ourselves as strangers. I trust to your honour as a Gentleman that you will not reveal anything that may have passed between us. I shall feel obliged by your bring me my letters and Likeness on Thursday eveng. at 7 – be at the Area Gate and C.H.[4] will (take) the parcel from you. On Friday night I shall send you all your letters, Likeness, &ca. I trust you may yet be happy, and get one more worthy of you than I. On Thursday at 7 o'C. I am &c.

M.

You may be astonished at this sudden change – but for some time back you must have noticed a coolness in my notes. My love for you has ceased, and that is why I was cool. I did once love you truly, fondly, but for some time back I have lost much of that love. There is no other reason for my conduct, and I think it but fair to let you know this. I might have gone on and become your wife, but I could not have loved you as I ought. My conduct you will condemn, but I did at one time love you with heart and soul. It has cost me much to tell you this – sleepless nights, but it is necessary you should know. If you should remain in Glasgow or go away, I hope you may succeed in all your endeavours. I know you will never injure the character of one you so fondly loved. No Emile, I know you have honour and are a Gentleman. What has passed you will not mention. I know when I ask you that you will comply. Adieu.

Emile was shattered. His suspicions had been proved right, in spite of Madeleine's claim of there being 'no other reason for my conduct'. He knew that the real reason was William Minnoch. But Emile also knew he now had the whip hand. Madeleine had asked for the return of her letters with a telltale urgency, and involving her servant, Christina Haggart. Emile had saved all Madeleine's letters, nearly two hundred in all, and they were dynamite. There was no way, at this stage at any rate, that Emile was going to make Madeleine a present of them. Christina Haggart waited in vain at the area gate, Thursday at seven, and Emile waited for the inevitable note from Madeleine. When it arrived it said:

I attribute it to your having cold that I had no answer to my last note. On Thursday evening you were, I suppose, afraid of the night air. I fear your cold is not better. I again appoint Thursday night first same place, Street Gate, 7 o'c.

M.

If you can not send me or bring me the parcel on Thursday please write a note saying when you shall bring it, and address it to C. H. Send it by post.

Emile sat down and wrote a reply, telling Madeleine that he regarded her as his wife. He then primed a timebomb, telling Madeleine that he would show her letters to her father, who would be particularly interested in those which proved 'criminal intimacy' between them. He posted the note, and sat back to await Madeleine's response. It came by return:

Monday Night. – Emile, I have just had your note. Emile, for the love you once had for me do nothing till I see you – for God's sake do not bring your once loved Mini to an open shame. Emile, I have deceived you. I have deceived my Mother. God knows she did not boast of any thing I had said of you – for she, poor woman, thought I had broken off with you last Winter. I deceived you by telling you she still knew of our engagement. She did not. This I now confess – and as for wishing for an engagement with another, I do not fancy she ever thought of it. Emile, write to no one, to Papa or any other. Oh, do not till I see you. On

Wednesday night – be at the Hamiltons at 12, and I shall open my Shutter, and then you come to the Area Gate, I shall see you.

It would break my Mother's heart. Oh, Emile be not harsh to me. I am the most guilty, miserable wretch on the face of the earth. Emile, do not drive me to death. When I ceased to love you, believe me, it was not to love another. I am free from all engagements at present. Emile, for God's sake do not send my letters to Papa. It will be an open rupture. I will leave the house. I will die. Emile, do nothing till I see you. One word tomorrow night at my window to tell me or I shall go mad.

Tuesday morning. – I am ill. God knows what I have suffered. My punishment is more than I can bear. Do nothing till I see you, for the love of heaven do nothing. I am mad. I am ill.

Emile might have permitted himself a wry smile of satisfaction on reading Madeleine's desperate entreaties. The boot was now on the other foot. He pondered now on how best to seize the advantage. Instead of appearing at Madeleine's window, as asked, he sent a note telling her he would do nothing until he saw her the following night. At midnight, Madeleine was sitting up in bed, possibly the worse for drink, writing furiously:

Emile, I have this night received your note. Oh, it is kind of you to write to me. Emile, no one can know the intense agony of mind I have suffered last night and today. Emile, my father's wrath would kill me; you little know his temper. Emile for the love you once had for me do not denounce me to my P/. Emile, if he should read my letters to you – he will put me from him, he will hate me as a guilty wretch. I loved you, and wrote to you in my first ardent love – it was with my deepest love I loved you. It was for your love I adored you. I put on paper what I should not. I was free, because I loved you with my heart. If he or any other saw those fond letters to you, what would not be said of me. On my bended knees I write you, and ask you as you hope for mercy at the Judgment do not inform on me – do not make me a public shame.

Madeleine rants and rambles on for several more pages. She had evidently been at the sherry. 'I grow mad,' she writes at one point. 'I have been ill, very ill, all day. I have had what has given meet a false spirit. I had to resort to what I should not have taken, but my brain is on fire. I feel as if death indeed would be sweet.'

The following day, Wednesday 11 February, Madeleine instructed the Smiths' page boy to go to Dr Yeaman's surgery in Sauchiehall Street with a note asking for 'a small phial of prussic acid' for her hands. The man behind the surgery counter shook his head, and explained to the lad that his mistress would need a proper prescription, since prussic acid was poison. Madeleine's reaction was calm. 'Very well,' she said quietly. 'Never mind.'

That night, at midnight, in Christina Haggart's room, Madeleine and Emile met for the first time since her letter breaking off the affair. There was a tearful reconciliation, Madeleine appearing suitably repentant and contrite. Whatever she told Emile, she omitted to tell him of her engagement to Mr Minnoch. Evidently, Emile did not press her on this point. At any rate, two days later, ominously Friday the thirteenth, the couple met again. That evening, Emile dined with Miss Perry and told her all his troubles. The following afternoon brought a note from Madeleine:

Saturday. – My dear Emile,
I have got my finger cut, and can not write, so dear, I wish you would excuse me. I was glad to see you looking so well yesterday. I hope to see you very soon . . . Write me for next Thursday, and then I shall tell you when I can see you. I want the first time we meet, that you will bring me all my cool letters back – the last four I have written – and I will give you others in their place.

Bring them all to me. Excuse me more; just now it hurts to write, so with kindest and dearest love, ever believe, yours with love and affection,

M.

The day of the great reconciliation, Emile had begun to keep a sketchy diary in a small pocketbook. The entry for Thursday 19 February is brief, but portentous:

Saw Mimi
a few moments
was very ill during the night

The fleeting moments with Madeleine must have been snatched last thing at night, for she had spent the evening at the opera with William Minnoch and his sister. They saw a performance of *Lucrezia Borgia*. A couple of days later Emile's landlady, Mrs Jenkins, knocked on the door of his room. A weak voice asked her to enter. Emile was still in bed. 'I have been very unwell,' he told her. 'Look what I have vomited.' Mrs Jenkins looked. Whatever it was, it was green. 'I think that's bile,' she said.

On Saturday morning, 21 February, Madeleine walked briskly from Blythswood Square to the druggist's shop on Sauchiehall Street owned by the Murdoch brothers. She paid sixpence for an ounce of arsenic, explaining to George Murdoch that the poison was for the garden at Rowaleyn. That night, Emile wrote bleakly in his diary:

don't feel well

The following day, the entry was bleaker still:

Sun. 22 Feb. – Saw Mimi in Drawing Room
Promised me French Bible
Taken very ill

Emile was sick again during the night, and wrote to Madeleine telling her of his illness. Her response was to pay a second visit to George Murdoch, the druggist, to ask if arsenic should not be white. Murdoch explained that by law arsenic had to be mixed with a colouring agent. The arsenic he had sold to Madeleine the previous week had been mixed with soot. Madeleine thanked him and left.

Towards the middle of March, Emile was taking tea with the elderly Miss Perry, and talking inevitably of Madeleine and his recent poor state of health. 'I can't think why I was so unwell,' he said, 'after getting that coffee and chocolate from her.' And then, as an afterthought: 'If she were to poison me, I would forgive her.' Miss Perry was to recall this odd remark some months later.

Meanwhile, Emile was thinking hard about Madeleine and her Mr Minnoch. 'Mimi, dear,' he wrote:

Place yourself in my position and tell me I am wrong in believing what I hear ... Answer me this, Mimi – Who gave you the trinket you showed me. Is it true it was Mr Minnoch. And is it true you are, directly or indirectly, engaged to Mr Minnoch or to anyone else but me. These questions I must know ...

If Emile was expecting a straight answer to a straight question, he was disappointed.

My sweet, dear pet, [Madeleine wrote] I am so sorry you should be so vexed – believe nothing, sweet one, till I tell you myself – it is a report I am sorry about – but it has been six months spoken of ... I will tell and answer you all questions when we meet. Adieu, dearest love of my soul – with fond and tender embraces, ever believe me, with love and kisses, to be your own fond, dear, and loving

Mini

Sealing the envelope, Madeleine strolled to the post office, mailed the letter, bought a further supply of arsenic (from a different druggist this time) and discussed plans for her wedding in June with an old schoolfriend who was to be Madeleine's bridesmaid. Her husband, Madeleine explained airily, was to be one Mr William Minnoch.

Having briefed the bridesmaid, Madeleine left Glasgow to travel to Bridge of Allan for a short holiday. It was there, on 12 March, that she and William Minnoch set the date of their wedding. It would be on 18 June.

Madeleine returned to Glasgow on 17 March. Emile had been kept in the dark about the details of her itinerary, and was unaware that Madeleine was already back at Blythswood Square when, two days later, he set off himself for Bridge of Allan. Madeleine, meanwhile, had been buying arsenic again. On the day Emile left town, Madeleine wrote to him at his lodgings. The letter was forwarded, as was a second which arrived two days later. The next day was a Sunday, 22 March. Emile's landlady, Mrs Jenkins, was surprised when he turned up, footsore and weary, at about 8 P.M. that evening. 'The letter you sent me brought me home,' he explained, adding that he had walked fifteen miles from Bridge of Allan. Mrs Jenkins gave him some tea and toast, and Emile asked for a passkey. 'I am not sure,' he said, 'but I may be late.'

At 9 P.M., as the Smith family were gathering for family prayers at Blythswood Square, Emile L'Angelier left his lodgings in Franklin Place. In the next half-hour he was seen at various spots in the city, apparently dawdling, killing time. But then he suddenly vanished. For five hours he could have been anywhere. We don't know where. The next we know is that at two-thirty the following morning he was tugging at the front-door bell at his lodgings asking Mrs Jenkins to open up. Mrs Jenkins pulled on a dressing gown, went downstairs and opened the door. Emile was almost collapsed on the step. He was clutching his stomach and groaning. The landlady helped him up to his room, and gave him a glass of water. Emile drank it greedily and asked for some tea. When Mrs Jenkins returned with a tray, Emile was half-undressed and in bad shape, complaining of chillness. Mrs Jenkins brought hot-water jars and blankets and put Emile to bed. As dawn broke, and seeing he was no better, she called a doctor, who applied a mustard plaster. 'I am far worse than the doctor thinks,' Emile muttered when the physician had left. The doctor called again a couple of hours later. Mrs Jenkins told him that Emile seemed at last to be sleeping. The doctor went in to his room. Emile was dead in bed.

Mrs Jenkins, distraught, sent for William Stevenson from Huggins, Emile's employers, and asked him to take charge. Stevenson started with Emile's clothes which were lying scattered on a sofa. In one of his pockets was a letter. 'This explains all,' said William Stevenson when he had read it. The letter, of course, was from Madeleine Smith.

Why my beloved did you not come to me. Oh beloved are you ill. Come to me sweet one. I waited and waited for you but you came not. I shall wait again tomorrow night same hour and arrangement. Do come sweet love my own dear love of a sweetheart. Come beloved and clasp me to your heart. Come and we shall be happy. A kiss fond love. Adieu with tender embraces ever believe me to be your own ever dear fond

Mini

Some time after lunch the same day, Madeleine Smith heard a servant admitting a visitor at 7 Blythswood Square. It was Miss Mary Perry, the elderly lady who had entertained Emile and Madeleine at her home. This time her manner was distinctly unfriendly. Madeleine received her, but it was Madeleine's mother that Miss Perry had come to see. 'Is anything wrong?' asked Madeleine. 'I wish to see your mamma and I will acquaint her with the object of my visit,' came the sharp reply. Alone with Mrs Smith in the drawing room, Miss Perry told her of the sudden, agonizing death of Pierre Emile L'Angelier. A bewildered Mrs Smith called for smelling salts and went straight to bed.

There was a second unexpected visitor to Blythswood

Square that day. An official of the French Consulate in Glasgow, M Auguste de Mean, who had known L'Angelier for three years, called to see Madeleine's father. M de Mean said he thought Mr Smith should know about a large number of letters which had passed between his daughter and the dead man. He might want to take steps to secure them. James Smith, too, promptly took to his bed. Madeleine, meanwhile, seemed unmoved by the news of Emile's death. A day or two later, she swore to M de Mean: 'I have not seen L'Angelier for three weeks.' Next morning she disappeared from home. William Minnoch found her on board the steamer for Helensburgh and Row, and brought her back to Glasgow in a carriage. On the way home Madeleine explained she had left home because she knew her parents would be angry with her over the relationship with Emile.

On the day after his death a post-mortem examination of Emile's body established that he had been poisoned. By the end of the week, medical experts were able to say that Emile had swallowed enough arsenic to kill forty men. But by this time he had been buried, and his body had to be exhumed to allow the medical men to carry out a fuller examination. The day following, Madeleine admitted to William Minnoch that she had recently bought arsenic, but for cosmetic purposes only. She had learned at her finishing school that a solution of arsenic was supposed to be good for the complexion. That afternoon, Madeleine Hamilton Smith was arrested and charged with murdering Pierre Emile L'Angelier by poisoning him.

Her trial opened three months later at the High Court of Justiciary in Edinburgh. Feelings about the case were running too strong to risk a trial in Glasgow. The Glaswegian bourgeoisie were largely sympathetic to Madeleine; even supposing she had murdered L'Angelier, he was nothing but a counter-jumper who had seduced the girl then tried to blackmail her over the return of the letters. Less well-to-do folk felt differently; Madeleine was a spoilt little rich girl who had despatched a poor but honest lover in order to marry a rich man.

The trial was nothing less than sensational. No fewer than sixty of Madeleine's love letters to Emile were read in open court. The crowds crammed into the public gallery were agog. The Lord Justice Clerk, one of three judges hearing the case with a jury, was clearly shocked by Madeleine's brazen use of the word 'love' to mean the sexual act. 'Would to God it were to be by your side,' said the letter which caused the most offence on the judicial bench. 'I would feel well and happy then. I think I would be wishing you to *love* me if I were with you – but I don't suppose you would refuse me. For I know you will like to *love* your Mimi. Adieu, sweet, love, kind pet husband my own true Emile. I am thine for ever, they wife, thy devoted, thy own true Mimi L'Angelier.'

To the scandalized consternation of the assembled judges, Madeleine had underlined the word 'love' three times in that letter.

Fifty-seven witnesses gave evidence for the prosecution, whose case took a full five days to present. The defence was more succinct, and lasted just two days. Madeleine's advocate, the Dean of Faculty, made a spectacular closing speech, the first sentence of which is still quoted in legal circles as a model one: 'Gentlemen of the jury, the charge against the prisoner is murder, and the punishment of murder is death; and that simple statement is sufficient to suggest to us the awful solemnity of the occasion which brings you and me face to face.' At the end of the speech the Dean of Faculty sat down to thunderous applause from the spectators. Finally, it was the turn of the Lord Chief Justice to sum up before turning the case over to the jury. They did not deliberate for long. It was less than half an hour before the bell outside the jury room rang, signalling their imminent return. The verdict was peculiarly Scottish: Not Proven on all counts. And for the first time in the entire nine-day hearing, Madeleine appeared moved.

'Scots law is different from English law,' Jack House explained to me. 'And one of the differences is that the Scots have three different verdicts, instead of the two available in England and Wales: Guilty or Not Guilty. In Scotland there is a third verdict: Not Proven. It's rather a strange verdict. According to some cynics, it means: Go away and don't do it again!'

Whatever the truth of the matter, Madeleine displayed a remarkable degree of sang-froid throughout. Four days after the verdict she wrote dismissively, not of Emile (whom she ignored), but of William Minnoch, who by now had followed Mr and Mrs Smith in the direction of a sick bed. 'I hear he has been ill,' she wrote, 'which I don't much care.'

Before the trial, William Minnoch had declared he would stand by Madeleine throughout, and would marry her in the event of her being free to wed. In fact the couple never met again. The case ruined James Smith and his family, both socially and professionally: he never received another important commission. Madeleine left Scotland and, calling herself Lena Smith, married a bohemian art teacher, George Wardle, in London in 1861. Two years later her father died a broken man. His wife followed him to the grave three years later. Neither seemed to have recovered from the shock of the case. Madeleine, meanwhile, was moving among the glitterati of the radical set led by the socialist William Morris and became a fashionable Bloomsbury hostess. There were two children of the marriage, which ended in 1889 when George Wardle emigrated to Italy, leaving Madeleine effectively widowed. What happened to her next is not entirely clear; she is supposed to have lived for a time in Staffordshire, but in 1916, when she was eighty, she decided to follow her son Tom to America. There she was married a second time, to an elderly man called Sheehy, and called herself Lena Wardle Sheehy. Old Mr Sheehy died in 1926 in New York. Two years later, on 12 April 1928 in the Bronx, Lena Wardle Sheehy – Madeleine Smith of Blythswood Square, Glasgow – died of kidney disease at the age of ninety-three. She is buried beneath a simple headstone inscribed Lena Sheehy.

Many years after Madeleine's death the diaries of W. Somerset Maugham were published, in which the celebrated novelist recalled an odd event involving his old friend, the criminologist H. B. Irving. It had happened in 1907. Maugham, writing in 1919, recalled it thus:

'H. B. went down to stay in the country. His next-door neighbour was a very quiet prim old lady; becoming acquainted with her, he gradually connected her with the heroine of a celebrated murder case which had excited the world fifty years before. She had been tried and found not guilty [*sic*] but the evidence was so damning that, notwithstanding the verdict, the general opinion was that she had in point of fact committed the crime. She discovered that he had found out her identity, taxed him with it, and presently said to him: "I suppose you want to know whether I did it or not. I did, and what's more, if it were all to happen again I'd do it again." '[5]

It is well over a century since Madeleine Smith finally turned her back on her home at 7 Blythswood Square and left Glasgow for good. Her bedroom, which she shared with her younger sister, Janet and where she canoodled with the poor, doomed Emile, still has its basement windows which open on to Blythswood Street. Some years ago, when the building housed the West of Scotland Agricultural College, the room was converted into a men's lavatory, a function of which Madeleine may or may not have approved. But her ghost, moving with the faintest rustle of crinoline among the young seedsmen and their pesticidal poisons, must surely have felt as though it had come home.

2 Dalton Square, Lancaster

She was not beautiful. She had buck teeth, her nose was too big and her chin too firm. Yet even as a teenager, the young Miss Isabella Kerr was strangely attractive to men. At cosy soirées in Edinburgh, where she grew up, they seemed to flit to her side. Perhaps it was her figure, fashionably slender, or her lilting Scottish small talk, and her tinkling laugh. Whatever her secret with men, she knew she had it. She was an outrageous flirt. At the restaurant in Princes Street where she worked as a waitress she encountered many eligible young men. And in 1919, aged just twenty, she married a Dutch sailor called Van Ess. But the marriage was not a success, and the couple drifted apart after only a few weeks. Isabella continued with her work at the restaurant, and eventually became manageress. In 1927, a handsome and dapper young Indian doctor swaggered into the restaurant and ordered a meal. Mrs Van Ess eyed her new customer with interest. He was slim, with dark, piercing eyes and a bush of glossy, black hair which fell appealingly over his forehead. He was immaculately dressed in a smart, expensively cut three-piece suit, and his skin was the colour of chocolate, smooth and milky. Isabella struck up a conversation. His English was slightly halting; even so he spoke rapidly and excitedly. He told her he came from Bombay, and that his name was Captain Gabriel Hakim. He belonged to a wealthy and highly respectable Parsee family in Bombay; he had achieved the rank of captain during his days with the Indian Medical Corps. Now, at the age of twenty-eight, he was studying for a Fellowship at the Royal College of Surgeons in

Edinburgh. He impressed Mrs Van Ess with a recital of his medical qualifications from the Universities of Bombay and London. But Captain Hakim forgot to mention that he also had a wife, whom he had left behind in India.

The couple tumbled headlong into an affair. Hakim proved a dashing lover, the experienced Isabella a passionate mistress. Hakim was soon spending more time and energy on his rapturous new girlfriend and less on his surgical studies. As a result, he failed his Fellowship exams. Early the following year, 1928, Isabella Van Ess became pregnant. She gave up her restaurant job and went to London to live with Hakim, having by now divorced her husband. At about this time Hakim decided to change his cumbersome Indian name by deed poll; henceforth Bukhtyar Rustomji Ratanji Hakim was known simply as Buck Ruxton. It was a strutting, vainglorious-sounding name. It suited him.

Although Ruxton and Isabella lived as man and wife and had three children, they were never legally married. Nevertheless, Isabella styled herself Mrs Ruxton and asked their new friends to call her Belle. Buck and Belle Ruxton. New names for a new life.

London did not last. For some reason the Ruxtons moved north in 1930 to the ancient county town of Lancaster. Dr Ruxton had by now abandoned his ambitions of a career as a surgeon and had turned to general practice. He bought a substantial Georgian house at 2 Dalton Square, a fine double-fronted building in a terrace directly opposite the town hall. He converted two ground-floor rooms into a surgery and a waiting room. He was a good doctor and worked hard. The practice prospered. Within two years his panel had grown to seven thousand patients, the largest in Lancaster. Dr Ruxton was particularly popular with the factory people of the town, and became known as The Working Man's Doctor. He was always prepared to see patients on a Sunday; working people appreciated this, since attendance at the surgery during the week invariably meant losing a day's wages. In the days when the provincial GP was almost invariably white and middle-class, Ruxton, the high-born Parsee, concerned himself with the welfare of ordinary folk, making house-calls at all hours of the day or night, chatting cheerfully to patients he met in the street, and earning a reputation as a caring doctor who never pressed for payment (in those pre-National Health Service days) when he knew that hardship would follow; he habitually added small amounts to the bills of wealthier patients to cover the amounts owed. The other doctors in Lancaster disliked Ruxton and disapproved of the way he ran his practice. They were suspicious of this young coloured upstart from London, and resented his success. 'The local establishment couldn't cope with a popular Indian doctor,' said Arthur Thompson, a local historian. 'They resented this inferior being beating them at their own game.'[1]

The social life of Lancaster between the wars was lived according to a set of unwritten but scrupulously observed rules governing the social pecking order. Everyone knew their place. At the top of the heap were the members of the so-called town hall set (council members and senior officials, professional people, and leading Rotarians and Freemasons) plus a handful of other assorted nabobs and nobodies who considered themselves a cut above the rest. These people seemed to have formed themselves into a kind of charmed circle; this meant that somebody like Belle Ruxton, who was socially ambitious, had to ingratiate herself in order to count. She certainly tried hard. She threw dinner parties and drinks parties, taking care to invite only the right people. She hosted children's parties and supported all the right charities. She took care to be seen in all the right places. 'There's no doubt she tried to get into local society,' said retired journalist Harry Aked who covered the case, 'but in a county town like Lancaster, which in those days was a little more particular than it is now, people just didn't accept her.'[1]

However hard she tried, the fact was that Belle Ruxton's social credentials were crucially flawed. It wasn't that she was the wife of a mere doctor. What mattered was that she was the wife of a *coloured* doctor. Moreover, she was the target of some lurid gossip linking her name with that of at least one young man. Although no evidence of a liaison was ever produced, the tattletales of Lancaster had a high time dishing out the dirt. 'Belle Ruxton undoubtedly had a strange kind of sexual magnetism,' recalled one old-timer, 'and she attracted quite a lot of men. Buck Ruxton always resented this. And after so many years, it has to be said that she appears to have been a generous woman with her sexual favours.'[1] This view, however, is still keenly disputed in Lancaster. A woman who knew Belle insists that she was a good woman, a model wife. 'Ruxton was the difficult one. She was just a doormat really.'

The early Thirties were exciting times in the Ruxton household. Their first child, Elizabeth, was followed by a second daughter, Diana, and finally a son, Billy. In 1933 the Ruxtons hired a nursemaid to look after the children, an attractive, blue-eyed girl of eighteen called Mary Rogerson. During the week, Mary lived with the Ruxtons at 2 Dalton Square, returning home at the weekends to her family at nearby Overton, on the Lune estuary. To the neighbours in Dalton Square the Ruxtons presented a perfect picture of domestic contentment. But behind the imposing front door and Dr Ruxton's brightly polished brass plate, some extremely odd things were going on. 'You've got to remember that Ruxton was Indian,' said Captain Henry Vann, who was then chief constable of Lancaster. 'His attitude to women was quite different to the attitude we know in England. He expected Belle to be always subservient, submissive. After his arrest, I visited Ruxton's house. At one end of the lounge was a platform, on which was a large chair, rather like a throne. I was told that if Belle Ruxton ever misbehaved or incurred the doctor's displeasure, she would have to kneel before him and beg his pardon!'[1]

Ruxton's own diary entries for this period reveal something of the ups and downs of life with Belle, their passionate devotion and their bitter quarrels. 'We were the kind of people who could not live with each other and who could not live without each other,' he said later, adding the French proverb: 'Who loves most chastises most.'[2]

'Belle came across one morning,' a former neighbour recalled, 'and said that Ruxton had thrown a vase at her during a row. She'd bruised her shoulder. She didn't deserve such treatment.'[3]

Ruxton's problem was his thunderflash temper and his uncontrollable and morbid jealousy of Belle. He flew into violent fits of rage at the least provocation, and often without any provocation at all. At times he turned on Belle and beat her, accusing her of flirting and even sleeping with other men. Belle's response was to threaten to leave Ruxton. On at least one occasion she actually did leave, taking all her clothes with her. 'She will not come back alive!' Ruxton ranted. 'I will bring her back to the mortuary!' But when his temper cooled, Ruxton was repentant. 'Every time a quarrel arose I paid dearly for it,' Ruxton recalled.

Against this provincial background of jealousy, mistrust and prejudice, the boiling instability between Buck and Belle Ruxton came to a climax in the first week of September 1935. Belle went home to Edinburgh for the weekend, intending to stay with her sister. With her on the trip went some friends from Lancaster, Mr and Mrs

Edmondson and their children, Barbara and Bobby. In the event, the entire party of five stayed – in separate rooms – at the Adelphi Hotel. Bobby Edmondson was a good-looking young man in his mid-twenties, employed as an assistant solicitor in the town clerk's department at the town hall, across the square from Ruxton's house. Ruxton, in his characteristic way, had been suspicious of young Edmondson for some time, and when he got wind that he and Belle were in Edinburgh together he drove to Scotland to find out what was going on. He tracked the party to the hotel and came away convinced that Bobby and Belle were having an affair. Later, when he challenged Bobby's father about the visit, Ruxton broke down in tears. (It should be made clear that at no time in the case was any shred of evidence produced to back up Ruxton's hysterical and paranoid interpretation of the Edinburgh trip.)

On Saturday 14 September, just a week after the visit to Edinburgh, Belle Ruxton left Dalton Square and drove to Blackpool to meet her two sisters. This trip to see the illuminations was an annual event in Belle's social calendar. The outing was a great success, and the three sisters spent the whole evening walking up and down the seafront admiring the lights. Belle was not back in Lancaster until well after midnight. She parked Ruxton's Hillman Minx car at Dalton Square and let herself in with her latchkey. Ruxton was waiting for her, beside himself with rage. We can only imagine exactly what happened during that dreadful encounter. But we can safely assume that Ruxton, in an exploding temper and a torrent of abusive accusations concerning Bobby Edmondson, seized Belle by the throat and strangled her. Her cries were probably heard by the nursemaid, Mary Rogerson, who, unusually, was sleeping that Saturday night at Dalton Square. Mary must have ventured down in her nightclothes in the direction of the commotion. As she poked her head blearily round the door of the kitchen she was just in time to see Ruxton throttling Belle. Mary must have known from that moment that her fate too was sealed. Hurling Belle's lifeless body to the ground, Ruxton pounced, dragged Mary into the room and bludgeoned her to death. Dragging the bodies upstairs, Ruxton manhandled each one into the bath and took up his surgical saw. The failed surgeon worked with speed and skill; by sunrise the bodies lay hacked to pieces behind the locked bathroom door.

At 6.30 A.M. Ruxton was standing, unshaven and bedraggled, on the step of a house a couple of miles from Dalton Square in a less elegant district of Lancaster. This was the home of one of Ruxton's charladies, Mrs Agnes Oxley. It was Mrs Oxley's husband who answered the door. 'Tell Mrs Oxley not to bother to come down this morning,' Ruxton told a rather surprised Mr Oxley. 'Mrs Ruxton and Mary have gone on a holiday to Edinburgh, and I am taking the children to Morecambe.' With that Ruxton climbed into his car and drove off, leaving the Oxleys to enjoy an unexpected Sunday lie-in.

Back at Dalton Square, Ruxton gave his three children their breakfast. (One of the minor mysteries of the case is how the youngsters slept undisturbed through the appalling events of the night.) During the morning, Ruxton dealt with several callers: a girl delivering newspapers, a woman delivering milk, and a man calling with a copy of that day's *Sunday Graphic*. Ruxton opened the door to the first two callers, but ignored the knocking of the third, so the delivery man pushed the newspaper under the door and left. At about 10.30 A.M. Ruxton drove his car to a nearby garage and bought two cans of petrol which he put in the boot. He then visited another garage and asked the attendant to put four gallons of petrol in the tank. When he got home there was a fourth visitor, a Mrs Whiteside, who had brought her son for a circumcision operation. The appointment had been for eleven o'clock. Ruxton opened the door slightly. He was wearing a grey suit, collar and tie. 'I'm sorry, Mrs Whiteside,' he said, 'but I can't perform the operation today. My wife is away in Scotland and there's just myself and my little maid and we are busy taking the carpets up ready for the decorators in the morning. Look at my hands, how dirty they are.' Mrs Whiteside looked, but saw only his left hand. The right hand was hidden by the door.

Shortly before midday Ruxton arrived in Morecambe, at the home of Herbert Anderson, a dentist. The children were with him. Ruxton was friendly with the Andersons, and occasionally left the children there when Belle and Mary were away, so Ruxton's request that Mrs Anderson look after them for the day was not particularly unusual. Ruxton explained that his wife and Mary Rogerson had gone away for a few days. Mrs Anderson noticed that Ruxton's right hand was bandaged. The doctor explained that he had cut it with a tin-opener while making the children's breakfast. While Mrs Anderson set about feeding three extra young mouths for Sunday lunch, Dr Ruxton was driving back to Dalton Square. There, for the next four hours, he was alone.

It was late afternoon when Ruxton turned his car into Bulk Road and drew up outside Mrs Mary Hampshire's house. She had been a patient of Ruxton's since his early days in Lancaster and knew the family well. She was surprised to have a visit from the doctor on a Sunday afternoon, and even more surprised when Ruxton asked her to return with him to Dalton Square to help tidy up the house. Decorators were coming in the morning, he explained. He had cut his fingers and needed help tidying the staircase, having managed to pull up the carpets on his own. Driving Mrs Hampshire back to Dalton Square,

Ruxton again explained his cut hand by saying he had had an accident opening a tin of fruit. He would not have troubled her at all, he added, but both his wife and the nursemaid were away.

At Dalton Square the obliging Mrs Hampshire may well have felt that something was wrong. The house was empty but the wireless was fully turned on. A meal for two, tea or supper, had been laid in the lounge: bread and butter, cakes, stewed blackberries, a fruit salad, a chocolate blancmange. It had not been touched. In the kitchen, an uncooked roast of meat lay in the meatsafe, still in its wrapping paper.

Other parts of the house attracted Mrs Hampshire's attention. The stair carpet had been pulled up, revealing dirt and straw from the hall to the top of the house. The landing carpets had also been removed. The bath was filthy. The enamel was coated with a thick, dirty, yellow scum, almost to the rim. Ruxton asked Mrs Hampshire to give it a good clean, and put a shilling (5p) in the meter for the hot water. Mrs Hampshire surveyed the mess again. There was too much here for one person, and she asked Ruxton if she could get her husband to help her. He agreed, and told her to use the telephone. At about half-past four Ruxton left Mrs Hampshire in the house, alone.

She wandered through the empty rooms and paid a second visit upstairs, stepping through the untidy wisps of straw which were strewn about. At the top of the stairs were two locked doors. Bits of straw were poking out beneath them. At the foot of the stairs someone had thrown an empty packet of Lux soapflakes. Mrs Hampshire passed on. In the waiting room, she noticed some rolled-up carpets, a blue suit and some stair pads. They were all stained with blood. She moved silently along the passage and through the kitchen. Outside, in the back yard, there were more carpets from the stairs and landings, clogged or stippled with blood. A man's shirt and some partly burned towels. All bloodstained.

It seems curious that poor Mrs Hampshire did not turn on her heel there and then and run across Dalton Square to the police station. In fact, she put on an apron, found a broom, and set to work. She swept the stairs from top to bottom, gathered up the straw and (another curiosity) put it in a bucket under the sink. She gave the bath a good scrub with hot water and Vim, but as hard as she scrubbed she could not shift the thick, greasy, yellow stain. The scrubbing was interrupted at about seven o'clock by the return of Dr Ruxton with his two daughters. He had brought them to collect their nightclothes, he explained, as they were going to spend the night with the Andersons in Morecambe. While Ruxton and the children were upstairs Mrs Hampshire's husband arrived. Ruxton reappeared and showed the Hampshires into the waiting room where he offered to let them have the discarded carpets and the suit, explaining the bloodstains by repeating the story about the cut hand and the tin of fruit. This offer was to prove damaging to Ruxton at his subsequent trial.

Leaving the Hampshires to their cleaning chores, Ruxton returned to Morecambe with the children, stopping at a chemist's shop on the way to buy 2lbs of cotton wool and a bottle of Dettol disinfectant. After a tour of Morecambe promenade to see the lights, Ruxton settled the children with Mr and Mrs Anderson and returned to Dalton Square at about eleven o'clock. He found that the Hampshires had finished the cleaning and had taken the carpets and the suit from the waiting room. (They had left the carpets in the yard because they had become waterlogged with the heavy rain which had fallen for most of the day.) Ruxton collapsed, exhausted, into bed.

After a night and day of murderous activity, and tortured by the pain in his injured hand, it was hardly surprising that Ruxton passed a sleepless night. As he lay turning over the events of the weekend in his mind it struck him that the gift to Mr Hampshire of his bloodstained suit might have been a mistake. Accordingly, at nine o'clock the following morning (Monday), Ruxton called at the Hampshires' house. He looked ill and he had not shaved. He wore neither collar nor tie, and had on an old raincoat. He asked Mrs Hampshire for the return of the suit so that he could send it to the cleaners. She replied that as he had already been so generous she must insist on paying for the cleaning herself. Together they examined the suit. 'I did not realize how dirty it was,' remarked Ruxton, in a rare moment of candour. 'Anyway,' he added, 'it is very undignified for a man to wear another man's suit and for people to know about it.' Then, pointing excitedly to his name written on a tab in the jacket pocket, he asked Mrs Hampshire to cut it off, crying 'Burn it! Burn it now!' This she did, to Ruxton's evident relief. The doctor had one more request. Could Mrs Hampshire come to Dalton Square later in the morning to open the door to patients? Ruxton explained that his charwoman was ill. Mrs Hampshire, apparently for the first time in this whole bizarre episode, finally plucked up the courage to ask a question. Where was Mrs Ruxton? She should be sent for, since Ruxton looked so ill. Ruxton replied that she was in Edinburgh and he didn't wish to spoil her holiday.

As soon as the dishevelled doctor had driven away Mrs Hampshire, becoming more curious by the minute, took another look at the bloodstained suit. She decided that the waistcoat was so saturated with blood that she could do nothing with it, so she burned it. Mrs Hampshire now turned her attention to the bundle of stair carpet and found it was not only bloody but still damp with blood. She manhandled the bundle out into her backyard and threw twenty or thirty buckets of water over it to get it clean, but without success. All that happened was that the water running off was itself the colour of blood. Finally she hung the carpet on the line and took a scrubbing brush to it, but the blood, now congealed, would not be shifted.

When Ruxton arrived home from Mrs Hampshire's he found Mrs Oxley waiting for him on the step. (She had been trying, unsuccessfully, to get into the house to start work since seven o'clock.) She made him some coffee and helped him bandage his injured hand. When Ruxton left the house in the middle of the morning Mrs Oxley cleared up the uneaten meal in the lounge and got on with her cleaning, noticing the appalling state of the bath and the heap of burned material in the back yard. She finished her work and let herself out of the house. Shortly afterwards Mrs Hampshire arrived and let herself in. There was no one in the house and the two rooms at the top of the stairs remained locked. She saw that someone had finished off the cleaning and, finding no doctor, no patients, in fact nothing whatever to do, she wandered round the house for over an hour. Finally she heard the key turn in the lock and Ruxton appeared at the door of the waiting room. Mrs Hampshire looked at him inquiringly. Why had she been sent for when there was no work to do? Ruxton's reply was ominous. 'I sent for you because you give me courage.'

Mrs Hampshire's suspicions were finally starting to take root. She sat him down in the lounge and questioned him further about his wife's whereabouts. This time Ruxton told her she was in London. Mrs Hampshire did not believe him and said so. To her astonishment, the doctor put his head in his hands and broke down weeping.

'You're right. I'm not telling the truth. I'm the most unhappy man in the world. My wife has gone off with another man and left me with the children,' he sobbed. 'You make a friend of a man, you treat him as a friend and

he eats at your table, and he makes love to your wife
behind your back. It's terrible.'

Mrs Hampshire was unprepared for this soul-baring,
and sat in discomfited silence for some minutes while
Ruxton continued to distress himself. 'I can forgive extravagance or anything else,' he moaned, 'but infidelity *never*.'

Monday was dustbin day at Dalton Square, and the men
arrived in mid-afternoon. In the back yard they found a
large pile of debris, bloodstained carpets, bloody and partly
burned towels and a shirt, part of a blue silk dress with
glass buttons, fragments of oilcloth and a hamper of straw.
One of the binmen asked Ruxton about the bloodstains.
Ruxton said he had severed his finger opening a tin. The
doctor told the men to take everything away except the
carpets (promised to Mrs Hampshire) and a child's toy car
which was lying in a corner of the yard. One of the men
swept the yard out.

That evening Ruxton drove again to Morecambe and
asked the Andersons if the children could stay another
night. They agreed. Mr Anderson noticed an injury to
Ruxton's right hand. There was a gash across three fingers,
exposing bone. Ruxton again claimed the wound had been
caused by a tin-opener. A peculiar kind of tin-opener, said
Mr Anderson, adding he would like to see it. Ruxton said
he had seen enough of it and had thrown it away.

The next day was Tuesday. Ruxton spent the morning
sorting out some clothes for the children, taking them to
school, and calling at the home of a decorator who was
supposed to have started work at Dalton Square the
previous day but hadn't shown up. At lunchtime we find
Ruxton driving his car at Kendal in the Lake District, and
colliding with a man on a bicycle. The man was not badly
hurt, but Ruxton failed to stop and the cyclist took his
number. At one o'clock Ruxton's car was stopped by a
policeman at Milnthorpe. Ruxton admitted the accident,

and became very agitated, almost incoherent. The puzzled constable allowed Ruxton to go on his way, and the doctor arrived back at Dalton Square shortly after two. Ruxton asked his cook, Mrs Elizabeth Curwen, to take his son Billy out as Mrs Ruxton and Mary Rogerson were 'on holiday in Edinburgh'. And he told one of his cleaners, Mrs Mabel Smith, to start stripping wallpaper at the top of the stairs. This was a big job, and Mrs Smith didn't finish until the afternoon of the following day, Wednesday. In the course of the stripping, she noticed blood on the curtains of the landing window and two bloody marks in the bathroom. She pointed the curtains out to Mrs Curwen and Mrs Oxley, who took them down and put them in the linen basket to be washed. But Ruxton was unhappy about this. Tearing off the bloodstained part, which he burned, he gave the rest of the curtains to the cleaners for dusters.

That afternoon Ruxton paid another visit to Morecambe, where the children were still lodged with the Andersons. It was the week of the Morecambe carnival, and his eldest daughter, Elizabeth, was taking part in the procession. He and the two youngest children went along to watch the festivities, accompanied by Mrs Anderson. That evening, back at the Andersons' house, the exhausted Dr Ruxton fell asleep in his chair and didn't leave until 1 A.M. The children slept a fourth night at the Andersons.

On Thursday morning Ruxton was up early, asking Mrs Oxley to get breakfast quickly and announcing that he was going to see a specialist about his injured hand. Mrs Oxley, working in the kitchen, heard Ruxton make several journeys between the upstairs rooms and his car, which he had brought to the back door. (She heard but could not see, since Ruxton had made a point of closing the kitchen door.) At 8 A.M. Ruxton left the house and drove off. Mrs Oxley now found that the bedroom doors which had been mysteriously locked since Sunday were now unlocked.

Another curious thing was an unpleasant smell coming from Ruxton's bedroom. Ruxton himself commented on the nasty smell the following day over lunch and asked Mrs Curwen to buy a spray and a bottle of eau-de-Cologne. This she did, and Ruxton sprayed the house from top to bottom.

Over the weekend, Ruxton was in and out of Dalton Square, attending to a number of different chores. The man who had been expected to start decorating the house was proving difficult to pin down; eventually he told Ruxton he was too busy and suggested he hired someone else. The children, now returned from Morecambe, were being looked after by one of Ruxton's helpful patients, Bessie Philbrook. On Monday evening Mary Rogerson's brother, Peter, called at Dalton Square to ask where his sister was. Ruxton explained that she and Belle had gone touring and he was uncertain how long they would be away. Peter Rogerson seemed satisfied with this, and left. Miss Philbrook arrived to put the children to bed, and Ruxton himself spent the evening watching *Clive of India* at the cinema.

On Tuesday 24 September Ruxton paid a visit to the police station, not in connection with the continued absence of his wife and servant but with the unexplained death of a woman at Morecambe called Mrs Smalley. Apparently, Ruxton had heard that Mrs Curwen, his cook, had been questioned in connection with the Smalley case. Ruxton was in a state of high dudgeon. 'Look here, Inspector Moffat,' he snapped. 'What the hell do the police want inquiring about my private affairs for?' The inspector listened patiently as Ruxton reeled off his troubles: his injured hand, and his belief that other doctors in Lancaster were jealous of his success. Finally, Ruxton became agitated. 'I am the most miserable man on earth,' he cried. 'My wife leaves me, now you come bothering me. I come home from visiting my patients a fortnight ago; I go into my study and call her name. No answer. I go to her room; I find a note. It says: "I am going away, don't worry." Leaves me with the three kids crying for their mother and I do not know where she is. She is supposed to have gone to Scotland. I wish she would come back. It's driving me crazy.' Ruxton put both hands to his head, took hold of his hair and shook it violently. 'And then you come to inquire about my private affairs. I know nothing about Mrs Smalley and I was never out of my house that Thursday night.' Inspector Moffat tried to calm Ruxton, and explained why Mrs Curwen had been interviewed. Ruxton was implacable. 'It is professional jealousy,' he stormed, 'and you will hear more about it.' At which point he stalked out of Moffat's office.

Ruxton paid a visit the following day to Mary Rogerson's stepmother at Overton. He told her that Mary had been different lately, and that she had been seeing a laundry boy. Did Mrs Rogerson know that Mary was pregnant? Mrs Rogerson was stunned; she knew nothing of any laundry boy nor of any pregnancy. When Ruxton repeated this tale to Mary's father, he was unimpressed. 'That girl must come back whatever her condition,' was James Rogerson's blunt response. What was more, unless Mary was home by the following Saturday he would report her to the police as missing. Ruxton viewed this threat with characteristic sang-froid. He told Mr Rogerson that he would have his daughter back by Sunday, and asked him not to go to the police.

As it turned out, the following Sunday was to provide the turning-point in the case. But not in the way Ruxton had promised.

The day dawned bright and dry in the small town of Moffat in the Scottish Borders. Miss Susan Johnson, a visitor from Edinburgh, took a walk out of the town along the main Edinburgh–Carlisle road. Presently she came to a bridge where the road crossed the Gardenholme Linn, a stream running into the River Annan. Pausing to look down into the ravine below, Miss Johnson suddenly recoiled in horror. Sticking out of some wrapping was a human arm. She ran as fast as she could back to her hotel to alert her brother. He returned to the spot and found a number of human remains wrapped in newspapers and a sheet. The police were called. In all they found four grisly bundles containing the remains of two bodies. These included the heads, one of which had been wrapped in a pair of child's woollen rompers. Sheets of newspapers had been used in the wrapping including, crucially, pages from a special 'slip' edition of the *Sunday Graphic* dated 15 September 1935, which contained pictures of the Morecambe carnival. This 'slip' page had circulated only in those editions of the newspaper delivered in the Morecambe and Lancaster areas.

The task of identifying the remains was not an easy one. For one thing, all recognizable features and identifying marks had been brutally hacked away. Whoever had killed these people had done a thorough and skilful job – so much so that at first the police were led to believe that one of the bodies was that of a man. When a report to this effect appeared in the press a couple of days later, a certain reader in Lancaster was jubilant. 'Listen to this, Mrs Oxley,' said Dr Buck Ruxton, pointing to a report of 'The Ravine Murder' in his *Daily Express*. He read the story out, barely concealing his elation. 'So you see it is a man and a woman; it is not our two.' And he began to laugh.

On Friday 4 October, nearly three weeks after the disappearance of Belle Ruxton and Mary Rogerson, Dr Ruxton again called on the police at Lancaster. This time he spoke to a detective constable, John Winstanley. 'She can't have any love for the children,' said Ruxton of his wife. 'Not even a postcard to Elizabeth.' Ruxton said he believed young Bobby Edmondson knew where his wife was, and became excited, banging his fist on the table and shouting, 'The blighter, I could murder him!'

The police had another visitor on Wednesday of the following week, 9 October. This was Mrs Jessie Rogerson, who gave detectives a description of her stepdaughter to be circulated to other police forces. Ruxton, meanwhile, had gone to Edinburgh to see Belle's sister, Mrs Jeannie Nelson. Mrs Nelson had heard of the gruesome discovery at Moffat and challenged Ruxton to his face. 'I would not harm a hair on her head,' cried Ruxton, indignant. 'I love her too much.'

When Ruxton arrived back in Lancaster early the next morning, a police inspector met him at the station and drove him to Dalton Square. On the way Ruxton explained he had been to Scotland to try to find his wife and to see her sister. Getting out of the car he turned to the inspector and told him: 'You inquire of Mr Edmondson at the town hall, and he will be able to tell you where my wife and maid are.'

But the trap was beginning to close, and Ruxton knew it. He went to Mrs Hampshire and asked about the bloodstained suit he had given her husband. She told him it was upstairs. 'Do something about it. Get it out of the way. Burn it,' said Ruxton. Mrs Hampshire could see the panic in the little doctor's eyes. When Ruxton again asked her to stand by him, she must have realized the awful truth about the fate of the two women. Ruxton left saying he was going to make a statement to the police. Yet still he refused to face up to the inevitable, and it was in his usual spirit of bluster that he confronted Detective Constable Winstanley later that evening. 'Winstanley, all this damned nonsense is ruining my practice,' said Ruxton, speaking of the rumours linking him with the bodies at Moffat. 'Can nothing be done to stop this talk?' Next day, Ruxton went again to the police, this time brandishing a copy of the *Daily Express*. 'Look at this,' he cried, 'ruining my practice. Why do they not accuse me of the Moffat murder? Someone will be putting a dead baby on my doorstep and I will be accused of killing it.' Later Ruxton made a similar complaint to the chief constable of Lancaster himself, Captain Henry Vann. 'My dear Vann, can't you do something about these newspaper reports? Look at this.' He pointed to the *Daily Express*. 'This newspaper says that this woman has a full set of teeth in the lower jaw, and I know, of my own knowledge, that Mary Rogerson has at least four teeth missing in this jaw.' But before Vann could reply, Ruxton launched into an impassioned tirade. 'This damned Bobby Edmondson is ruining my home,' he shouted angrily. Ruxton spoke of intimate telephone conversations between Bobby Edmondson and his wife, and of an exchange of letters between them. He asked if the police could not intercept letters in the post. Vann explained the police had no such authority, and tried to calm Ruxton, but now the doctor was weeping openly and very distressed. Finally, recovering some of his composure, Ruxton asked if it was not possible for the police to publish a statement that there was no connection between the bodies at Moffat and his wife and maid. Vann promised to do so, once he was satisfied that this was the case.

Saturday 12 October was to be Buck Ruxton's last day of freedom. Realizing that his arrest was inevitable, he spent much of the day visiting people to whom he had spoken since the night Belle and Mary were murdered. He asked several of them to revise their recollection of events, saying to Mrs Oxley, for example, 'Oh, Mrs Oxley, about that [first] Sunday morning, tell them I came for you at seven o'clock and told you not to come, and that I came again at nine and you came down till eleven.' Naturally, Mrs Oxley said she could not say this, as it wasn't true.

It was mid-evening when the telephone rang at 2 Dalton Square. Ruxton answered. It was Captain Vann. Could Ruxton please step across the square to the police station? Leaving Bessie Philbrook to babysit, Ruxton walked smartly over to the town hall and into the police station. He was surprised at how many officers were present. Some were from Scotland. Vann sat the doctor down and told him he thought he might give some useful help in finding his missing wife and maid. He proposed to ask the doctor to account for his movements between 14–30 September. To this Ruxton replied that he would be only too pleased. When Vann formally cautioned him, Ruxton – to the astonishment of the officers – reached into his jacket pocket and produced a sheaf of papers headed 'My Movements', on which he had written a kind of itinerary of events. Vann took it and scanned the pages. It would not do, he thought. It would not do at all. 'Dr Ruxton,' said Vann quietly. 'We are going to need a proper statement from you.'

It was a very long night. But Vann and the other officers were in no hurry. They began by asking Ruxton about the events of Saturday 14 September, the night his wife visited the Blackpool illuminations with her sisters. Ruxton explained that he and Belle were using separate bedrooms ('Last intercourse was Christmas 1934,' said Ruxton ruefully). 'I had gone to my room and was in the room when Mrs Ruxton came back from the garage. I heard her come up the stairs and go to her room. As she passed she said, "Goodnight Pa."' For a provincial doctor, Ruxton was a fair romancer. This is his version of events on the Sunday morning, when in reality he had spent the night mutilating the bodies of two women:

'She [Belle] got [up] about a little after 6 o'clock. She knocked on my door and entered. She came to the bed and in a coquettish manner said "Want to go anywhere, Pa?" There was no definite arrangement as to place but we would go from the house.

'She said "Get up, Pa" and she seemed very anxious to get me out of the house.

'I got up and it would be about six or quarter past. I tell you why I got up and dressed slowly and went for the car. When I was about to go for the car she said that I should go to Mrs Oxley, asking her not to come today. Mrs Oxley comes on Sunday at about 8 A.M. and on weekdays at 7 A.M. She comes every day.

'When I came back with my car in Dalton Square, I purposely looked at the clock, and it was just gone quarter past seven. When I got back to the house, Mrs Ruxton was in the room previous to the kitchen, and Mary was in the kitchen.

'I again went to my bedroom for no special reason, and I reclined on my couch and I went there to await my coffee and toast. I waited in vain for about three quarters of an hour and went to the children's room where Mrs Ruxton also sleeps. She was dressing. The children were asleep. I offered to help with getting the children ready and she said there was no hurry, just to put me off. I went to the bathroom. I had my grey suit on and this suit I afterwards got cleaned ... I took off my coat and waistcoat and I sat on the lavatory. I was sitting and thinking. When I was there, Isabel comes into the bathroom to powder and make up. The lavatory is in the bathroom. She was making up and talking to me as she had to look in the mirror.

'The first mean action now. "Do you mind if I go to Edinburgh today instead of tomorrow?" I said, "Have you made up your mind?" because she had made me get up, get the car and lose my sleep. Anyone would get sarcastic with her ... I said, "You can do what you like, you are not running away with my car again," as the car was then outside the house. I went to the bedroom, took off my shoes and I took my coat and waistcoat from the bathroom and carried them in my hand. I put the suit down. I took my trousers off and vest and reput my pyjama trousers on. My shirt was still on and I lay on the bed. I went again to the bathroom to make water. They were then ready to go and while I was in there she said, "I am taking Mary with me." I was rather glad because she couldn't abscond having Mary with her. She knocked and said, "Toodleoo Pa. There is a cup of tea on the hall

table." That was the only breakfast I got that morning. I heard
them go out and the catch of the door fall.'[4]

The statement ran to more than a dozen pages. Captain
Vann wrote in longhand at Ruxton's (often imperfect)
dictation, passing the statement sheet by sheet to his typist
next door. It was nearly four in the morning when the job
was done. Ruxton read the statement and spent over an
hour laboriously making handwritten corrections. Then he
signed it. Vann and the other officers held an on-the-spot
conference and agreed that there were sufficient grounds
for charging Ruxton and arresting him there and then.
Dawn was just beginning to break at twenty past seven
when Vann charged Dr Buck Ruxton with murdering Mary
Rogerson. 'Most emphatically not,' was Ruxton's reply.
'Of course not, the furthest thing from my mind. What
motive? And why?'

By the time Buck Ruxton's trial opened at Manchester
Assizes the following March, the police had spent many
long hours pursuing answers to these questions. But their
chief concern was to prove that the bodies found in the
ravine near Moffat were in fact those of Ruxton's wife and
nursemaid. And on this crucial point the police sought
expert help. They brought in a top Scottish anatomist,
Professor James Brash, and Professor John Glaister, Regius
Professor of Forensic Medicine at Glasgow University.
Their brief was unprecedented in medico-legal history:
piece these remains together and prove conclusively that
they are those of Isabella Ruxton and Mary Rogerson.

Two heads had been found, but the killer had taken care
to mutilate all recognizable or identifiable features. For
example, Mary Rogerson had a slight cast in one eye: her
eyes had been removed. Mrs Ruxton had a noticeably large
nose: the nose had been cut off. So had the lips and ears
and, as with Mary, the eyes had been taken out. The tip of

Belle's tongue had been sliced off. In life she had worn a denture and her teeth protruded: whoever murdered her had extracted most of her teeth after death. And although Mrs Ruxton had been scalped, enough traces of hair remained to reveal its colour: light to medium brown.

But Professor Brash's greatest triumph was to show to an astonished court life-size photographs of the heads of the women when alive and photographs of the skulls found at Moffat. Superimposed one over the other, they matched exactly. And if further proof were needed, Professor Brash showed that one of Isabella Ruxton's tiaras fitted perfectly over her skull.

The trial was a marathon. It lasted eleven days. There were more than a hundred witnesses for the prosecution, but only one for the defence: Dr Buck Ruxton himself. Some two hundred exhibits were carried in and out of the court, including a scale model of 2 Dalton Square complete with furnishings and Ruxton's brass nameplate. Each juror was issued with an album of 130 photographs of the various remains found in Scotland. Mrs Hampshire fainted in the witness box and had to be carried out for some fresh air. 'She'll be all right,' Ruxton exclaimed from the dock.

The Crown's case, in essence, was that the murder of Isabella Ruxton had been witnessed by the unfortunate Mary Rogerson. She too had been murdered, hit over the head (her skull had been fractured) and probably finished off with a knife, judging by the copious amount of blood found on the stairs. In his opening speech for the prosecution, Mr J. C. Jackson KC told the jury how Isabella Ruxton had gone to Blackpool for the evening and had returned late to Dalton Square. 'Remember the prisoner's violent temper and jealousy!' he said. 'What do you think was in his mind when she came home?' he added darkly.

Ruxton's defence lawyer, Norman Birkett KC, knew he had a formidable task. He pinned his hopes on courtroom strategy, and advised Ruxton against calling any other witnesses in his defence. This move entitled Birkett to the last word to the jury before the judge summed up and asked for a verdict. 'Any other course,' Birkett wrote, 'would be absolutely fatal.' Ruxton agreed. 'I wish to give evidence on my own behalf and I also note that it is not in the interest of defence that further evidence should be called.' Accordingly on the ninth day of the trial, with the Crown case complete, Birkett stood facing Mr Justice Singleton and said quietly: 'My lord, I call the prisoner.'

Birkett wasted no time. 'I want to put the question plainly and directly,' he said, fixing Ruxton in the eye. 'It is suggested by the Crown that on the morning of Sunday after your wife had come back you killed her?'

Ruxton at once burst into tears. 'It is a deliberate, fantastic story,' he wept. 'You might just as well say the sun was rising in the west and setting in the east!'

Birkett pressed on. 'It is suggested that upon that morning you killed Mary Rogerson?'

'It is absolute bunkum with a capital B, if I may say so,' sobbed Ruxton. 'Why should I kill my poor Mary?' Ruxton poured out his story, his tale of how, having suggested a family day out, Belle had changed her mind and decided to go to Edinburgh instead. 'I couldn't help getting annoyed,' said Ruxton, 'because I was asked to get up and dress . . . I was annoyed at her making a monkey out of me by making me get up early and changing her mind at the last moment.' At any rate, said Ruxton, he agreed that she could go, but without the car. Belle had decided to take Mary with her, and the doctor had seen them leave the house together between 9.15 and 9.30, leaving him with the children. He had searched for something for their breakfast, and found a tin of peaches. He tried to open it but the blade of the tin opener was bent and he cut his hand trying to bang the blade in. On his way up three flights of stairs to the bathroom, the cut bled profusely.

His other explanations were no less disingenuous. He blamed other bloodstains on the carpets on Belle's miscarriage some time previously, and claimed he often bought petrol in tins to burn household rubbish in the back yard. As for the suit he gave to Mrs Hampshire, he denied ever telling her to cut off the name tab and burn it.

'So far as Mrs Ruxton is concerned,' said Birkett, 'did you do any violence of any kind to her on the morning of Sunday, September 15?'

'Never, never, sir,' blurted Ruxton.

'If she was strangled, had you any part or lot in it?'

'Sir, I have never done it.'

'So far as Mary Rogerson is concerned, did you do any violence to her?'

'Never. Let alone doing it, I never thought of it. She has always been a dear child to my heart.'

'If Mary Rogerson is dead, had you any part in bringing about her death?'

'Certainly not. A most ridiculous thing to suggest.'

'Apart from what you have just told us about their departure on the morning of Sunday, 15 September, do you know anything else about their disappearance?'

'No,' said Ruxton, 'I do not.'

During his examination-in-chief Ruxton had, for the most part, remained comparatively calm. Certainly, his composure up to this point was in marked contrast to his hysterical outburst at one of the remand hearings at the police court, when Ruxton's wild-eyed ravings ('It is one damned thing after another! Is this court crazy? That damned man has wrecked my happy life! That damned rascal! Damn and blast the man! My blood is boiling now!') had caused the magistrates to retire for five minutes while the prisoner calmed down. Old hands on both sides agreed that during Birkett's questioning Ruxton had made a good showing; moreover, he had stood up well to the early part of Mr Jackson's cross-examination on behalf of the Crown. But when this cross-examination resumed on the tenth morning of the trial Ruxton seemed a changed man. His blustering self-confidence had deserted him. His old excitability had returned, and his replies to Mr Jackson were in turn hesitant, testy, incoherent and ambiguous. Birkett stole a baleful glance at the jury. Already he feared the worst.

Ruxton got himself into a terrible tangle during Jackson's questioning over the bloodstained suit he gave to Mrs Hampshire. The doctor agreed that there were 'two or three years'' accumulation of blood on the jacket, explaining that he always wore it for messy jobs. 'It was always put on in anticipation of a confinement or some such work,' said Ruxton.

Mr Jackson peered at his notes, then at Ruxton. 'Did you hear Professor Glaister say that no respectable doctor would ever wear a suit in that condition?'

At this, Ruxton lost his temper altogether. 'Out of two hundred and thirty cases of confinements in Lancaster, Dr Ruxton has never written a death certificate,' he raged.

'You would not agree with Professor Glaister when he said that suit would be a potential source of infection?'

'May I say one word?' said Ruxton, angrily. But before he could go on, the judge leaned forward and interrupted him. 'Just listen to the question,' he told Ruxton firmly.

But Ruxton would not listen. He turned to the judge. 'Has my learned friend read the life of Jonathan Hunter, the great surgeon?'

The judge ignored the question. 'Just attend to me for a minute,' he snapped.

Again, Ruxton ploughed on. 'It's a disgrace,' he shouted. 'It's a reflection on my professional capabilities.'

Mr Justice Singleton had just about had enough of Dr Ruxton. 'It will be better for you and for every one in this court if you will listen to the question,' he said, eyeing Ruxton severely. The doctor, who had pitched forward in the witness box during this outburst, now shrank back.

'Forgive me,' he muttered. 'I am sorry. I humbly beg your pardon. Can't you see how I am feeling? Everybody is cornering me, and trying to get me into a corner.'

Birkett rose at this point. 'Will you remember this?' he said quietly to Ruxton. 'I am watching the case for you and I will deal with all these matters.'

'I am grateful to you,' replied Ruxton, calmer now.

Birkett sat down, and Mr Jackson continued his cross-examination, carefully prying Ruxton's story apart little by little. The final question was perhaps the deadliest of all. Mr Jackson pointed to a section of bedroom sheeting displayed among the exhibits in the well of the court. 'If that is the sheet from your wife's bed,' he asked, 'can you explain how it got round those bodies at Moffat?'

Ruxton, of course, could not explain. 'How could it be, sir?' was his lame reply.

Birkett, in his re-examination, could only recapitulate on Ruxton's declaration of innocence. 'Did you at any time do any act of violence at all to Mrs Ruxton?' he asked.

'No,' said Ruxton. 'God is my judge.'

'Did you make any journeys to dispose of any remains?'

'No sir, I say as God is the judge above.'

The jury took just over an hour to bring in a verdict of guilty. 'Have you anything to say why sentence of death should not be passed according to law?' asked the judge. Ruxton raised his right hand, palm forwards, in a weird salute. His words were mumbled and garbled: 'Subject to the point that I be allowed to appeal . . . in the administration of justice. I submit that to your lordship and the jury. I want to thank everybody for the patience and fairness of my trial. I have never attempted to pass any special restrictions. I should like to hear whatever his lordship has to say about it.'

The judge, however, had only one thing left to say, and sentenced Ruxton to death. As his words trailed away, Ruxton again raised his hand and saluted the judge. Then he bowed slightly and walked quickly out of the dock looking strangely unmoved.

Six weeks later, his appeal was dismissed, and Ruxton's execution date was set. In Lancaster, however, many people remained unconvinced that Ruxton's guilt had been proved, and six thousand townspeople signed a petition calling for a reprieve. But the Home Secretary refused to intervene, and the eve of execution found Ruxton in the condemned cell at Strangeways Prison, Manchester, resigned to his fate.

'Thanks awfully, old man, for all you have done,' he wrote to Birkett that evening:

Please accept a trivial token of gratitude I have left you in my will. I am sure your wife will be delighted with it.[5]

May I beg a favour of you? If there should be any litigation re my estate, will you kindly give your services as a favour to a dying man?

I am leaving three bonnie little mites behind.

If you can, please be good to them. They are intelligent and good looking.

May you reach the highest pinnacle of the Legal Pedestal.

I'll bless you from above. Try your best to get in touch with Mr Gardner now and again and do your best for my children.

God bless you and yours,

Yours very sincerely,

BUCK RUXTON[6]

Ruxton also wrote that evening to Captain Henry Vann, chief constable of Lancaster:

May I make a dying request? Oh please do be good to my children. Mr Gardner, my solicitor, is their trustee. You will not fail me, will you? These children have never known a mother's love, and they have lost a father's care . . . You have children of your own. In your lifetime please make a practice of enquiring after my children and seeing to their welfare at least once every six months. It is not asking too much, is it?

Promise me, a dying man, you will be good enough to take an interest in the wellbeing of my three children. Be a friend to them, dear Vann, I implore you, I beseech thee. I will bless you and yours from above if simply you be good to my children.

I don't bear the slightest spite against you. Shake hands. Remember me to all . . .

Yours,

BUCK RUXTON'

In the absence of any reported confession on the scaffold the following morning, these might well have been Ruxton's last recorded words. But his execution on Tuesday 12 May 1936, was followed five days later by a sensational confession, published in the *News of the World*. It seems that the day after his arrest, Ruxton had been visited in his cell at Lancaster by a *News of the World* reporter. Ruxton had handed him a sealed envelope. 'Take great care of this,' he said. 'They have charged me with murder, and I, in turn, charge you to place this envelope in safety and security. On no account must it be opened until my death, if to die I am. If I am acquitted – and I think I must be acquitted – you will give it back to me.'

Towards the end of his trial, Ruxton saw the reporter again. He repeated his instructions, adding that in the event of his death, the envelope was to be handed unopened to the editor. Accordingly, on the day Ruxton was hanged, the envelope was opened. Inside was a single slip of paper on which Ruxton had scrawled a five-line note:

Lancaster
14.10.35

I killed Mrs Ruxton in a fit of temper because I thought she had been with a man. I was mad at the time. Mary Rogerson was present at the time. I had to kill her.

B. Ruxton

This spectacular scoop for the *News of the World* was unique. No one could recall another case of a signed confession being entrusted to a newspaper by a doomed man.

The legacy of this, one of the grisliest, most horrible murder cases in British legal history, is briefly told. Captain Vann fulfilled Ruxton's dying wish that he should see to the welfare of the three children. For some years after the case they were placed in the care of Lancashire County Council. Evidently, all of them made good, and as far as I am aware, all are still living. One of the daughters, Diana, qualified as a doctor and is still working in an English hospital as a pathologist.[8]

Bobby Edmondson left Lancaster after the trial, hounded out by the gossips, although his reputation had been completely vindicated by the trial judge. He eventually set up his own legal practice in London, and now lives in prosperous retirement in the south of England.

The contents of Ruxton's house, 2 Dalton Square, were sold off, and the house itself remained empty for many years. Plans were announced to convert it into a sports centre, then a night club, but they both fell through. By the late 1970s both the house and the adjoining former cinema had become so delapidated that the town council decided to spend £18,000 on giving it a facelift. Finally, in 1982, the council's own planning department moved into the building. The shades of the little Indian doctor and his tragic victims have been replaced by high-tech offices, computers, concealed lighting, glass doors and pot plants. The original front door round which Ruxton poked his head on that fateful Sunday morning is now a fire escape.

Both the kitchen and the bedroom above it have been demolished, as if to expunge the memory of the terrible events of September 1935. The back yard, where Ruxton burned his murderous debris, remains. When it was resurfaced as part of the refurbishment programme, workmen had to tear up the original stone flags. Beneath one of these heavy stones, they found a large well, probably a relic of medieval times, measuring about a yard in diameter. The city planning officer, Charles Wilson, led me to the rim of the well. We threw handfuls of gravel and listened for the splash. 'It's about twenty feet to the water,' he said, 'and there's about twelve feet of water in the well. The joke nowadays is that had Ruxton known of the existence of the well in his own backyard the disappearance of his wife and maid might never have been solved.'⁹

Traffic noise fills Dalton Square. Old men sit on benches in the public gardens that surround the monument to Queen Victoria and gaze across at the freshly sandblasted façade of Ruxton's old house.

Why did he do it?

'He had the stresses of a husband whose wife was playing around,' said Arthur Thompson. 'He was alone in a foreign country. All their friends were recruited by Belle, and he resented that, although being a great stickler for protocol, he recognized that it was his duty to entertain people. But the fact was that he was entertaining people who were only there because of Belle, and who were laughing at him behind his back. That's where the resentment came in.'⁹

The man who arrested Ruxton, police chief Henry Vann, made his name on the strength of the case. Ambitious and dynamic, he eventually became chief constable of Maidstone. He lives alone in a private hotel on the south coast. He is an old man now, and thinks of the case 'very seldom'.

A few miles from Lancaster, at the headquarters of Lancashire Police near Preston, visitors to the mounted branch stables are startled by a macabre relic of the Ruxton case. The bath, which was ripped out in the course of the investigation, has been cleaned and preserved, and now stands in a corner of the stable yard where it serves as a horse trough. Above the bath is small metal plaque. The inscription reads:

This bath was used by Dr Buck Ruxton when mutilating the bodies of his wife and his maid on an unknown date between the 14th and 29th September 1935 at 2 Dalton Square, Lancaster. Ruxton was hanged for these murders on 12th May 1936 at Strangeways Prison, Manchester.

3

The Homestead, 339 Devonshire Road, Blackpool

In the early spring of 1953 Britain was a more optimistic place than it had been for a generation. The clouds of war had lifted, and now the long, grinding years of austerity, rationing and shortages were rolling away too. As if stepping from shadow into sunlight the nation stood on the threshold of the New Elizabethan age, and looked forward with keen anticipation to the coronation of the young Queen Elizabeth II in June. In the Lancashire seaside resort of Blackpool, hoteliers and landladies were preparing for Easter and a bumper summer season. The coronation would be good for business. The jobs columns of the local newspapers were jammed with vacancies for seasonal workers, cleaners, waitresses, cooks and chamber-maids for the hotels and boarding houses; sugar-boilers, wrappers and rollers for the scores of rock stalls that lined the resort's famous Golden Mile. On Tuesday 10 March, this innocent-sounding advertisement appeared in the Situations Vacant column of the *West Lancashire Evening Gazette*:

HOUSEKEEPER/COMPANION for one lady, small, modern and attractive home in Norbreck. Refs. essential. Car driver an advantage. Age 35 to 50.

The advertisement had been placed by Mrs Sarah Ann Ricketts, a cantankerous and awkward old woman of seventy-nine, who lived alone in her neat, double-fronted bungalow in Norbreck, a nobby district on Blackpool's North Shore. The Homestead in Devonshire Road was a genteel, ten-minute tram ride from the brawling clamour of the holiday crowds. But in Mrs Ricketts' case this was academic, for the old woman never went out, and spent most of her time in bed, swathed in shawls and combinations, listening to the wireless and swigging from bottles of stout which were delivered every week. Partially paralysed, she could scarcely walk and hadn't cooked herself a meal for years, surviving on a diet of breakfast cereals and tinned fruit. The house was small, with only two bedrooms, but even so it had become too much for the old woman to manage single-handedly, and though fiercely independent by nature, Mrs Ricketts had been persuaded by her daughter that she needed help with the cooking and cleaning. The advertisement, with its promise of comfortable accommodation in a salubrious district, attracted no fewer than fifty applicants. With conspicuous haste (the swiftness of events is a feature of the entire case), old Mrs Ricketts made her choice with scarcely a second thought, and the following day gave the job to Mrs Louisa Merrifield, a dumpy, boot-faced woman of forty-six, and her unlikely third husband, Alfred, a white-haired simpleton of seventy. The Merrifields moved themselves and their belongings into The Homestead the very next day.

We do not know what commended Louisa Merrifield to old Mrs Ricketts, since it is difficult to point to a single redeeming feature in either. It may have been their common experience of having buried two previous husbands. Mrs Ricketts' first husband, a plumber, had put his head in the gas oven during the war; husband number two, William Ricketts, a retired farmer, also committed suicide in the kitchen at The Homestead by turning on the gas and waiting for death seated in a deckchair. Mrs Merrifield, the daughter of a Wigan collier, had also been widowed twice. Her first husband had died of tuberculosis; three months later she married a man of eighty who dropped dead with a heart attack after only eight weeks. But where Mrs Ricketts had settled for the melancholy dignity of widowhood, her new housekeeper had hastened to the altar a third time, on this occasion with old Alfred Merrifield, a retired maker of sanitary ware, who followed the ceremony with difficulty through a large and inefficient electric hearing aid. Their arrival at the bungalow signalled a welcome change of fortune for the Merrifields. Since their marriage in 1950 the couple had lived frugally on Alfred's state pension, with his wife taking the odd cooking and nursing job to supplement their income. Times were hard. So much so that the day before spotting Mrs Ricketts' advertisement Mrs Merrifield had been forced to pawn Alfred's light-grey suit at a shop in Blackpool. But now, with a new job and a new and comfortable place in which to live, the future offered fresh hope and financial security. Two days after moving in with Mrs Ricketts, Mrs Merrifield was able to redeem the suit on the strength of a cash advance on her wages.

The Merrifields lost no time in ingratiating themselves with their elderly employer. The bungalow was washed and swept from top to bottom, and the kitchen cupboards cleaned and stocked. Alfred Merrifield tidied up the garden, while his wife busied herself in the kitchen preparing hot, nourishing meals to serve to the bedridden Mrs Ricketts on a tray. The Merrifields would invariably eat with the old woman as she lay propped up in the day bed in the living room, wisps of white hair falling over the shoulders of her red bed jacket. The couple seemed to enjoy her company, sharing with her the gossip from the local shops, and enquiring solicitously about her state of health. On fine afternoons the Merrifields got Mrs Ricketts dressed and pushed her in her wheelchair down to the promenade for an airing. Within a matter of days Mrs

Ricketts had taken the Merrifields entirely into her confidence, and had told Mrs Merrifield to take charge of her money for household expenses, scrawling notes to the bank giving Mrs Merrifield authority to cash her cheques. In Louisa Merrifield Mrs Ricketts felt she had found more than a caring, efficient housekeeper. She felt she had found a trusted friend and confidante, someone whom she now wished to reward with a promise of security after her death. The reality, however, was cruelly different.

For in Mrs Ricketts, Louisa Merrifield had found a vulnerable victim for a wicked and ultimately deadly deception. Lacking the skill and patience to nurse the old woman properly, Mrs Merrifield quickly grew tired of her demanding and difficult patient who ruled her life day and night. Like many elderly and eccentric invalids, Mrs Ricketts seemed cranky and wilful. She began turning away her food, calling instead for a pot of blackcurrant jam from the chest beneath her day bed which she would mix with glycerine and eat with a spoon. This would invariably be accompanied by a tot of rum. Although the Merrifields kept a coal fire burning in the room Mrs Ricketts complained constantly of being cold, and demanded extra layers of blankets. At night, she insisted on a final covering of newspapers, saying they kept her warm. Settling the old woman down at night was a particular trial. Having spent a good half-hour making her comfortable Mrs Merrifield would retire to her own room, only to hear the old woman getting out of bed to poke the fire. This was not what Mrs Merrifield had bargained for. It was bad enough having to cope with a deaf and daft elderly husband. On top of that, the exasperating habits of a bedridden old crone were just too much to handle. Mrs Merrifield determined that something drastic must be done.

Less than two weeks after moving in at The Homestead, Mrs Merrifield called at the offices of a Blackpool solicitor,

Mr William Darbyshire, and instructed him to draw up a new will for Mrs Ricketts, naming herself as sole beneficiary. With a resigned shrug, Mr Darbyshire did as he was asked. He knew that the old woman was not on friendly terms with her two daughters and cared little for her small circle of friends. He had also heard that Mrs Ricketts had at various times promised her money to different tradespeople, so her apparent decision to will her estate to her housekeeper seemed, on the face of it, a more acceptable one. Accordingly, a week later Mr Darbyshire and his clerk called on Mrs Ricketts at her bungalow where the new will was duly signed and witnessed. There was just one alteration: Mr Merrifield was named joint beneficiary with his wife. 'I'm looking after them that are looking after me,' Mrs Ricketts explained to a sceptical doctor who called a few days later. The doctor asked if she knew what she was doing. 'Definitely,' the old woman replied.

Four days later, Mrs Ricketts was dead. Killed by rat poison.

There was already plenty of news to go round, and it was perhaps just as well that the Blackpool police sat on the story for four full days, leaving room in the newspapers for other matters of moment. There was Chancellor R. A. Butler's budget (Mrs Ricketts died on Budget Day, Tuesday 14 April), the launching on Clydebank of the Royal Yacht *Britannia* by the Queen, and the appearance at Clerkenwell magistrates' court of one John Reginald Halliday Christie, on a charge of murdering his wife and three other women at 10 Rillington Place, Notting Hill. As details of all these events were bruited the length and breadth of Britain a post-mortem examination on a silent mortuary slab in Blackpool revealed that Mrs Sarah Ann Ricketts had swallowed a fatal dose of yellow phosphorus mixed with bran, of a type used in a brand of rat poison called Rodine. The bewildered doctor who had queried the old lady's new will only days before told police that Mrs Ricketts had been perfectly well. Equally baffling, he added, was the reaction of Mr and Mrs Merrifield. Neither had seemed in the least concerned about their employer's sudden and unexpected death. A glance at Mrs Ricketts' will convinced the police that she had been deliberately murdered by her own beneficiaries.

Local journalists finally got wind that a major sensation was in the offing, and broke the story over the weekend. They reported that the Blackpool borough police (ill-equipped in those pre-reorganization days to handle a full-scale murder investigation) had called in officers from Scotland Yard, led by Detective Superintendent Colin McDougall, the man who had succeeded the legendary Fabian in 1949. But exactly what the men from the Yard were investigating, and where and why, was not immediately clear. The story spoke of a suspected poisoning in the Norbreck district, but did not even name the victim. The local chief constable, doubtless under instructions from London, was singularly uncommunicative. 'I have nothing to tell you,' he growled at reporters, 'and I will have nothing to tell you later today.' Only when the inquest on Mrs Ricketts was formally opened and adjourned the following Monday did the press coverage begin in earnest. Now armed with an address, journalists descended on the small, double-fronted bungalow in Devonshire Road to interview its new owners.

They discovered that Mrs Louisa Merrifield, the dumpy, bespectacled housekeeper, was more than willing to talk. 'Murder?' she laughed. 'Impossible. How could it happen? I admit it's strange, but all this fuss is ridiculous.'

Next day, the police arrived with a mine detector and started combing the garden. Others using shovels, forks and rakes dug and probed among the daffodils. Mrs Merrifield offered them tea. The detectives declined. Asked by reporters what she thought they were looking for, she roared with laughter. 'Not the slightest idea,' she replied, 'unless it's old Mrs Ricketts' money.' In fact the police were searching for a tin of rat poison which they thought might have been buried in the garden. They found nothing. In a display of nonchalant defiance Mrs Merrifield left them to their digging and went out shopping.

'I don't know what the hell's going on, or why they're bothering me,' she told one journalist as he sipped nervously on a cup of tea brewed by Mrs Merrifield. 'Everyone's saying Mrs Ricketts was an old angel. But that's not true. She was a difficult and eccentric old so-and-so. And what a drinker! She had cases of rum and stout delivered regularly. A proper old toper.'

Mrs Merrifield, in her conversations with both police and press, made no secret of the fact that she cared little for her ageing husband. Her face fixed in a taut expressionless mask of contempt, she spoke freely of the old man's failings. She even accused him of having been 'a damn sight too friendly' with Mrs Ricketts. 'I used to be suspicious when he spent a long time massaging her leg and making her comfortable in bed,' she said to one reporter, as Alfred sat smiling vacantly a few feet away fumbling with his deaf-aid. From time to time he tried to join in the conversation but Mrs Merrifield would turn on him and order him to be quiet. 'I'm sorry I ever teamed up with him,' she muttered as he left the room. 'It was only because he kept calling on me and pestering me to marry him. I'm fed up with it.' She glared at the retreating figure shuffling towards the kitchen. 'How would you like to live in the same house as a bore like him?' she said. 'I don't know how I stand it. I've had three husbands and I've had to work for them all.'

As she held court in the living room at The Homestead, with husband Alfred loping back and forth from the kitchen with trays of tea for the thirsty reporters, Mrs Merrifield, her face and neck flushed with excitement, made blunt and pungent comments on the police investigation. 'The buggers can come as often as they like,' she exclaimed. 'They've searched the place high and low for whatever it is they're looking for. Why should I worry? I've nothing to fear from anyone, Scotland Yard and all.' She spoke without sorrow about the death of Mrs Ricketts. 'She was all right when I first came here,' she said, 'but towards the end the blasted old cat made my life hell. Whatever I did for her she wasn't satisfied. She used to have me getting up to her at all hours of the night.'

Detective Superintendent McDougall, meanwhile, had also sought an interview with Mrs Merrifield. In a lengthy statement she described how she and her husband had moved into The Homestead to find Mrs Ricketts ill and unable to cope alone. The Merrifields had found no food in the house, only bottles of stout and spirits. Mrs Ricketts had asked Mrs Merrifield to take over everything, even the money to run the house. Mrs Merrifield admitted speaking sharply to the old woman about her eating habits, and had suggested spending more money on food than drink. In April the Merrifields had witnessed a decline in Mrs Ricketts' health. She was keeping them awake at night, moaning and complaining of stomach pains. It was as a result of this that Mrs Merrifield had called in Mrs Ricketts' doctor, Dr Burton Yule. In fact, the men from Scotland Yard learned that in the week leading up to Mrs Ricketts' sudden death, Mrs Merrifield had visited no fewer than three different doctors. It was true that she had contacted Dr Yule, but there had been no mention of stomach pains. Mrs Merrifield had asked the doctor merely to confirm that when the old woman had changed her will she had been mentally sound. This he had done, and found her perfectly *compos mentis*. Four days later Mrs Merrifield appeared at the surgery of Dr Albert Wood with the news that Mrs Ricketts was seriously ill. Dr Wood hurried round to the bungalow and found the old woman sitting up in bed, suffering from nothing more than a mild attack of bronchitis. But the following day Mrs Merrifield left a message for Dr Ernest Page, Dr Wood's partner, asking him to call urgently at Devonshire Road. When he arrived at midday he found Alfred Merrifield tucking into his lunch at a table which had been pushed up against Mrs Ricketts' day bed. Dr Page took one look at Mrs Ricketts and saw that she was dying. There was nothing he could do for her. Dr Page sent for Dr Yule, who arrived at ten to two to find Mrs Ricketts dead.

Other witnesses came forward to shed more light on this strange sequence of events. The most important, from the police point of view, was a white-haired old lady called Mrs Elizabeth Barrowclough. She told a puzzling story. On the afternoon before Mrs Ricketts died, Mrs Barrowclough had been standing in a bus queue when Mrs Merrifield – a complete stranger – had struck up a conversation. Mrs Barrowclough listened politely, but with growing incredulity. Mrs Merrifield said she was looking after a very sick old woman. 'She has left me a bungalow between me and my husband,' Mrs Merrifield continued. She had been so worried about her patient's condition that she had been down to the town to consult her solicitor. She had returned to find her own husband in bed with the ailing woman. That, snorted Mrs Merrifield, had got her vexed. 'I know what I will do for that,' she snapped. 'If he does it again I'll poison the old bitch and him as well.'

The post-mortem on Mrs Ricketts had shown clearly that she had died from swallowing phosphorus and bran of a type used in a brand of rat poison called Rodine. The detectives needed to show that Mrs Merrifield or her barmy husband, or both, had recently purchased Rodine, and a team of officers spent many weary hours trudging the streets of Blackpool and neighbouring towns making inquiries at chemists' shops where the poison was sold (quite openly and legally) over the counter. These inquiries drew a blank, and it was only as a result of newspaper publicity that the source of the Rodine was traced to a chemist's shop in Manchester, fifty miles from Blackpool. The shop was owned by Henry Hague, who remembered an ill-matched couple asking for a tin of Rodine some time in the middle of March. (Their visit had stuck in his mind because the white-haired man with the deaf-aid had spoken to him about his ulcerated leg.)

On Thursday 30 April a small convoy of black, official-looking cars drew up outside The Homestead. Detective Superintendent McDougall and his team of officers marched up the path with scarcely a glance for the reporters who had been posted at the garden gate awaiting the arrest of the Merrifields. A few moments later Mrs Louisa Merrifield came out of the bungalow wearing a raincoat and hat. With her were her husband and her solicitor. At the police station Mrs Merrifield was formally charged with the murder of Mrs Ricketts. She replied: 'Not guilty'. The following morning she made a brief appearance at the magistrates' court to be formally remanded in custody. As she was led from the dock her husband, who had been sitting in the front row of the public gallery, sprang to his feet and dashed forward, shouting, 'Keep your chin up, Louie!'

News of Mrs Merrifield's arrest had caused the inevitable sensation in Blackpool, and a crowd of more than a hundred, mainly women, had gathered outside the court. The entire town was in a state of hyper-tense anticipation, both at the outcome of Mrs Merrifield's inevitable trial and at the result of the Cup Final to be played at Wembley the following day between Blackpool and Bolton Wanderers.

(Blackpool, whose team included the legendary Stanley Matthews, won 4–3.) The public clamour reached even greater heights when, two weeks later, Alfred Merrifield too was arrested. He was held while visiting his wife in the police cells, and charged with murder. His appearance in court the following morning had an unusual and melancholy sequel. The prosecution announced that it needed to call evidence from Dr Albert Wood, but that the doctor was too ill to attend court. So the magistrates adjourned the hearing, and reconvened it an hour later in a small waiting room next to Dr Wood's consulting room, complete with the Merrifields, police, lawyers and court officials. The hearing lasted less than an hour. The defendants sat quietly on chairs near the window, as though waiting for an appointment. Dr Wood shuffled in, wearing his red leather carpet slippers, grey suit and a hand-knitted jersey. He gave his evidence in a very low whisper, and it was clear that he was very ill indeed. In the event, Dr Wood died before the case came to trial.

The committal hearing against the Merrifields took place in Blackpool at the end of May. Even *The Times*, at the height of pre-coronation fever, devoted a full column to the case every day. After three days of detailed evidence on behalf of the prosecution the Merrifields were sent for trial at Manchester Assizes. For the moment, the odd couple dropped from public view, and national attention focused on the pageantry at Westminster Abbey as the new Queen was crowned amid scenes of jubilation and rejoicing. By the time the Merrifield trial opened in late July, however, the public was ready for it, a savoury counterpoint, as it were, to the confection of a coronation. Their appetite had been keenly whetted by the news that, such was the importance of the case, the Attorney-General himself, Sir Lionel Heald QC, would lead for the Crown. The judge would be Mr Justice Glyn Jones, only recently promoted, who had never tried a capital case before. He was, however, a qualified chemist.

Hair neatly waved, and wearing a light-blue gaberdine coat over her favourite woollen dress, Mrs Louisa Merrifield stared blankly from the dock at Manchester Assizes as the Attorney-General rose stiffly to make his opening speech. By contrast, Alfred Merrifield, sitting alongside his wife wearing his (only) brown suit, stiff white collar, striped shirt and red tie, seemed unconcerned, and smiled and waved towards the reporters jammed into the press benches. Sir Lionel's speech lasted most of the morning. He told the jury of the sudden demise of Mrs Ricketts, and the discovery in her body of yellow phosphorus and bran, both ingredients of Rodine rat poison. A one-ounce tin of Rodine, he explained, cost a shilling (5p) and contained ten grains of yellow phosphorus, enough to kill five people if used skilfully.

Sir Lionel told the jury how the Merrifields had gone to live with Mrs Ricketts, and how she had drawn up a fresh will in their favour. However, the day before she died, the old lady had shown signs of going back on the Merrifields, because there had been some disagreement between them, which had been overheard by a tradesman calling at the door. Mrs Ricketts had been upset, and had told the Merrifields they would have to go. So, said the Attorney-General, the Merrifields had an obvious interest in the old lady's death, and no reason to wish her to live any longer than necessary. There was an unrivalled opportunity for the Merrifields to make away with Mrs Ricketts if they wanted to do so. It was, he added, an exclusive opportunity, because they were alone in the bungalow with her.

A van driver for a firm of wine merchants, George Forjan, said he used to call on Mrs Ricketts every Monday with her regular order of a bottle of rum. Once a month he also delivered a dozen bottles of Guinness. On the day before she died he made his regular call and found Mrs Ricketts scrabbling round for money to pay him. She had spoken darkly of the Merrifields. 'I don't know what they're doing with my money,' she had told him. 'I can't pay you.' Mr Forjan added that Mrs Ricketts had complained to him about the food being served up by the Merrifields. 'They are no good to me,' she had told him. 'They will have to go.'

The Manchester chemist and his sales assistant both identified Mr Merrifield as the man with the deaf-aid who had come into their shop in mid-March, accompanied by a woman, to buy a tin of Rodine. A police pathologist, Dr George Manning, described experiments he had made to see if it were possible to slip some Rodine powder into someone's food and drink undetected. He told the court that rum masked the garlic aroma and flavour, and that brandy masked the taste but not the smell. Blackcurrant jam, he added, masked both taste and smell.

Mrs Merrifield herself spent a mammoth nine hours in the witness box giving evidence in her own defence. She was led through her version of events by her barrister, Mr Jack di V. Nahum QC, who asked her bluntly if she had given rat poison to Mrs Ricketts. 'No, sir,' she replied.

'So far as you could observe from the actions or words of your husband, did he ever administer anything of a poisonous nature?'

'No, sir.'

Mrs Merrifield gave a lurid description of Mrs Ricketts' final few days, in which she had complained of stomach pains and a nasty taste in her mouth. The old woman had swabbed her mouth out with cotton wool soaked in glycerine. 'I asked her if she was sick,' Mrs Merrifield told the court, 'and Mrs Ricketts said "No, I'm all right. Don't bother about me. It'll be all right."' Mrs Ricketts had dosed herself with a variety of concoctions, such as cereal and jam, and jam mixed with liquid paraffin. She also, according to Mrs Merrifield, took her customary tot of rum, swigged neat from an egg cup. On the night before she died Mrs Ricketts had been up and down to the bathroom several times, crying bitterly. 'I got her into bed,' said Mrs Merrifield. 'She seemed to go a bit quieter. Next thing I heard her up again and she was in the hall on the floor. I picked her up, and got her into bed. She said she thanked both my husband and me for what we had done for her. Those were the last words she spoke.'

The entire court listened intently as the dumpy figure in the witness box described the last hours of Mrs Ricketts. 'She had apparently lost her speech at that time,' said Mrs Merrifield. 'Her teeth came out and I pushed them back and found she had about five pink cough lozenges in her mouth at once. She seemed to go quieter. She had a bottle of rum on the table, her egg cup full of brandy or rum. She had her tongue out. She could not speak. I just gave her a sip out of the egg cup which she had prepared herself the night before. She also had a small bottle of brandy on the table. I gave her nothing,' she added, 'until the time when she lost her speech.'

Mr Nahum was anxious to refute suggestions by at least two people that Mrs Merrifield had pre-empted Mrs Ricketts' death by boasting of her inheritance while the old lady was in fact still alive. Mrs Merrifield was indignant. 'I never told anyone that Mrs Ricketts had died before she died,' she snapped. What about the threatening remark to Mrs Barrowclough, the woman in the bus queue? asked Mr Nahum. 'I spoke to a woman in a bus queue,' Mrs Merrifield conceded, 'but it was not her. The woman I spoke to didn't have white hair.'

The Attorney-General rose to cross-examine, and pursued the point. Three days before Mrs Ricketts' death, Mrs Merrifield had told a Mrs Jessie Brewer that the old woman had died leaving her the bungalow. Sir Lionel peered at his notes. 'You used this language: "We are landed. We were living with an old lady and she has died leaving me a bungalow worth £4,000."' But Mrs Merrifield was unshakeable. 'I have never told anyone that Mrs Ricketts was dead before she died,' she insisted.

Sir Lionel turned to the question of the old lady's will. Mrs Merrifield said it was not true that she had wanted the bungalow from the moment she and her husband moved in to The Homestead. On the contrary, it was Mrs Ricketts herself who had been determined to bequeath it to the Merrifields. Asked if she knew that Mr Merrifield had 'got talking' to Mrs Ricketts about the will, Mrs Merrifield replied: 'No, I don't think he would.'

The Attorney-General fixed Mrs Merrifield with his sternest eye. 'Was it true that at that time you thought that Mr Merrifield was getting too friendly with the old lady?'

Mrs Merrifield dropped her gaze. 'Well, everybody has their suspicions. She was fond of him.'

'You were afraid,' said Sir Lionel, 'that Mr Merrifield might so please the old lady that she might alter her will and you would be left out altogether?'

'No,' Mrs Merrifield replied, 'not at all.'

Making his point crystal clear, Sir Lionel said icily: 'If you had poisoned both of them, you would have had the bungalow to yourself.'

But Mrs Merrifield was not being drawn. 'I never had any intention to poison anyone,' she replied.

Mrs Merrifield's evidence spread across three days. She was followed into the witness box by her husband, Alfred, still wearing his hearing aid and vacant smile. It was clear at once that Mr Merrifield's memory was as defective as his hearing. He told Mr Nahum, his counsel, that yes, he remembered going to see old Mrs Ricketts about a job but that no, he did not remember much of the conversation as most of it had been conducted by his wife. However, he did recall, in word-for-word detail, a remark he claimed Mrs Ricketts had made to him at her bedside. 'My word, Mr Merrifield,' she was supposed to have said, 'you are being good and kind to me . . . I will make it so that you will always have a home here the longest day you live.' Mr Merrifield was unable to recall the alleged trip to Manchester in March to buy rat poison with his wife. 'Definitely not, sir. I've never been in Manchester for five solid years. I've never left the precincts of Blackpool.' Had he ever seen Mr Hague, the chemist? 'Never, sir, definitely not.' Or Miss Atkinson, his assistant? Never. He had no idea where their shop was, and, what was more, he had no knowledge of Rodine. As for the suggestion that he and his wife gave Mrs Ricketts rat poison to kill her, that was 'an outrageous, false statement'.

Mr Nahum coughed politely and shuffled his papers. 'From time to time in this case,' he said, 'it has been suggested that you were guilty of some impropriety with Mrs Ricketts.'

All eyes turned to the shambling old man in the witness box.

'A more infamous statement has never been made in a court of justice,' barked Mr Merrifield, clutching his deaf-aid with indignant excitement. 'It is definitely not true, sir. Outrageous!' He began waving his arms. 'Fancy,' he shouted, 'an old woman of eighty years of age, paralysed down one side. It's definitely not true, sir. Outrageous! Look at my wife. A young woman. Fancy me getting into bed with an old woman of eighty!'

Mr Nahum sat down. He wondered what kind of a show the old man would make against the Attorney-General, who now rose to cross-examine. Sir Lionel's opening questions were vague and soft-centred. Had Mr Merrifield been fond of old Mrs Ricketts? Yes, very fond, because 'I had a good, comfortable home and nothing at all to worry about'. Why then, if he was so fond of her, had he not gone for help when Mrs Ricketts was taken ill? Mr Merrifield now played his sympathy card. 'I am a cripple,' he croaked. 'It is definite that I should have my rest.' He turned his pale, rheumy eyes towards his wife, sitting nervously in the dock. 'Not only that,' he added, 'but there was a capable lady there, my wife, to attend to her.'

Sir Lionel Heald paused for a moment and pulled the long sleeves of his gown behind his back. He looked scornfully at the pathetic old man leaning on the witness-box rail. It was time for the wily Attorney-General to pull a stunt of his own. He referred Mr Merrifield to his wife's handbag, reminding him of a remark during an interview with the police that he thought it might be dangerous. 'Now, Mr Merrifield,' he said quietly. 'What would the danger be?'

Without pausing to consider the answer Mr Merrifield replied, 'My own safety.'

The Attorney-General raised his eyebrows in mock surprise. The jurors saw this, and leaned forward. The sleeves of Sir Lionel's gown billowed behind him.

'Were you afraid it might be something like this?' exclaimed the Attorney-General, producing a tin of Rodine from behind his back. A gasp echoed through the court. Mr Merrifield quickly turned his head away.

'Don't let me look at it!' he cried. 'I've heard so much about it this last four months, I see it in my sleep!'

Sir Lionel held the tin aloft like a prize trophy. 'You have seen something like that before?' he asked sternly.

'No,' cried Alfred Merrifield, still averting his gaze, 'unless it's been in some shop or chemist's.'

The wretched Mr Merrifield was followed into the witness box by the defence's expert witness, Professor J. M. Webster, director of the West Midland Forensic Science

Laboratory. Examined by Mr Nahum, Professor Webster said that, in his opinion, Mrs Ricketts died not of phosphorus poisoning but of necrosis – fatty insufficiency – of the liver. A poor diet or lack of food could cause necrosis.

Professor Webster had a rough ride at the hands of the judge. When the professor said he accepted that phosphorus poison had been found in Mrs Ricketts' body, the judge asked him how he thought it had got there. 'I make no point about that,' the professor replied. 'I think it entered by the mouth.'

The judge looked puzzled. 'Would you suggest any form, as far as you know, in which it could have entered the body by the mouth save in the form of Rodine rat poison?'

Professor Webster looked uncomfortably at Mr Nahum, and then at the judge. 'Let me be quite frank and honest about that,' he replied. 'I think it is the most likely way in which phosphorus entered the body.' It might have been that Mrs Ricketts ingested phosphorus fifteen minutes before she died. On the other hand, it could have been as long as five hours. Assuming that Mr Merrifield was right, that he saw her at nine o'clock and that she was dying, he thought it was reasonably possible that the old woman could have administered rat poison to herself after 7 A.M. But, he added, without having seen the case, he was not in a position to express an opinion.

Mr Justice Glyn Jones sniffed loudly. 'You have not hesitated to express vigorous and, I can almost say, even dogmatic opinions on the strength of what you have seen and heard. Do you feel unable to express an opinion on whether or not it was possible for this woman to have administered rat poison to herself after seven o'clock in the morning?'

Professor Webster returned the judge's stare. 'I must not dodge the issue,' he replied. 'I don't think it impossible.'

Agreeing with the professor that an accidental dose of Rodine could be ruled out in this case, the judge had one final question for him. 'Is it the suggestion that Mrs Ricketts liked it so much that, after seven o'clock in the morning, she helped herself to more?'

From Professor Webster there was no reply.

On the ninth day of the trial Mr Nahum rose to make his closing speech for the defence. It lasted just over four hours. Turning to the jury, he said that suspicion had, not unnaturally, accumulated against the Merrifields, and that this had been engendered by Mrs Merrifield's own foolish talk. 'But in this country, people aren't convicted of murder on what they say, but on what they do,' he said. Mrs Merrifield's reported conversations before the old lady's death were nothing more than the stupid vapourings of a woman who couldn't wait to tell everybody that she had been left a lovely little bungalow, said Mr Nahum. 'If Mrs Merrifield was a murderess about to kill her victim, what would be the two subjects she would avoid most in conversation? They would be death, and death in connection with Mrs Ricketts!'

Turning now to the dock, Mr Nahum indicated Mr Merrifield, still fiddling with his hearing aid. 'A tragic simpleton,' he said, 'and no more capable of concocting or taking part in this scheme than a child.'

Mr Nahum's speech was no impassioned plea. Rather it was a low-key recital of rebuttals, underpinned by warnings of the danger in a capital case of convicting on circumstantial evidence. The prosecution, he told the jury, had failed to prove a case with the correct standard of proof. There were loopholes everywhere. For the Crown, Sir Lionel Heald was equally undynamic, reviewing the medical evidence with clarity and precision before turning to the Merrifields themselves. 'There they were,' he said, 'both in the same house, both standing to gain from the old lady's death, both thoroughly callous about her, both more concerned with what they could get out of it than with any other consideration.'

The judge's summing up on the final day of the trial lasted nearly four hours. It was a hot, sticky Friday afternoon, the last day of July. Everyone was tired and impatient for the case to end but the judge, although summing up against the Merrifields, presented a very fair review of the evidence on both sides. At one point he gave his own opinion of Mrs Merrifield ('a vulgar and stupid woman with a dirty mind') but pointed out that this should not necessarily lead to a conviction for murder. 'Use your practical common sense,' he said as he turned the case over to the jury.

The mammoth trial lasting eleven days was nearly over. All afternoon, the sun had streamed into the court; now, the last of the daylight filtered through the windows and the court lights were switched on. After the oppressive heat of the afternoon, the court was pleasantly cool. As the evening dragged on, the panelled courtroom lost something of its dignity as the spectators, tired and hungry but not daring to go for refreshments in case the jury returned, waited patiently. There was a subdued chatter. Some people munched at sandwiches they had brought in, picnic-style; one man lolled casually in the witness box leafing through an evening paper. Finally, at just after half-past nine, the court usher appeared and signalled the return of the jury. They had been out for nearly six hours. Lawyers, witnesses, reporters and onlookers settled noisily back into their places, and stood as the judge resumed his seat. Almost unnoticed, Louisa and Alfred Merrifield were led silently back into the dock from the cells below. Mrs Merrifield, pale-faced but calm, made as if to sit down, but she was checked by the restraining arm of a prison official. Her husband, his white hair slightly awry, his face flushed, looked dazed, as if he had just been awoken from a deep sleep. He adjusted his deaf-aid as the clerk called for the verdicts: the jury had found Mrs Merrifield guilty, but had been unable to agree in the case of her husband. The judge ordered his retrial and Alfred Merrifield disappeared down the steps from the dock, leaving his wife standing alone, flanked by a woman prison officer and a nurse. As she tried to shake them off, her lips moved as if to say: I am all right.

There was dead silence as the chaplain placed the black cap on the head of Mr Justice Glyn Jones. Passing the death sentence, the judge said Mrs Merrifield had been convicted 'on the plain evidence of as wicked and cruel a murder as I have ever heard tell of'. Mrs Merrifield stared steadfastly at the judge as he intoned the words that would seal her doom, glancing down only as he spoke of 'death by hanging' and the final 'may the Lord have mercy on your soul'. She was led below without uttering a word.

The split verdicts caused an immediate and unprecedented legal tangle. Mrs Merrifield's lawyers announced that she would appeal, but would she be allowed to give evidence at her husband's retrial? Even though she had been convicted of murder she remained, under criminal law, a competent witness, and could be called by her husband to give evidence in his defence. But, as her solicitor, Mr John Budd, pointed out, 'It would be a most painful decision to have to reach.' The provisional date for Mrs Merrifield's execution was set for 18 August, but the judge had ordered a second trial for Alfred Merrifield at the next Manchester Assizes, which were not scheduled to open until early October.

If Mrs Merrifield's appeal were dismissed, would the execution be postponed so that she could give evidence on her husband's behalf? Failing that, could the evidence be taken in advance?

In the event, these questions were rendered academic with the announcement, a week later, that the murder charge against Mr Merrifield had been dropped on the personal decision of the Attorney-General, Sir Lionel Heald. Sir Lionel issued a *fiat* of *nolle prosequi* (literally 'unwilling to prosecute'). The effect was to end the proceedings against Alfred Merrifield without any action being necessary by a court. No official reason was ever given for this decision. Nor was such a reason even necessary. The decision, as the *Daily Telegraph* explained, was taken entirely on the responsibility of the Attorney-General who, as principal law officer of the Crown, did not have to consult the Home Secretary in such a case. The paper pointed out, however, that because it was still within the power of the Crown to take fresh proceedings, the *nolle prosequi* did not rank as an acquittal.

Alfred Merrifield emerged blinking into the August sunlight at lunchtime the same day, clutching the key to Mrs Ricketts' bungalow. He was driven from Strangeways Gaol to Blackpool, pursued by a pack of reporters who saw him lope cheerfully up the short drive to the bungalow. Once inside, the curtains were drawn, to the disappointment of a crowd of some two hundred sightseers who had gathered on the pavement outside the house. The reporters, anxious for an interview, had to be content with a hastily scribbled statement pushed outwards through the letter box by Mr Merrifield's companion. 'Mr Merrifield says he will not make any statement to any pressmen as long as his wife's appeal is pending,' it said. 'He is very tired and wants to rest. He is going to live very quietly for a while. He will see his solicitor very soon again. He must rest and consider whether he wishes to remain in Blackpool.'

That evening Alfred Merrifield came out of the bungalow holding a handkerchief over his face and carrying a silver-headed walking stick. He was led down the drive, through the barracking reporters, and into a taxi which drove him away.

Mrs Merrifield's execution was deferred and her appeal heard in early September. Her lawyers claimed the trial judge had misdirected the jury on points of law and on the evidence. But the presiding appeal judge, Mr Justice Cassells, rejected this argument. 'The jury understood the situation with regard to the onus of proof, and the summing up properly directed the jury to the evidence, medical and otherwise, that they had to consider,' he declared. 'This court is satisfied that there was no miscarriage of justice.' Mrs Merrifield, who had listened intently to the proceedings with her podgy hands folded in her lap, now stood in the jury box supported on either side by prison wardresses. As she heard the judgement, she wrenched her arm free and stretched it high above her short, plump figure. Her fist opened and closed spasmodically. For the first time during the two-and-a-half-day hearing, her face lost its impassivity. She fixed her eyes intently on Mr Justice Cassells, and once turned her gaze swiftly over the crowded court. When the judge had ended, she allowed her arm to be pulled down. Then she was led away. A fresh date was announced for her execution, 18 September. Two days before the execution, Mrs Merrifield heard that the Home Secretary had rejected her application for a reprieve.

'I have learned from bitter experience that she is a wicked woman,' declared Alfred Merrifield in an interview with the *Daily Mail* on hearing the result of his wife's appeal. 'She has absolutely no moral sense, and she has done many things to show that she had no feeling for the old man she married.

'In the short while we were together she dragged my good name in the mud. She ill-treated me so badly and so often that my health broke down and I had to go into hospital. She showed no pity, not even ordinary womanly kindness.

'Not for all the money in the world would I live in the same town, never mind the same house, as Louie again.'[1]

Although she had three times refused to see her husband in the days following her unsuccessful appeal, the news that there would be no reprieve prompted a change of heart in Louisa Merrifield. The governor at Strangeways Gaol sent for Mr Merrifield, who arrived by car, sitting in the back with a raincoat over his head. He paid two further visits to his wife on the day before she was hanged. Her last words to him as he left were: 'Goodbye, Alfie. Look after yourself. God bless you.'

At 9 A.M the following morning Mrs Louisa Merrifield was hanged. The *Manchester Guardian* sent a reporter to cover the scenes outside Strangeways:

It is a long time since hangings were a public spectacle, but their removal behind closed doors has not killed morbid curiosity. Perhaps it has kindled it. At all events public imagination seemed to be fertilized by yesterday's dreary scene, empty as it was of all action, and even sound, if one excludes the drone of passing motors and lorries. Close on nine o'clock several hundred people had gathered outside the gates to await the hour and the moment of crescendo when the notice was posted to the effect that sentence had been duly carried out.

It was in the main a down-at-heel crowd – mentally as well as sartorially. It stood in silent rows. Women made the majority, and many of them had brought their infants – folded in arms or held absent-mindedly by the hand. If there were any abolitionists present they did not make themselves known, but one gentleman extracted a moral from the occasion by bearing aloft a banner: 'Thus saith the Lord. Be sure your sin will find you out.'

A few minutes after nine some creak or minute movement indicated that the wicket gate was about to be opened. This was clearly the moment for which all had been waiting; the moment of completion, of release perhaps. The crowd rushed across the road, stood on tiptoe, and craned upwards to read the final official words. Sentence had been carried out: justice was done. Meanwhile, during this sickly hour, Mr Merrifield was in the Cathedral.

Legally, no doubt, it is necessary to make public the date and hour of an execution. One wonders if some other means could be found under which the hour of execution would be as private as the act itself.[2]

Alfred Merrifield travelled home to the empty bungalow in Blackpool. He lived there, alone, for the next three years while the will of Mrs Ricketts was disputed in the courts by the old woman's daughters. Eventually, in 1956, the probate court declared the will valid, and awarded Mr Merrifield one-sixth of Mrs Ricketts's estate of £2,000. At the same time, the judge ordered that he should give up the bungalow. Before moving out, Mr Merrifield complained to a reporter that he ought to have been awarded at least half the estate. He died, lonely and friendless, in a Blackpool hospital in June 1962, aged seventy-nine.

The Homestead still stands in Devonshire Road, Norbreck, but the present owners have renamed it Inglewood. It is a pretty, double-fronted bungalow, smartly painted in black and white, looking every inch the highly desirable retirement home sought by the middle-classes from Manchester and Merseyside who cruise along Devonshire Road in search of their individual Dunromins. Glancing through the neat white window nets of Inglewood, few would guess that the cruel events witnessed by that house in the spring of Coronation year helped turn the tide of public opinion against capital punishment. For the execution of Mrs Louisa Merrifield, that 'vulgar and stupid woman' who carefully plotted the agonizing death of a frail, defenceless and slightly potty old woman, was not an edifying moment in British criminal annals. In the event it took the case of another, much younger woman, Ruth Ellis, two years later, to convince people that hanging women, however wicked, was no real remedy in a country claiming to embrace civilized values.

4
Mayfield, Hay-on-Wye

Afternoon tea was served in the drawing room. The two men sat on opposite sides of a small oval table. The maid had laid out the best silver service. There were sandwiches, thinly cut and served on the finest porcelain plates. There was currant loaf. And there were buttered scones.

Through the window, dusk was drawing on. Damp leaves carpeted the autumn lawn. It was Wednesday 26 October 1921.

Major Herbert Rowse Armstrong, solicitor and clerk to the magistrates in the small Welsh border town of Hay-on-Wye, peered at his guest over his pince-nez. Oswald Martin, his rival solicitor in Hay, sipped his tea politely. Martin thought he'd been invited up to Mayfield to discuss a property deal in which he and Armstrong were involved. But Armstrong had scarcely mentioned it. Instead the conversation was rambling and polite. Armstrong spoke of being lonely since the death of his wife the previous February. Martin was suitably solicitous. The two men smoked: Martin lit a cigarette; Armstrong puffed on his pipe. A fire crackled agreeably in the grate. They were alone.

Armstrong poured Martin a second cup of tea. Then he leaned over, took a buttered scone from the cake-stand and placed it on Martin's plate.

'Excuse fingers,' said the Major, smiling and helping himself to the currant loaf.

George Orwell might well have had this scene in mind when, a quarter of a century later, he lamented the passing of the golden age of the English murder, 'our Elizabethan period, so to speak'. It was set in the kind of house, the kind of town that might have been made for murder. Mayfield, pinched and brooding villa on a hill, prim, fussy and double-fronted. Hay, hushed and ambiguous, cradled by mountains, half in England, half in Wales, a slumbering brook marking the border. Mayfield stands in England, in a straggle of Hay called Cusop. It has a large garden, and is approached from the road by a sweeping gravel drive. In Armstrong's time it boasted a tennis court. Armstrong enjoyed the occasional game of tennis, but he was a mediocre player. The garden was his favourite pastime but, being a pernickety type, he worried greatly about weeds. These he dosed with a homemade brew of weedkiller concocted from several chemicals including arsenic, which he bought from time to time from the local chemist. Many of the chemist's customers purchased arsenic, for most earned their living from the land, Hay being the business centre of a thriving agricultural area.

Think of it: a provincial, small-town setting between the wars, with one main street, a clock tower, and few cars.

Picture the little solicitor, button-neat, and his miserable pinned-back wife staring wire-rimmed, solemn and mute through burned-out monochrome. The big house, three children, housekeeper, maids and gardener.

Hear the clamour of cattle and sheep in pens on market day, and the beery, wagging tongues of shopkeepers, estate agents and farmers in the all-day saloon bar.

Imagine arsenic signed for in a register. High-collared constables and doctors on horseback. Buttoned-up spinsters, steam trains and whispers of syphilis. Strong, sweet tea and buttered scones carried stiff-capped along half-lighted passageways. The Armstrong case is the quiddity of English murderousness.

Darkness was falling in Hay as Oswald Martin made his way home from Mayfield. That evening, after dinner,

Martin was violently sick. He was so ill during the night with vomiting and diarrhoea that early next morning his wife telephoned for the doctor.

When Dr Tom Hincks arrived, Mrs Martin explained that although she and her husband had eaten the same dish at dinner, she felt perfectly well. The doctor looked at Martin, lying queasily in bed.

'What did you have for tea?' asked Dr Hincks.

'A currant bun and two cups of tea,' he replied, explaining that he had been entertained by Major Armstrong at Mayfield.

Thursday was market day in Hay, and the busiest day of the week for almost everyone in the town, including Dr Hincks, a bluff, red-faced man known affectionately by his patients as Dr Tom. By mid-morning the waiting room at his surgery in Broad Street was full. Far-flung farmers and their families who only came to Hay once a week on market day tended to save up their minor ailments for Thursdays. The doctor had just dealt with the last patient of the morning. He was getting ready to walk to the King's Head for lunch when the small, dapper figure of Major Armstrong appeared at his surgery door. 'You were up at Oswald Martin's this morning,' said the Major. 'What's the matter with him?'

'Oh,' said Dr Hincks, 'he's got a bilious attack.'

In the afternoon Hincks had a second visitor. It was Martin's father-in-law, John Fred Davies, a local dispensing chemist. 'Are you sure it's a bilious attack?' asked Davies. 'Are you sure he hasn't been poisoned?'

'Poisoned?'

Hincks was mildly vexed at the blunt tone of this question, and wanted to know why Davies had asked it. Davies replied that he knew his son-in-law had taken tea at Mayfield with the Major the previous day.

'I wouldn't trust Armstrong a yard,' said Davies. Dr

Hincks looked surprised. It was not the sort of opinion normally expressed in small towns about a local solicitor and clerk to the magistrates.

Seeing the doctor's puzzled reaction, Davies went on to explain that he had sold several packets of arsenic to Armstrong. The Major had complained that the garden at Mayfield was plagued with dandelions; the arsenic would be an effective weedkiller. That was how Davies had logged Armstrong's purchases in the poisons register: for use as weedkiller.

'So?' Dr Hincks was sceptical.

'Don't you see?' exclaimed Davies excitedly. 'Armstrong buys arsenic and the next thing you know his business rival goes down with some kind of poisoning. Suspicious, that's what I call it.'

Dr Hincks sniffed loudly. He was unimpressed. He repeated his opinion that Oswald Martin was suffering from nothing more than biliousness. 'Still,' he added as Davies was leaving, 'I'll bear in mind what you said.'

Davies the chemist was convinced that his son-in-law had been poisoned, and confided his theory to the Martins that evening. He warned them that the poisoner might try again, and told them to be suspicious of any gifts, especially anonymous gifts. Oswald and Constance Martin looked startled.

'What is it?' asked Davies.

'You mentioned anonymous gifts,' said Oswald Martin uncomfortably. 'The fact is we've already had one.'

Davies rocked forward in his chair. 'What? Tell me,' he said.

Martin glanced nervously at his wife. 'Chocolates. A box of chocolates.'

'When?' asked Davies, incredulous.

Oswald Martin thought for a moment. 'About five weeks ago.'

Martin explained that the one-pound box of Fuller's chocolates had arrived anonymously by post in mid-September. Neither he nor his wife were particularly fond of chocolates, so the box had been put aside and almost forgotten. But then, nearly three weeks later, Constance Martin had offered some of the chocolates to a party of dinner guests; one had been violently unwell, complaining of sickness and diarrhoea. The woman had recovered completely, however, and had put the attack down to a severe chill.

'Where are the chocolates now?' asked Davies.

'I think I still have them,' replied his daughter.

Next day Davies the chemist took the box of chocolates to his dispensary and locked the door. Carefully he turned each chocolate over with a pencil. He saw that at least two chocolates appeared to have been tampered with; the ends looked as though they had been drilled out 'and I noticed minute particles of white powder adhering to them', he reported later. John Davies wasted no time. With the agreement of Dr Hincks he persuaded Oswald Martin to supply a sample of urine, which was sealed in a clean bottle with a fresh cork. The bottle and the box of chocolates were carefully parcelled up and despatched to a laboratory in London for clinical analysis.

Major Herbert Rowse Armstrong, meanwhile, continued about his daily business, unaware that he was the object of suspicion. Every morning he left Mayfield to walk briskly down to his office in Broad Street, the main thoroughfare in Hay. He was a neat and well-proportioned man of fifty-two, but small and insignificant-looking. As if to compensate for this his manner was pompous and self-important. And, like many small men, Armstrong was vain and fastidious about his appearance. Every morning he put on a clean, high-wing collar, waxed the ends of his moustache, and bought a fresh buttonhole for his lapel. On cold

days one of the maids would help him into his thick
overcoat, a grey British warm with a deep fur collar which
Armstrong liked to think gave him a military appearance.
Behind his pince-nez flickered eyes of bright, piercing blue.
Everyone in Hay knew Major Armstrong. He was as much
a part of the local scenery as the River Wye and the Black
Mountains beyond. But he was not a native. He was
actually born in Plymouth, and had worked in Liverpool
before moving to Hay in 1906, as managing clerk to Mr
Cheese, a solicitor with offices in Broad Street. He took an
interest in church affairs, and joined the local Freemasons.
Four years later Mr Cheese offered Armstrong a partner-
ship, and he and his wife moved from their modest house
at Cusop to a larger, more imposing home nearby. This
was Mayfield, set back from the road in extensive grounds
where the Armstrongs' three children could play.

In 1914 two events occurred which dramatically
improved Armstrong's fortunes even further. In the spring,
old Mr Cheese suddenly died and Armstrong inherited the
practice outright. Then, in the summer, came war. At the
age of forty-five Armstrong was too old to be conscripted,
but he needed no second bidding. His previous military
experience as a captain in the Territorials, combined with
his legal training, admirably fitted him for the post of
adjutant, and Armstrong spent most of the war as a
glorified pen pusher. Promoted to the rank of major, he
served briefly in France in the summer of 1918, returning
to England shortly before the Armistice. He was
demobbed in May 1919 and awarded the Territorial Decoration the following November. Armstrong was burstingly
proud of his war service and delighted with his decoration,
which he had sought assiduously since realizing he had not
been mentioned in despatches. When he was officially
retired from the Army in 1921 the War Office wrote saying
he could retain his rank; from that day forward Armstrong

used his rank whenever he could. To him, it was more than a label. It was a weapon of self-defence, an instrument of self-aggrandizement. Henceforward, Armstrong announced himself as Major, signed himself Major, and caused it to be known in Hay and beyond that he expected to be addressed as Major.

When Armstrong returned to Hay in 1919 to pick up the threads of his legal practice, he found several distressing changes in his domestic and professional circumstances. At home his wife was behaving rather oddly. And his legal practice, run down and neglected during the war years, was facing an unexpected challenge literally from across the street.

Like most small towns Hay boasted two firms of solicitors: H. Rowse Armstrong and Robert Griffiths, whose offices faced each other in Broad Street. At war's end, the ageing Griffiths had taken a partner, Oswald Martin, a young solicitor who had been wounded in France and invalided out of the Army. Martin was youthful and dynamic, and his appointment gave Griffiths' practice a definite edge over the moribund firm headed by Armstrong. Martin specialized in tax affairs, and wealthy farmers flocked to him from miles around for advice on preparing their tax returns. Business boomed as a result. Armstrong could only brood on the success of his rival across the street. The situation was hitting both his pride and his pocket. Something had to be done.

Meanwhile Armstrong had equally pressing problems at home. His wife Katharine, always a difficult woman, had become even more domineering since his return from the war. True, she was a good homemaker and a conscientious mother, but she was becoming an impossible wife. She ruled her diminutive husband with a rod of iron, forbidding him the few worldly pleasures that Hay had to offer and humiliating him in front of servants and strangers. She even made him remove his shoes at the front door.

To the people of Hay, the Armstrongs seemed an ill-matched couple. She was not particularly tall, but she was taller than him and people called them 'Mutt and Jeff' because of this disparity in height. She was an unlovely lady, spare and sallow with staring, protruding eyes and wire-rimmed spectacles. The couple were hopelessly incompatible, the popinjay Major and his dragon of a wife who never missed an opportunity to belittle her husband in public. He enjoyed the occasional drink and a smoke; she forbade him alcohol totally and only allowed him to smoke in one room of the house. At other people's dinner parties she would curtly dismiss the servant with the instruction, 'No wine for the Major.' She repeatedly humiliated him in front of the domestic staff at Mayfield by telling him off for being late at his own table. On one celebrated occasion she hauled him home in the middle of a tennis match, reminding him loudly that it was his bath night. Armstrong knew better than to argue; meekly, he picked up his racket and followed dumbly in his wife's wake.

Armstrong sought refuge from this wifely tyranny in his work and his outside interests, the Army, the Church, the Freemasons, and his garden. No one ever heard him complain; on the contrary, people remarked how he indulged his wife with every consideration. But as time went by, Mrs Armstrong became increasingly eccentric and withdrawn. She indulged her chronic hypochondria with a passionate interest in homeopathic medicines. But in May 1919, at around the time her husband was demobbed, Katharine Armstrong paid a visit to Dr Hincks, complaining of a pain in her right arm and numbness in the fingers. Hincks diagnosed neuritis and wrote a prescription which seemed to clear up the problem straight away.

It was over a year before Dr Hincks saw Mrs Armstrong again. In August 1920 he visited her at Mayfield and was shocked at the state she was in. It was evident that she was now mentally ill, and that her general health was beginning to fail. She was suffering from delusions and her speech was affected. Indeed, Hincks was so worried that he sought a second opinion from another doctor. 'Mrs Armstrong was pale and thin,' he wrote in a note to Dr Hincks, 'and presented a very sad picture. She was very listless and seemed to take no interest in my conversation with her. I had some difficulty in getting her to speak at all, and when I did succeed I came to the conclusion that she was of unsound mind.' The two doctors conferred, and agreed that Mrs Armstrong should be certified insane there and then and committed to Barnwood, a private asylum near Gloucester. She stayed there for six months.

While his wife was a patient at Barnwood, Armstrong took the opportunity to indulge in furtive pleasures such as an occasional visit to the pub and the odd dance. But by January 1921 Armstrong told Dr Hincks that he was anxious to have his wife back home at Mayfield. Against the advice of the medical superintendent at Barnwood she was brought back to Hay. At once her condition deteriorated, and she began talking openly of suicide. Two days after Katharine Armstrong's forty-eighth birthday in early February a visitor found her in a terrible state. She looked wasted, and her skin was of such a pallor that the visitor, a trained nurse, assumed she had jaundice. She was complaining to Dr Hincks of a curious sensation in her feet, as though springs were pressing her up from the ground. She told him of constant pains in her stomach. It was clear she was seriously ill.

Dr Hincks was now calling at Mayfield every day. A professional nurse had been brought in, and she worked around the clock, helped by the housekeeper, Emily

Pearce, and Armstrong himself, who cut short his working day to spend more time at his wife's bedside. But Mrs Armstrong was sinking. Hincks administered morphia to ease the pain, but she was alarmingly weak and was vomiting constantly. She was desperately thin, and too weak even to sit up in bed. Her skin turned a dark copper colour. Hincks warned Armstrong to expect the worst.

In the early hours of Tuesday 22 February, shortly before losing consciousness, Mrs Armstrong spoke quietly to the nurse. 'I am not going to die, am I? Because I have everything to live for.' Dr Hincks was summoned but he told Armstrong there was nothing more he could do. He did not think she would last the day. He was right. Katharine Armstrong died at ten past nine that morning.

The Major was at his office when the nurse broke the news on the telephone. His first act on returning home was to throw open all the curtains that had been drawn by the housemaid as a mark of respect.

Armstrong's demeanour following the death of his wife changed completely. Less than a month after the funeral he left England for a holiday in Europe, spending twelve days in Italy before cruising on to Malta. He wasn't short of female company, as his diary records:

1 April	*Rigoletto* with Susan
6	*La Traviata* with Miss B
7	10 A.M. Miss Buchanan
8	10 A.M Miss Buchanan
	11 Miss McRae
9	Motor ride S Paul's Bay. I and Miss B.
15	'Billeted' with Miss B.

Armstrong returned to London via Rome and Paris. He wrote to a friend a few days later:

Once more I am back – arrived home a week ago and I am glad to say quite fit again. You wouldn't know me for the same person, and I can now face the future with a correct sense of proportion which I had temporarily lost.

On returning from his Continental spree, Armstrong travelled to Bournemouth to visit a well-to-do woman he had met while stationed on the south coast during the war. Throughout the case this woman was known simply as Mrs X. Armstrong's purpose in visiting Mrs X was to propose marriage. She promised to think it over. Back in Hay, meanwhile, Armstrong embarked on a life of gay abandon, cramming in as many social activities as his work allowed, taking dancing lessons, travelling, and entertaining at Mayfield. He became a regular figure in the bar at the King's Head near his office, and smoked as much as he liked. He certainly cut quite a dash as the merry widower, and there was an extra pleasure to come. It seemed that his late wife had altered her will a few months before she died, leaving all her money – more than two thousand pounds – to him.

This was all very well, but bigger and blacker clouds were looming over Major Armstrong's professional life. At the centre of his problems stood the young solicitor from over the street, Oswald Martin. Martin had started pressing Armstrong in the matter of the Velinewydd estate at Brecon. This large estate had been sold in 1919, with Armstrong acting on behalf of the vendor. The contract of sale should have been completed early in 1920, but now, more than eighteen months later, completion still hadn't taken place. The buyers, who had lodged a deposit of £500 with Armstrong, were becoming restive, and instructed Oswald Martin to see the matter through. 'Will you please let us know,' wrote Martin to Armstrong, 'if possible by return, the exact position of this matter, and the reason why completion has been delayed for such an excessively long time?' Armstrong knew that this was a serious matter, and realized that he was being backed into a corner. He faced a simple alternative: complete the sale or return the deposit money. In the event, Armstrong's hand was forced, and Martin wrote a second time rescinding the contract and demanding the repayment of the deposit plus costs and expenses.

It was at this critical point in Armstrong's affairs that he invited Oswald Martin up to Mayfield for afternoon tea. And it was as a result of Martin's sudden illness that a sample of his urine was sent to London for analysis. The result was several weeks coming, but when it came it confirmed the growing suspicions of Dr Hincks and John Davies, the chemist. The analyst reported finding one thirty-third of a grain of arsenic in Martin's sample. As for the chocolates, they had indeed been tampered with. Someone had drilled out the ends and filled the little holes with white arsenic. It was true. Someone was indeed trying to poison Oswald Martin.

Dr Hincks was dismayed. And not just by the case of Oswald Martin, who was completely recovered and back at work. The doctor's heart sank as he recalled the symptoms of poor Mrs Armstrong during her fatal illness six months before, symptoms which, he now realized, could have been caused by arsenic. And there was another, rather delicate matter that reinforced Dr Hincks's suspicions. He was loath to discuss it with Davies the chemist, since it was a confidence between doctor and patient. But the fact was that, during Mrs Armstrong's stay at Barnwood, Hincks had been treating her husband for a dose of syphilis. The treatment had involved a course of injections, and Armstrong had asked if the drug in the syringe contained arsenic. Dr Hincks had said it did, and Armstrong had asked how much arsenic would constitute a fatal dose. Dr Hincks had told him: two or three grains. To which Armstrong had replied: 'Would not one be sufficient?'

As Dr Hincks pondered the appalling possibilities, Armstrong – unaware of the suspicions of the doctor, the chemist and his fellow solicitor – issued a further string of invitations to Martin to take tea. Almost daily the telephone in Martin's office would ring, and it would be Armstrong, suggesting that Martin step across the road for a cup of tea and a scone. At first Martin managed to deflect these invitations with plausible excuses ('I have to attend a meeting', or 'I have to finish some important letters') but these were soon exhausted. Not wishing to appear rude by flatly declining, Martin eventually resorted to taking tea early in his own office, so that he could truthfully say that he was already refreshed.

Meanwhile, the wheels of officialdom were slowly beginning to turn.

By now, Dr Hincks's initial scepticism had evaporated, and he was convinced that Major Armstrong had not only murdered his wife but was now trying to poison his rival. Having sent Martin's urine and the chocolates to London for analysis, he sat down and wrote a letter to the Home Office outlining his suspicions. He said that in his opinion the symptoms of Mrs Armstrong's fatal illness were not those of nephritis and gastritis after all, but of arsenical poisoning. Mr Martin, he added, had undoubtedly been poisoned after taking tea with Major Armstrong. There was also the case of a land agent who, after dining with Armstrong, had died, apparently of peritonitis. This so alarmed officials at the Home Office that they quickly arranged for the tests to be carried out by their own senior analyst, who submitted his report to Whitehall in early December. A senior Home Office civil servant notified the test results to the Director of Public Prosecutions, and it wasn't long before a representative of the DPP was hurrying down to Hereford to interview Dr Hincks in the office of the local chief constable. The doctor made a full and lengthy statement, scarcely concealing his fears about what Armstrong might do next. 'Mr and Mrs Martin are becoming ill from strain,' he said. 'They are both convinced that Armstrong will "do him in" sooner or later.'

The man from the DPP looked up from his notes. 'Tell me about Major Armstrong,' he said.

'I've been his doctor since his return from the war,' said Hincks. 'In my opinion he is of abnormal mentality, very clever and well-read. He runs after women. No particular woman that I know of, but I'm told he goes to the village dances and pesters the girls there.' Dr Hincks thought for a moment. 'Armstrong keeps a revolver by his bed,' he added. 'I think this man is a homicidal maniac. And if he finds out he's under investigation, he may well use it. On himself. On his children. On Mr Martin. And on me.'

Hincks' dramatic prognostication immediately convinced the Director of Public Prosecutions, Sir Archibald Bodkin, that something sinister was indeed afoot at Mayfield. On Bodkin's instructions Scotland Yard briefed one of its top detectives, Chief Inspector Alfred Crutchett, with orders to go to Hay to find out exactly what was going on. Crutchett, accompanied by his assistant, Sergeant Walter Sharp, arrived in Hay on the morning of 11 December. Their first stop was the home of the chemist, John Davies.

The two detectives impressed on Davies and his wife the need for absolute secrecy. If Major Armstrong got wind of their presence in the town heaven knows what would happen. Mr and Mrs Davies nodded grimly. They would tell no one. Crutchett and Sharp spent several days undercover in Hay, posing as tourists. They moved around the town mainly after dark, taking statements from Oswald Martin and his wife, and their dinner guest who had become ill after eating the contaminated chocolates. Crutchett knew that if he could identify Armstrong as the sender of the chocolates, the case against him would be clinched. But this proved an impossible task. The brown paper in which the box had been wrapped had been destroyed, and Mrs Martin could remember little about the postmark except that she thought it had ended in 'ford'. The post office kept no records, and neither the local postman nor the stationmaster could remember handling any such parcel. In London, a police officer was despatched to the Fuller's chocolate factory with the box and the uneaten chocolates, but the makers had no record of where they had been sent after packing.

In the absence of a definite link between Major Armstrong and the poisoned chocolates, the two men from the Yard turned to other possible leads. They obtained from Somerset House a copy of Mrs Armstrong's will, dated July 1920, in which she left everything to her husband. They were struck by the fact that less than a month after his wife's slow and agonizing death, the Major had applied for a passport to travel to Europe on holiday. They checked Oswald Martin's story against the versions of Dr Hincks and John Davies. It was a convincing one. And there was Armstrong's mystifying remark to Oswald Martin, a few days after the incident with the buttered scone. 'It seems a queer thing to say,' Armstrong had remarked to Martin, 'but you will be ill again soon.'

Crutchett and Sharp reported the results of their inquiries to the Director of Public Prosecutions. They listed the facts: Dr Hincks's suspicion that Mrs Armstrong's symptoms were consistent with arsenical poisoning; Oswald Martin's poisoning after tea at Mayfield; Armstrong's business worries, and the death of his wife by which he inherited £2,000; his proposal of marriage to a woman of substance in Bournemouth; his recalcitrance in the Velinewydd affair in which Martin was pressing him for payment. Bodkin was at once persuaded that Dr Hincks's original suspicions were well-founded. On Christmas Eve he summoned Sir William Willcox, the Home Office's medical adviser, and outlined the facts to him. The two men agreed that there were disturbing similarities between the strange events in Hay and the case of another solicitor, Harold Greenwood, in not-so-far-away Llanelly. Greenwood had been tried the previous year for the murder of his wife by poisoning. But the evidence had failed to convince a jury and Greenwood was acquitted. Bodkin was anxious to avoid a similar debacle; Willcox nodded his agreement. But when Sir William's report on the Armstrong case landed on Bodkin's desk the day after Boxing Day, the DPP finally determined to act. He ordered the Major's arrest.

New Year's Eve 1921 was a bitterly cold Saturday in Hay. As usual, Armstrong had walked down from Mayfield to his office in Broad Street, clad in his familiar British warm, riding breeches and boots. With his customary 'good morning' to the clerk and office girl, Armstrong strode through the downstairs general office and climbed the stairs to his own private office on the first floor. He had scarcely taken off his coat and settled at his desk when he heard the clatter of several heavy boots on the stairs. A moment later, without knocking, three burly police officers filed into the room. Armstrong recognized only one, the deputy chief constable of Herefordshire, Superintendent Albert Weaver. It was Weaver who spoke first, introducing his companions as Chief Inspector Crutchett and Sergeant Sharp of Scotland Yard. Armstrong was visibly shocked, and for a moment was lost for words. It did not matter, for Crutchett had stepped forward and was reading from a prepared statement. 'Inquiries . . . sudden illness of Mr Oswald Martin . . . taking tea with you . . . later seized with sickness . . . specimen of urine . . . arsenic . . . box of Fuller's chocolates . . . tampered with . . . arsenic put into them . . .' Armstrong's mind must have been racing as Crutchett glanced up from his notes. 'It may be,' said

Crutchett finally, 'that you would like to make a statement as to your own actions . . . why Mr Martin was asked to tea . . . and whether you bought any chocolates. But I must tell you that anything you do say will be taken down in writing and may be used in evidence.' The chief inspector folded his piece of paper and looked grimly at Armstrong, sitting white-faced at his desk. Armstrong, the trained lawyer, knew that his reaction at this moment would be critical. He thought for a moment. Sergeant Sharp's pencil was poised. Armstrong took a deep breath. 'Certainly,' he said. 'I will help you all I can.'

For two hours Armstrong spoke about his version of events in a statement which Sergeant Sharp took down in longhand. Superintendent Weaver then charged Armstrong with administering arsenic to Oswald Martin at Mayfield with intent to murder him. 'I am quite innocent,' replied the Major. Armstrong was made to sit on a chair in the centre of the room while the officers searched the office and told him to turn out his pockets. In his jacket the officers found a bundle of love letters, written on light-blue notepaper and signed 'Your loving Marion'. They also found a neatly wrapped packet of arsenic, just enough to stir into Mr Martin's cup should he care to come to tea.

Shortly after midday Armstrong left his office for the last time and walked with the detectives to the local police station where he was searched. His watch, ring, cufflinks, pen and pocket knife were taken from him and he was led to a small cell with a single barred window set high in the wall. But before he was locked up he telephoned a fellow solicitor, Thomas Matthews, in Hereford, explained briefly what had happened, and asked Matthews to act for him. That night, alone in his cell, Armstrong heard the bells of Hay ringing in the new year. He must have realized that his chances of seeing out 1922 were far from good.

As in all small country towns, news in Hay travels fast,

and the news that Major Herbert Rowse Armstrong, solicitor and clerk to the justices, had been arrested on a charge of attempted murder hit the townspeople like an express train. William Lloyd's reaction was typical. 'Good grief!' he exclaimed to a friend when he heard. 'What's he done?' Mr Lloyd still tingles at the recollection of it. 'It was a shock, you see. Major Armstrong! Can you imagine it? A solicitor, a well-read man, a well-educated man? That he could do such a thing?'[1]

By the time Armstrong appeared in his own police court the following Monday morning the whole of Hay and most of Herefordshire had heard the news. The tiny courtroom behind the police station was jammed to choking point. The first thing the magistrates did when they filed in was to appoint a temporary clerk, in the ancient form of eighty-two-year-old Mr Cambridge Phillips. The hearing was short. Superintendent Weaver gave evidence of arrest, and the magistrates remanded Armstrong in custody for a week. The Major was led away to Worcester Gaol, and the focus of events switched from the stuffy, overheated courtroom to the chill bleakness of Cusop churchyard, just over a mile away.

Dr Hincks had told Chief Inspector Crutchett that he might have been wrong in ascribing the death of Katharine Armstrong to gastritis. The attempted poisoning of Oswald Martin had strengthened his suspicion that Mrs Armstrong too had been poisoned; reviewing her symptoms in the light of Martin's illness he was forced to admit that they closely resembled those of arsenical poisoning. Dr Hincks was not alone in this view. John Fred Davies, the chemist, had also expressed unease, having on several occasions sold arsenic to Major Armstrong. Crutchett decided that there was only one way to settle the matter for once and for all: the exhumation of Mrs Armstrong's body.

The exhumation took place at Cusop churchyard on the

day Armstrong first faced the local magistrates. The sexton worked alone behind canvas screens. By late afternoon a large mound of dark-coloured earth was heaped up along-side the opened grave, scab-like on the snow-covered ground. Across the road from the churchyard a small, whitewashed cottage had been commandeered to receive the coffin, which was wheeled from the graveside on a hand-bier as darkness fell. The post-mortem was performed the following day by the Home Office pathologist, Dr Bernard Spilsbury, who removed a number of organs and body samples for examination. The law required that an inquest be held on the exhumed body, and the jury of twelve men had the unpleasant task of viewing the body. The hearing was adjourned, and the body of Katharine Armstrong was returned to its resting place the following morning. At his laboratory in London Spilsbury found that the dead woman's organs were unusually well-preserved, in particular the liver, kidneys, stomach and intestines. When these were analysed by a Home Office scientist arsenic was found in every one. Samples of Mrs Armstrong's bone, skin, muscle, hair and even fingernails also contained traces of arsenic. In all, the body was found to contain 208 milligrams of arsenic; the liver alone contained the equivalent of a fatal dose. Ten months after her death, Katharine Armstrong's body was still riddled with arsenic. The worst suspicions of John Davies and Dr Hincks were finally confirmed. And when Major Herbert Rowse Armstrong made his next appearance at Hay magistrates' court, he faced a further charge. Mr St John Micklethwait, appearing for the Director of Public Prosecutions, rose to address the bench. 'It now becomes my duty,' he began, 'to prefer against the prisoner, Major Armstrong, another charge of a more grave and more serious character even than the charge of attempting to murder Mr Martin. The prisoner is now charged with the wilful murder of his wife by poisoning her with arsenic.'

Armstrong in a sense faced two trials, the first at the magistrates' court for the attempted poisoning of Oswald Martin, the second at Hereford Assizes for the murder of his wife. The hearings at the lower court extended over a period of weeks, and were fully reported in the newspapers circulating in the Hereford area. At the outset of Armstrong's trial for murder the judge, Mr Justice Darling, had to rule on a crucial point of law: whether to admit evidence relating to the attempted murder of Oswald Martin. The judge's decision to allow this evidence was subsequently upheld in the appeal court. But it undoubtedly wrecked Armstrong's chances of an acquittal.

The importance of the Armstrong case was reflected in the DPP's decision to brief the Attorney-General, Sir Ernest Pollock KC, for the Crown. The prosecution took six days to present its case. The evidence against Armstrong was totally circumstantial: there was no proof that the little Major had administered with his own hands any kind of food or drink to his wretched wife, but the jury was satisfied that he had had the means and the opportunity to do so. As the Attorney-General explained, direct evidence in a poisoning trial is practically impossible. 'In this case,' he told the jury in his opening speech, 'we know that Mrs Armstrong died from arsenic poisoning. This body of evidence which will be called before you will be directed piece by piece, circumstance by circumstance, pointing to a conclusion that it was the prisoner at the bar who killed his wife.

'She died from arsenic poisoning. Who had the means, who had the opportunity – in August [when she was admitted to the asylum at Barnwood] and in February [on her return] – and who had the motive to administer the poison?

'You find the means with the prisoner. You find the opportunity – the one man who was at Mayfield both in August and in February. You find the motive in the will referred to.'

One of the greatest advocates of the day, Sir Henry Curtis-Bennett KC, was briefed for the defence. He put up a brilliant fight, managing to cast even the smallest fact in the most favourable light. The thrust of the defence case was that Katharine Armstrong, suffering from melancholia and delusions on her return home from the asylum, had committed suicide. In fact the defence did not dispute that she had died from arsenical poisoning. But Curtis-Bennett needed to show that she had taken a single, huge and fatal dose in the six days leading up to her death. He quoted the case of a French nobleman, the Duc de Praslin, who in 1846 had committed suicide by taking arsenic but had lived for six days after taking the fatal dose. The theory was ingenious, but it was not borne out by the findings of the post-mortem examination. Curtis-Bennett suggested that most of the arsenic swallowed by Mrs Armstrong had become encysted, sealed up and enclosed in a sort of pocket on the stomach wall. His theory was that after six days the cyst broke, flooding the woman's system with arsenic.

Unfortunately for Armstrong the theory remained only a theory. The jury was more inclined to believe the testimony of Dr Spilsbury, who said: 'From the amount of arsenic present, it is clear that a large dose, a possibly fatal dose, must have been taken within twenty-four hours of her death. And from the amount of arsenic found in the liver, over two grains, and from the disease of the liver as I found it, it is clear that arsenic must have been given in a number of large doses extending over a period of several days, probably a week, immediately before death.'

So how did Major Armstrong set about poisoning his

wife? It seems he intercepted her meals, taking trays from the servants and secretly sprinkling the deadly white powder into her food, and stirring it into her tea. The staff at Mayfield noticed how careful the Major was to wash his wife's crockery himself. The first large dose of arsenic appears to have been administered on the day she went into Barnwood, in August 1920. Dr Hincks, who had seen her in the morning, returned after lunch to fetch her and noticed she was much worse, running a pulse of 120, and vomiting. She was extremely sick in the car on the way to the asylum and this seems to have saved her. Once away from Mayfield, and the poisonous attentions of her husband, Mrs Armstrong began to improve. The Major himself, realizing this, determined to have his wife home again as soon as possible and began pressing the authorities at Barnwood to release her. At the same time he was buying a fresh supply of arsenic from Mr Davies's shop, explaining that the garden at Mayfield was overrun with dandelions.

Armstrong's story was that he had divided the arsenic into two halves. One half had been stored in a drawer of his bureau at Mayfield. With the other half, he had decided to try an experiment. Taking a penknife he had carefully split the remaining powder into twenty small parts. He had wrapped each part in a twist of paper. Armstrong explained that he had decided to treat each dandelion individually, boring a hole beside each offending plant and sprinkling in a single dose of lethal arsenic from one of the twenty small twists. This was Armstrong's explanation for the fact that a small packet of arsenic was found in his coat pocket when arrested. The coat in question was his gardening jacket. The packet found by the police, said Armstrong, must have been accidentally overlooked during his weeding blitz at Mayfield.

The Major spent nearly six hours in the witness box giving evidence in his own defence. In the face of a relentless cross-examination by Sir Ernest Pollock, Armstrong had scarcely faltered, and observers in the court were struck by the little man's confidence and self-possession. But all that changed when, just as Armstrong turned to step down, the judge leaned forward and, with five little words, changed the course of the entire trial.

'Wait a minute, Major Armstrong.'

Mr Justice Darling's voice cracked like an old, dry branch. He was glaring at the table in the well of the court on which, amid the other exhibits, lay the twentieth twist of arsenic powder which Armstrong had been carrying in his pocket on the morning he was arrested. The judge now looked up at Armstrong. 'Did you realize that it was just a fatal dose of arsenic, not only for dandelions but for human beings?'

'No,' Armstrong replied, 'I did not realize it at all.'

'You know now?'

'I know since the evidence in this case.'

'And you realize what you had given the dandelions was a fatal dose of arsenic for a human being?'

'I have realized it since. I did not know it at the time.'

The judge blinked. 'Why go to the trouble of making twenty little packets, one for each dandelion, instead of taking out the ounce you had got and making a hole and giving the dandelions something from the one ounce?'

Armstrong paused. 'I don't really know.'

'Why make up twenty little packets, each a fatal dose for a human being, and put it in your pocket?'

'At the time,' said the Major, 'it seemed to me the most convenient way of doing it. I cannot give any other explanation.'

The judge continued to pick away at Armstrong's story. Why, when he remembered this interesting experiment, had he not told the police? Why, when he remembered the unused two ounces in his desk drawer, had he not told the police? He was a man accustomed to criminal procedure. If he thought the police were certain to find the arsenic, as he said, would it not have been better to have made a clean breast of it, and take the credit of telling them himself?

'It didn't occur to me, my Lord,' said Armstrong, limply.

Some people still think that the Major was the kind of meticulous man who would have sat down at his desk with a penknife and carefully divided his arsenic into twenty little twists. But the real puzzle is why Armstrong told the arresting officers that the only arsenic he possessed at Mayfield was grey arsenic – arsenic mixed with charcoal. In fact there was some white arsenic at Mayfield, the unused half of the powder Armstrong had bought from Mr Davies in January 1921. When the little packet of white arsenic was found in the Major's pocket, the police had searched Mayfield looking for more but had failed to find the arsenic in the bureau drawer. The missing powder was eventually found by Armstrong's own solicitor, Mr Matthews, who found that the drawer had stuck. When he put his hand into the drawer and felt around he found the bag of unused white arsenic jammed at the back. Armstrong maintained that at first he had forgotten about this residue of arsenic, which is why in his initial statement to the police he had admitted only to having some grey (weedkilling) arsenic, 'the only poison in my possession'.

The jury was out for fifty minutes. Major Armstrong received the 'guilty' verdict standing at attention, heels together, body and arms ramrod-straight. As the words of the judge's death sentence and the chaplain's amen died away he turned smartly and disappeared down the dock steps. A month later his appeal was roundly dismissed, and he was hanged at Gloucester Prison at 8 A.M. on the last day of May 1922. It was Derby Day, and the sun shone.

It is hard to feel any sympathy for the little Major of

Mayfield. There is no doubt he murdered his wife, and although she was a deeply irritating and difficult woman to live with, she was also a loving wife and devoted mother. She surely did not deserve the lingering, agonizing death that Armstrong plotted in his effort to be rid of her, to inherit her money, and to remarry. And yet he deliberately and cold-bloodedly spread his poison out over several weeks, probably months, regardless of the presence in the house of his three uncomprehending young children. Her suffering must have been indescribable.

There was intense speculation at the time of Armstrong's trial about the identity of Mrs X – 'Your loving Marion' – with whom the Major had planned a new life. Her name was Mrs Marion Glassford Gale, a widow of fifty, who lived at Bournemouth with her elderly mother and a niece. For the sake of propriety her real name remained hidden throughout the entire case, and only with the publication of an excellent book on the Armstrong affair over half a century later did the full story emerge of how she and the syphilitic Major enjoyed a discreet if ill-starred dalliance.[2] Like so many innocent bit-players in the drama of murder, Marion Glassford Gale found her life shattered after the trial, and she eked out her days caring for her family. She died at Bournemouth in 1960, aged ninety-one.

Having survived Major Armstrong's fiendish attempt on his life over afternoon tea at Mayfield, Oswald Martin and his family left Hay and moved to East Anglia. But his ordeal continued to haunt him, and he suffered from depression for the rest of his life. He died of cancer aged only fifty-six in 1946.

Nearly seventy years after the Armstrong case the town of Hay-on-Wye has changed very little. The Major's old house is still there, and so is his office in Broad Street. Both are now occupied by another solicitor, Martin Beales, who spends much of his time at Armstrong's massive oak desk in the first-floor office that overlooks Broad Street. When I visited him in 1985 during the making of my radio series he proudly showed me Armstrong's old brass plate which he had discovered stored away in the office. At that time the Beales family were living, coincidentally, in the pretty whitewashed cottage opposite Cusop churchyard in which the post-mortem was performed on the exhumed body of Mrs Katharine Armstrong. But a year or two later when Armstrong's house came on the market Martin Beales bought it, so cementing the links between the modern-day legal practice and the home of his infamous precursor.

The older generation in Hay still talks of Major Armstrong, but by and large the town now concerns itself with tourists and the second-hand book trade. Above the town, in Cusop Dingle, the rooks call at dusk in the trees at Mayfield, now renamed The Mantles. And when a group of old-timers meet to talk of times remembered, and the sandwiches and cakes are passed round over tea, someone will always salute the memory of the treacherous Major Armstrong with a wry smile and a polite, if slightly laboured, apology: Excuse fingers!

5
The Priory, Balham

From the road you can hardly catch a glimpse. In fact, the finest prospect of The Priory is from the railway. Travelling through south-west London towards Victoria, it is suddenly there, on the left, a pink stuccoed marshmallow of a house peeping out of the brickwork on the fringe of Tooting Bec Common. The commonplace suburban train might be a time machine if you half-close your eyes for a moment. Can you see the phantom figures on horseback taking a Sunday ride on the common? Can you catch the chatter of fashionable ladies stepping from their carriages to take the air in what, a century or more ago, was the semi-rural fringe of London? Can you discern the wistful shade of Florence Bravo moving silently between the trees in the flaring gaslit dusk? For the story of The Priory is the story of the extraordinary Mrs Bravo, an attractive young woman who inherited a fortune on the death of her first husband in 1871. Being of independent means, she was free to indulge her taste for the good life and could afford the best clothes and jewellery. She was passionately fond of horses, and enjoyed continental travel. But there was talk of an illicit love affair with a married society doctor, and it was this taint of scandal that brought her instant notoriety when, in the spring of 1876, her second husband, Charles, died suddenly and mysteriously of poison.

She was beautiful. Chestnut hair and large, melting blue eyes that concealed a rather selfish and formidable temperament. She came of a well-to-do family. Her grandfather had made a fortune rearing sheep in Australia and her father, Robert Campbell, was a familiar figure in London society. He was a member of the Reform Club, and owned a large estate at Buscot in Berkshire, where he was a magistrate and later high sheriff. The Campbells doted on their eldest daughter. Florence studied with a private governess, and travelled extensively with her family. It was on a trip to Canada in the early 1860s that she met her first husband, a young officer in the Grenadier Guards named Alexander Ricardo. The couple married in 1864 when Florence was just nineteen and Captain Ricardo twenty-one. The marriage was a disaster. Florence discovered that her new husband was an alcoholic and, in the spring of 1870, on the advice of her mother, she took Ricardo to a fashionable water-cure establishment at Malvern in Worcestershire. Here, the brandy-sodden Ricardo was treated by the eminent Dr James Manby Gully, an old friend of Florence's family. Dr Gully, a man in his early sixties, remembered treating Florence as a girl of twelve. Now, meeting her again as a beautiful, poised woman of twenty-five, Gully immediately took an intense personal interest in her husband's case. At first, Gully's revolutionary regime of soaking sheets, sitz-baths and plunges seemed to be working, but within a fortnight Ricardo was at the brandy again. Finally, in June, he stormed out of their rented house in a drunken rage and caught a train to London, leaving no word of his whereabouts with his distraught wife. Dr Gully was quick to offer soothing words of comfort. He also offered Florence some salutary advice; he warned her that her own health might suffer under the strain of coping with a wayward husband, and proposed that she seek a separation. Florence agreed, and with Gully's help, signed the necessary papers in March 1871. But before the legalities were complete Florence received grave news from Germany. Captain Ricardo's body had been discovered at lodgings in Cologne where he had been living with a woman. He had succumbed to delirium tremens, the result of a massive drinking spree. Increasingly befuddled, Ricardo had failed to alter the settlement he had made on Florence at the time of their marriage, and his death meant that Florence was now the mistress of his £40,000 fortune.

Widowed at twenty-six, Florence faced the future alone, consoled on the one hand by the increasingly attentive Dr Gully and on the other by the prospect of an annual income of between three and four thousand pounds. Exactly when her affair with Gully began is not entirely clear. Florence later admitted that she was attracted by his undoubted personal charm, his avuncular wit and worldly wisdom. Her parents, scandalized and embarrassed at Florence's infatuation with a man more than twice her age, sealed their consternation by effectively disowning her. 'We became aware,' Mrs Campbell said later, 'of the frequent visits of Dr Gully. That intimacy met with our entire disapproval. I remonstrated with her over her infatuation for Dr Gully – but all to no purpose.' Florence's estrangement from her family had the effect of pressing her still further into the affections of Dr Gully, and the couple toyed with the idea of marriage. Gully, however, already possessed a wife, from whom he had been separated for some thirty years. She was even older than he was and, although over eighty and a chronic invalid, remained very much alive. In the circumstances, divorce was out of the question. So Dr Gully contented himself with retiring from his hydro at Malvern and moving to London, where he took a house opposite one that Florence had rented in Leigham Court Road, Streatham.

Within the strict confines of Victorian decorum, the romance between the wealthy young widow and the ageing doctor seemed to blossom. Each entertained the other to dinner, they took outings together and even foreign holidays. At first, wherever they travelled, discretion was observed; they stayed at the same hotels, but always in separate rooms under their own names and accompanied by their own servants. At length, however, in the summer of 1873, the couple took a holiday in the pretty Bavarian spa town of Kissingen, and it was there that they slept together for the first time. On their return to England, they again spoke tentatively of marriage. Florence agreed to a form of engagement, Gully having gallantly promised to step aside should she meet and fall in love with another man. Had the hardy Mrs Gully obligingly died at this point, it seems certain they would have married, in spite of Florence's parents. But the old lady clung to life, and Florence and Dr Gully remained steadfastly at their separate addresses.

Florence was single, but she did not live alone. Roosting with her at Leigham Court Road was the small, batlike figure of her lady's companion, Mrs Jane Cannon Cox. This sour-faced woman, sloe-eyed and swarthy-skinned, was to play an enigmatic but central role in the destiny of Florence Ricardo. It is hard to imagine a woman with so many unfeminine characteristics (by the standards of that time), ranging from a dogged independence to a severity of countenance that must have struck a chill in the heart of anyone making her acquaintance for the first time. She was born in Jamaica of Creole stock; this accounted for her sallow, taut skin and thick, coarse, jet-black hair, which she invariably wore scraped up beneath a black bonnet. A pair of slitted needle eyes darted behind a pair of steel-rimmed spectacles, watching the world with an unsettling inscrutability. She was in her thirties, but looked older, with the haunted, pinched features of a woman who had suffered some hidden grief or disappointment. In fact, like Florence, she had been widowed as a young woman, left

Right: Madeleine Smith sketched at her trial. (*BBC Hulton Picture Library*)

Below: 7 Blythswood Square, Glasgow, today.

Left: Dr Buck Ruxton.
(*Popperfoto*)

Below: Belle and Buck Ruxton
with one of their children.
(*Popperfoto*)

Right: Mary Jane Rogerson. (*Popperfoto*)

Below: Police in the Ruxton case searching the ravine near Moffat. (*Popperfoto*)

Left: 2 Dalton Square, Lancaster, today.

Below: Captain Henry Vann and the letter from Ruxton written on the eve of his execution.

Right: The Homestead, 399 Devonshire Road, Blackpool, today.

Below: Alfred and Louisa Merrifield. (*Popperfoto*)

Above left: Mrs Merrifield (second from left) leaves Manchester Assizes on the third day of her trial. (*Popperfoto*)

Below left: Mrs Merrifield and the bed in which she poisoned Mrs Sarah Ann Ricketts. (*Popperfoto*)

Right: Mayfield, Hay-on-Wye, today.

Below: Mayfield at the time of the Armstrong case.

Right: Katharine Armstrong.

Below: Major Herbert
Rowse Armstrong.

Above: Chief Inspector Walter Crutchett (1) and Dr Bernard Spilsbury (2) arriving at Cusop for the autopsy on the exhumed body of Mrs Armstrong. (*Popperfoto*)

Right: The Armstrongs on their wedding day. (*Popperfoto*)

Above: The Priory, Balham, today.

Right: Florence Bravo at the time of her marriage to Charles. (*BBC Hulton Picture Library*)

Below: The Priory, Balham in 1876 (*BBC Hulton Picture Library*)

Right: Providence House, Peasenhall.

Below: The Doctor's Chapel, Peasenhall.

Left: Frederick Henry Seddon. (*BBC Hulton Picture Library*)

Below: 63 Tollington Park, North London, at the time of the Seddon case. (*BBC Hulton Picture Library*)

Above: 63 Tollington Park, today.

Right: Miss Eliza Mary Barrow.

Above: Rear of the Villa Madeira, Bournemouth, at the time of the Rattenbury case, showing the French windows to the living-room, Mrs Rattenbury's bedroom (top left) and the neighbouring room occupied by George Stoner. (*Popperfoto*)

Right: The Villa Madeira, today.

Right: Alma Rattenbury leaving the Old Bailey. (*Popperfoto*)

Left: Alma Rattenbury in an autographed publicity picture signed Lozanne.

Below: Alma and Francis Rattenbury with their son John on the sands at Bournemouth. (*Popperfoto*)

Above: Miles Giffard (left) is led to court. (*Popperfoto*)

Right: Charles Giffard. (*Popperfoto*)

to raise three small sons in straitened circumstances; two of the boys were now registered at a school for distressed gentlefolk. She had earned a meagre living as a governess, and as the head of a dame-school in Suffolk, but she had returned to London to take a position as private tutor to the children of a wealthy family in Tooting. It was here that she met the newly widowed Florence Ricardo. The two women seemed to hit it off at once; Florence was struck by her evident loyalty and trustworthiness, her razor-sharp mind and quiet discretion. The impoverished Mrs Cox was attracted by the prospect of becoming a paid companion to a young woman of wealth and position who lived close at hand and in considerable style.

The months passed, and with Mrs Gully lingering defiantly in her sickbed Florence Ricardo became increasingly unsettled about her future. For some reason, seemingly to do with Victorian attitudes to social acceptability, she felt impelled to be married again. A spinster or a wealthy widow such as herself had a sort of taint about her, and this had to be corrected. To be sure, she had everything else the world could offer – wealth, the right sort of friends, influence, and a magnificent home. But what she lacked was the all-important signature of respectability: a husband. In response to these feelings, and to the need to distance herself, however slightly, from the pressing attentions of Gully, Florence looked around for somewhere else to live. She found it in The Priory, a castellated fifteen-room mansion on the fringe of Tooting Bec Common.

Built at the beginning of the nineteenth century, The Priory has been described as a 'perfect example in miniature of the Gothic revival'. Approached by an elegant carriage-drive flanked by two lodges, the house stood in a small estate of some ten acres on the fringe of Tooting Bec Common; today the estate has been shorn of most of its land, and the house now boasts only a large garden, with a lawn that sweeps down to the Common's edge. The house itself captivated Florence at first sight. With its crenellated roof and tiny turrets, its casement windows, orchards, lawns and paddocks, it combined style with amenity in a sylvan setting less than ten miles from London. Florence installed herself there in the spring of 1874, and proceeded to furnish it in the most luxurious and extravagant manner. The drawing room was draped in blue and richly furnished with suites of the most expensive satinwood and mahogany; rose-patterned chintz hung in thick folds at every window, and Florence's collection of rare Venetian glass and china glinted discreetly in massive display cases. In every room she set a profusion of valuable ornaments, pictures, clocks, and marble busts. Upstairs she installed exotic bedsteads from France and Arabia; outside on the lawns, pheasants and fantail pigeons strutted between the borders of rose bushes. In the stables she kept a pair of very expensive and beautifully matched little cobs to draw her phaeton. To clean, cater and care for herself and her possessions, Florence hired what by today's standards would be considered an embarrassingly large retinue of staff: a butler, footman, cook, three housemaids, gardeners, coachman and stablehands. Naturally, she appointed her trusted Mrs Cox as head of the household, a position of considerable influence and prestige. In addition to her duties as the senior servant Mrs Cox (by now on first-name terms with her young mistress) continued to accompany and advise Florence in her capacity as close confidante and chaperon.

In April 1875 Florence received word that her mother was seriously ill. Mrs Campbell had always hoped for a reconciliation with her maverick daughter and Florence knew that her entire family would welcome her back – provided she broke with Dr Gully. Fearful that her mother might die without their being reconciled, Florence determined to make the break, and she stuck to this difficult and courageous decision even after hearing that her mother was better. However, the pain of parting was eased by thoughts of a young man to whom she had been introduced (through Mrs Cox) in late 1874, a handsome, dreamy-eyed young barrister named Charles Bravo, who lived with his family in considerable style in a large house in Kensington.

Charles's stepfather, Joseph Bravo, was acquainted with Mrs Cox through a business partner in Jamaica; he had loaned her some money and given her some financial advice on her arrival in London. From time to time, Mrs Cox called on the Bravos at their huge, palatial house in Palace Green, and it was on one of these social visits shortly before Christmas 1874 that she had introduced Florence to Charles. There was no instant attraction, however, and it was nearly a year before they met again, this time on the seafront at Brighton where Florence and Jane Cox were enjoying a short holiday. Charles Bravo was almost the same age as Florence, tall and attractive, fiercely ambitious and a natural charmer. Florence, now more uncertain than ever about her prospects with Dr Gully, was captivated. Charmed by his silver-tongued platitudes, she saw in Charles a debonair, talented and amusing suitor; she did not yet see his dark side, his thunderflash temperament, his wantonness with women and money, his greedy, acquisitive nature. Charles, for his part, saw in Florence a dazzling vision of deliverance from the claustrophobic confines of his family circle, and in particular from his morbidly possessive mother. Marriage to the wealthy and beautiful Florence Ricardo would mean freedom, social position and respect. Moreover, it promised Charles Bravo the chance of achieving his greatest ambition: to abandon his law practice and stand for Parliament.

Florence was smitten. And when, a few weeks later, Dr

Gully returned from a trip to Europe (on which Florence had peevishly refused to accompany him), she abruptly told him that the affair was off. Florence's explanation was at least honest; she told Gully that she wanted to be reconciled with her family, but admitted that young Charles Bravo had been paying attention to her. Gully was wise enough to accept her decision without question and, true to his pledge, released Florence from any further obligation to him. When Florence and the doctor lunched together for the last time, she promised to heed his advice not to rush into any engagement, and so it came as a surprise to Gully to hear that Florence and Charles Bravo were to be married before the year was out. Gully's forbearance suddenly vanished, and he wrote Florence a hurt and angry letter, to which she replied in equally stinging terms, expressing the wish never to set eyes on him again. In a fit of pique, the wounded doctor ordered his servants to admit neither Florence nor Mrs Cox to his house in future.

Amid these rancorous exchanges, Florence Ricardo continued to encourage Charles Bravo. His proposal of marriage had put Florence in a difficulty; she told her ardent new suitor that she had been seeing Dr Gully since her husband's death, and that this had led to an estrangement from her family. Now that she had terminated the affair with the doctor, a reconciliation was imminent. To Florence's relief, Bravo did not flinch in the face of these unpleasant disclosures. On the contrary, he seemed to accept the affair with Gully philosophically and without fuss. However, Florence did not, at this stage, confess the whole truth, which was that she and Gully had regularly been sleeping together for the past two years, ever since their holiday in Kissingen in 1873. Neither did she mention the wholly unpalatable fact that as a result Dr Gully had attended her professionally in order to perform an abortion. Charles Bravo, for his part, was rather more openhanded, explaining clearly to Florence that he would need his mother's permission to marry, and this he had yet to seek.

'My dear Charlie,' Florence wrote a few days later:

After serious and deep consideration I have come to the conclusion that if you still *hope* and wish to gain my love we must see more of each other, and be quite sure that the solemn act of marriage will be for the happiness of us both.

This is what I think – you ought to *tell* your mother. I would never enter a family where I was not welcome. I have no fear of not gaining her affection, but of course she must see me and judge for herself. All I can say is that you have behaved in the noblest manner, and that I have no doubt of being happy with you; but of course before giving up my present freedom I must be quite convinced that it will be for our mutual happiness.

Now I must tell you that I have written to the Dr to say that I must never see his face again; it is the right thing to do in every respect.

Whatever happens, whether we marry or whether we do not, I shall ever have a great respect for you and take a deep interest in your welfare, for I think you are a very good man. Write and tell me what you think of this letter, and with every kind wish,
Ever your sincere friend

Florence Ricardo

Ten days later, Charles Bravo told Florence that his mother had (grudgingly, as it turned out) given her consent to the engagement. But before the news was made public Florence took Charles to one side and explained that she had not told him everything about her affair with Gully. Now she confessed it all. 'I told him that I had been constantly in Dr Gully's company; I told him we had travelled abroad together, and in England,' said Florence later. 'I told him all. I told him of the intimacy which had occurred between myself and Dr Gully at Kissingen in

1873. I told him that I had had a miscarriage [she could not bring herself to admit to an abortion], and that if he still wished to marry me, he married me in full knowledge of that fact.' Florence left Bravo to ponder these tidings alone, no doubt fully expecting an outburst of wounded indignation on her return. Instead, Bravo countered with a confession of his own. For the past four years, he explained sheepishly, he had kept a woman at Maidenhead, who had previously had a son by another man and who now had a daughter by him. Bravo now promised to give this woman up. As for Florence's indiscretions, they were forgiven. 'I am satisfied to make you my wife,' he told her, 'but, of course, you must never see Dr Gully again.'

Having given her word, Florence Ricardo married Charles Delaunay Turner Bravo on 7 December 1875.

They moved straight away to The Priory. By now, Dr Gully had also moved out of Leigham Court Road into an agreeable villa in Bedford Hill Road, not five minutes' walk from The Priory. But Gully was not part of Charles and Florence Bravo's new life. Her feelings for him had died in the flush of courtship and marriage, and Charles kept his promise never to rake up the Gully affair. In any case, the newly-weds had problems of their own. At the end of January 1876, not two months after their marriage, Florence had a miscarriage. 'We have had bitter trouble,' Charles wrote to Florence as she convalesced at the seaside, 'but I trust every day to come the sweet peace of our lives will not so much as be disturbed by memories like those . . .' But Charles was over-optimistic. Florence miscarried again early in April, and (evidently at her request) Charles moved from the marital bed into a neighbouring room while his wife recuperated. There were other, unexpected tensions, too. Florence was becoming irritated by Charles's meanness with money. His mother had ordered him to persuade Florence to economize by getting rid of two of her favourite ponies and one of the maids. Florence was furious, declaring that she had always lived within her income and that what she did with her money was her own business. Charles backed down, but continued to express concern about a different aspect of life with Florence: her growing fondness for drink. Mrs Cox had noticed it too, but it fell to Charles to issue a rebuke. Instead of her customary sherry, Bravo suggested that good red burgundy (his own tipple) would do her more good. Florence stonily ignored the suggestion.

Aside from these minor undercurrents of tension, life at The Priory in those early months of 1876 presented a picture of blameless, almost idyllic domesticity. 'Charlie is very well, and equally happy,' Florence wrote to her mother a few days after her April miscarriage. 'He has been so good and kind to me while I have been ill.' But just two days later Charles was sitting at his wife's bedside nursing his face and complaining of toothache and neuralgia. At Florence's suggestion he rubbed his gums with laudanum (the Victorian equivalent of oil of cloves) but this brought no relief, and he applied a little chloroform to dull the pain. The following weekend was Easter. The morning of Good Friday brought rain, and Charles, bored and still nagged by pain, paced restlessly through the house. The weather improved on the Saturday, and he was able to spend the morning exercising one of the horses. That afternoon Florence was feeling well enough to take an airing in the family coach, and Charles rode out alongside her. After lunch he and Rowe, the butler, put up a new lawn-tennis net in the garden and Charles played several vigorous games with Rowe and Osman, the gardener. Easter Sunday was too windy for tennis, and in any case, in Charles's own words, playing games on such a day 'might shock the good people of Balham and Tooting'. The holiday had brought Charles a respite from his neuralgia.

'I never saw him look so well,' commented Florence in a chatty letter to her mother. 'The country is life to him, and he walks about with a book under his arm as happy as a king.' Hardly had she penned these words, however, when Charles appeared in her room complaining that the neuralgia had returned. Florence recommended a hot toddy of brandy and lemon, which Charles drank alone in his room. By the evening of Easter Monday, he was in considerable pain. Florence's maid, Mary Ann Keeber, found him slumped in a chair by the fire, his face in his hands. The girl asked him what he was taking. 'I rub my gums with laudanum,' Charles replied, 'and sometimes chloroform.'

Charles Bravo took seriously ill the following evening, Tuesday 18 April. He had dined on fish, roast lamb, anchovy eggs on toast and bloater paste, a meal he shared with Florence and Mrs Cox. During dinner, Charles drank three glasses of burgundy; Florence and Mrs Cox between them finished off two whole bottles of sherry. Unsurprisingly, perhaps, Florence presently announced that she was feeling unwell, and retired to her room at about quarter to nine, asking a servant on the way to fetch her more sherry. This seems to have offended Charles, who (seeing they were within earshot of the staff) muttered something to her in French. Charles himself went upstairs about half an hour later, exhausted by a hair-raising ride he had had that afternoon when his horse bolted with him. A few minutes later he appeared at his bedroom door in his nightshirt shouting: 'Florence! Florence! Hot water!' Mrs Cox, who was sitting with the slumbering Florence in her room next door, heard the commotion and hurried to Charles's aid. She found him standing at the open window. His face was grey and sweaty. 'Hot water! Hot water! *Hot water!*' he cried, his voice rising to a scream. Then, leaning forward through the window, he was violently sick.

Mrs Cox acted quickly. She realized that Bravo urgently

needed an emetic to clear his system. He also needed a doctor.

Mary Ann Keeber, who had dashed upstairs on hearing her master's cries, was instantly despatched downstairs again for water, and to alert the other servants to send for a doctor. With the hot water she brought some mustard which she hurriedly mixed into a paste. Charles was now slumped on the bedroom floor beneath the open window, but Mrs Cox managed to force some of the mustard paste through his clenched teeth, and this caused him to vomit into a basin. Mrs Cox, keeping admirably cool under the circumstances, instructed the maid to set Charles's feet in a bowl of mustard and water and to rub them as hard as she could. This she did, breaking off at length to fetch some strong coffee from the kitchen and some spirits of camphor from her mistress's room, where she found Florence still sleeping. 'Oh, madam,' cried the maid, 'do come quickly. Mr Bravo's very ill.'

Florence opened her eyes and stared at the maid.

'What is it?' Florence sounded groggy with sleep.

Pulling a dressing gown around her shoulders, Florence hurried on to the landing. 'When I went into the room,' she said later, 'I found my husband lying on the floor near the window looking like death, and Mrs Cox rubbing his chest.'

Florence stared down in horror. She could scarcely speak for the tears. 'Has the doctor been sent for?'

Mrs Cox said that word had been sent to the family's regular physician, Dr Harrison at Streatham, two miles away. Florence was appalled at the inevitable delay this implied, and turning sharply she fled down the stairs, calling for Rowe, the butler. 'Get someone from Balham!' she screamed. 'I don't care who it is! Get someone!'

Rowe hurried off down the drive to fetch the local

doctor, Dr Moore, who arrived at half-past ten. With Rowe's help, Dr Moore managed to get Charles Bravo into bed. By now the patient was unconscious and breathing hard. His skin was cold, and the pulse so weak that Dr Moore feared it would cease altogether at any moment. 'He looked like a person under the influence of poison,' he recalled, 'but I could not identify any poison which would correspond with the symptoms. Mrs Bravo asked me if I thought his state was dangerous, and when I replied that I did not think he would recover she burst into a flood of tears. Her grief appeared to me altogether natural.' Dr Moore was presently joined at the bedside by Dr Harrison from Streatham. 'I'm sure my husband has taken chloroform,' said Florence, but Dr Harrison could smell no chloroform on Charles's breath. Both doctors now conferred anxiously and, suspecting heart failure, decided to inject Bravo with a mixture of brandy and water. They explained to Florence that they would value a third opinion, and she at once suggested sending for Bravo's cousin and closest friend, Royes Bell, a Harley Street surgeon. Bell arrived at half past two in the morning, bringing with him a colleague from King's College Hospital, Dr George Johnson. As senior physician at the hospital, Dr Johnson at once took charge of the case. Charles Bravo had now surfaced from his coma, and Johnson leaned over and asked him softly: 'What have you taken?'

'I rubbed my gums with laudanum for neuralgia – I may have swallowed some.'

'Laudanum will not explain your symptoms, Mr Bravo.'

'If it isn't laudanum,' Charles replied, 'I don't know what it is.'

The doctors looked at each other, and shook their heads.

It took Charles Bravo two more days to die.

Two further doctors were summoned, the eminent Sir William Gull and – as a last resort, and at Florence's request – the neighbouring Dr Gully. Each physician, suspecting poison, began by asking Bravo the same question: 'What have you taken?' But the patient doggedly insisted that he had taken nothing, merely that he had rubbed some laudanum on his gums to rid himself of toothache. With the family gathered at his bedside, Charles admitted he had never been a religious man but nevertheless he prayed and recited the Lord's Prayer with them. He made a brief will, leaving everything he owned to Florence, and implored his grief-stricken mother to take care of her. He died at half-past five on the Friday morning. A post-mortem examination showed the cause of death to have been a massive dose of some thirty grains of tartar emetic or antimony.

None of the baffled medical men was prepared to sign a death certificate, and the local coroner was obliged to hold an inquest. This took place in quite unprecedented circumstances, not in any public arena (as the law required) but, at Florence's invitation, in the dining room at The Priory. Anxious to spare the feelings of the Campbells, the coroner neglected to notify the press of the inquest, and tried to gloss over a sensational claim by Mrs Cox that Charles had confided to her that he had taken poison intentionally. In the face of an open verdict from a confused and suspicious jury, and mounting pressure from the press and outraged members of Bravo's family, the Attorney-General ordered a second inquest. This took place in even more bizarre circumstances than the first, being held in the upstairs billiards room of a local hotel, the Bedford, where the protracted proceedings – the hearing lasted twenty-three days – took on the air of a Roman holiday, with crowds of sightseers and ticket-touts jamming the streets below 'like a swarm of crows feasting on the dead body'. The result was an extraordinarily quirky verdict. Charles Bravo, the jury concluded, 'did not commit suicide . . . he did not meet his death by misadventure . . . he was wilfully murdered by the administration of tartar emetic, but there is not sufficient proof to fix the guilt on any person or persons.'

The Bravo case fired enormous public interest in Victorian England. For one thing, it was set firmly in the world of the upper-classes, and smacked deliciously of money, land, power and illicit sex. To the working masses, it was what we would now consider pure soap-opera. The enigmatic Mrs Cox provided a cliff-hanging twist to the plot with her claim at the second inquest that the dying Charles Bravo had confided to her: 'I have taken poison for Gully. Don't tell Florence.' Then there was the conflicting and puzzling evidence of Florence's former coachman, George Griffith, sacked on the orders of Charles Bravo only days before the wedding for careless driving. Sitting sullenly in the taproom of the Bedford Hotel on the morning of the wedding, he had prophesied Bravo's imminent demise, exclaiming with uncanny prescience: 'Poor fellow, he won't be alive in four months!'

Something else that was considered extremely newsworthy at the start of the second inquest was the exhumation of Charles Bravo's remains. By law, the jury had to view the body, so the coroner packed them off in a train to Lower Norwood cemetery. The coffin was raised and a small glass window, a sort of Judas-hatch, inserted in the lid. One by one the jurors filed solemnly past, pausing briefly to glance down at the blackened, decaying features of Charles Bravo.

Although the legal process was exhausted with the jury's inconclusive verdict at the Bedford Hotel, public suspicion festered on, inflamed by Mrs Cox's sensational revelations about the nature of Florence Bravo's relationship with Dr Gully. A popular jingle of the day, a parody of Goldsmith's

The Vicar of Wakefield, summed up the public's verdict on the case:

> When lovely lady stoops to folly,
> And finds her husband in the way,
> What charm can soothe her melancholy,
> What art can turn him into clay?
>
> The only means her aims to cover,
> And save herself from prison locks,
> And repossess her ancient lover,
> Are burgundy and Mrs Cox!

And yet there had emerged no shred of evidence that Florence Bravo had poisoned her wretched husband in order to 'repossess her ancient lover'. Indeed, no clear motive was assigned to anyone, although the prosecution did its best to denounce the beautiful young widow as a murderess as well as an adulteress. After her failure to appear at the first inquest except in the role of hostess, and faced with wagging tongues on all sides, Florence had signed a lengthy formal statement in early June in an effort to exonerate herself. This had contained a flat denial of any 'criminal intimacy' with Dr Gully, and described their relationship as 'quite innocent'. At the second inquest, solicitor George Lewis, on behalf of Bravo's family, tested this assertion with saw-edged implacability during the testimony of Florence's 'faithful' lady's companion, Jane Cox.

'You say you kept something back [from Charles Bravo] before marriage – what was it?'

'I kept back from him what Mrs Ricardo had told me after giving up her acquaintance with Dr Gully.'

'What was it she told you?'

'Of her intimacy with Dr Gully.'

'What do you mean,' asked Mr Lewis, 'by intimacy?'

Mrs Cox hesitated. 'You may draw your own conclusions.'

'No, I decline to do that,' retorted Mr Lewis, to the strained delight of the onlookers crowding the public seats. 'Tell me, madam, was it a *criminal* intimacy with Dr Gully that she told you of?'

Mrs Cox looked dumbly at the table in front of her.

'Answer my question, madam!'

'Yes,' Mrs Cox muttered, reluctantly. 'A criminal intimacy.'

Faced with this sensational disclosure, Florence had no option but to admit to a fully fledged sexual relationship with Gully when she entered the witness box herself a couple of days later. She chose to fight fire with fire, however, and at one point tearfully rounded on Mr Lewis as he probed relentlessly into the details of the affair:

'That attachment to Dr Gully has nothing to do with this case – of the death of Mr Charles Bravo!' Florence shouted angrily. 'As to that, I will answer any question. I have been subjected to sufficient pain and humiliation already, and I appeal to the coroner and to the jury, as men and as Britons, to protect me. I think it is a great shame that I should be thus questioned, and I will refuse to answer any further questions with regard to Dr Gully!'

Florence's anguished outburst prompted an approving round of foot-stamping from the gallery, but the wider world continued to gloat, relishing unreservedly the public and final humiliation of a woman whose honour had been ripped from her in raw strips. Next it was Dr Gully's turn. 'I have read Mrs Bravo's statement as to [our] intimacy,' he said, ruefully. 'I am sorry to say that statement is true and correct, and I feel my position most bitterly in having to stand here and say this.'

Mr George Lewis prepared to mete out the same rough treatment he had shown towards Florence. 'You knew,' he rasped at length, 'that she had given you her entire affections; given up for you her home, family and all – even to her good name?'

'I knew she had been given the chance of giving me up and had refused.'

That was not the answer Mr Lewis required, and he put the question again. 'You knew she had given up her name for you? Her good name? Her *honour*?'

'Well,' said Gully resignedly, 'she had given up her home, but what do you mean by her honour?'

Gully's counsel protested angrily to the coroner, but to no avail. The question had to be answered.

'There came a time,' Gully finally conceded, 'when she sacrificed her honour for me.'

The dishonouring of Dr James Manby Gully MD was complete. Victorian contempt, spite and envy – that a man of his years should have been to bed with a pretty young woman – had claimed him as a victim, and yet his testimony had contained not the slightest hint that he had connived in any way in the death of his mistress's new husband. So, if Charles Bravo was murdered, who murdered him – and how?

The answer seems to lie at the dying Charles's bedside.

It was Charles Bravo's lifelong habit to drink last thing at night from his water bottle placed on the washstand by a servant. 'I noticed,' said one of Bravo's roommates from his Oxford days, 'that before going to bed he always took a deep draught of water. He used to drink it straight from the water bottle in his room . . . without using a tumbler.' Dr Harrison, the first medical man to reach the stricken Charles's bedside, remembered seeing a water bottle on the table in the sickroom, about three-parts full.

Did someone tamper with the water in that bottle in order to poison Charles Bravo?

If so, who? And why?

In her four short months of marriage to Charles Bravo Florence suffered two traumatic miscarriages. The first occurred at the end of January 1876, about seven weeks after the wedding. Florence travelled to the south coast to recuperate, but without her husband, who seems to have moved back in with his mother at Palace Green while attending to his business affairs at his chambers in the Temple. Under his mother's malevolent influence Charles, on Florence's return to Balham, began urging his wife to economize in the running of The Priory. 'My *mother* thinks a lady's maid an unnecessary extravagance . . . My *mother* thinks three gardeners excessive . . .' Florence, who after all lived comfortably within her ample means, was deeply irritated by these unwarranted interferences, and announced that she proposed to confront old Mrs Bravo at Palace Green and 'have it out' with her mother-in-law. In the event, Mrs Jane Cox intervened and counselled caution; Florence's temper cooled, and she set out, not for Kensington, but for her father's mansion at Buscot. For a day or two she sulked. Then came a letter:

My darling wife,
Looking back on the weeks of our marriage I feel that many of my words, although kindly meant, were unnecessarily harsh. In future my rebukes, if it is necessary to say anything, which God forbid! shall be given with the utmost gentleness . . .
    Come back as well as you can to your devoted husband,
                                                                                    Charles

And then another:

I miss you, my darling wife, dreadfully. When you come back I will so take care of you that you will never leave me again.

Charles's passionate entreaties did the trick, and Florence returned to The Priory. But again her health faltered, and she was treated for depression and bouts of nausea.

She suggested that she might convalesce at Worthing 'for a change of air', but Charles was cool on the idea. He even prompted his mother to write to Florence seeking to dissuade her 'on the score of expense'. Florence was upset and angry at their attitude, and the incident triggered a violent quarrel in which Charles completely lost his temper. 'I said I would write [Mrs Bravo] such a letter that she would not interfere with us again,' Florence recalled. 'He was angry with me for saying that. He jumped out of bed saying: "I will go and cut my throat!" He rushed into his dressing room and I rushed after him ... His temper was like a frenzy ...'

In the heat of that frenzy, Charles struck his new bride a painful blow to the face.

Tears were streaming down Florence's cheeks as she hastened up to Mrs Cox's room on the top floor of The Priory. Mrs Cox listened to Florence's hysterical account of what had happened. Then, scenting possible scandal, Mrs Cox dressed hurriedly. 'I went downstairs,' she said, 'and saw Mr Bravo with his hat and coat on. He told me he was going away, took the bolt off the door and went down the drive. I followed him and begged him to come back again. I told him what a scandal there would be. "What would the world say?" I asked him.

'"Some will say it is her fault, and some will say it is mine," he replied.

'"What will your mother say?" I asked.

'"My mother! She will be only too glad to have me back at any price!"'

Mrs Cox took Charles by the arm and led him back into the house where the newly-weds kissed and made up. It was only a temporary truce, however, and the following morning, still smarting from the clout on her cheek, Florence packed her bags again and left for Buscot. Again, Charles decamped home to Palace Green, and again wrote pleadingly to Florence that 'I cannot be happy in the absence of my best of wives. My only object is to make you happy . . .'

Once more Florence relented. It was pointless to stay at Buscot; in any case, she had discovered she was pregnant again (hence the nauseous attacks), and her place was at The Priory with her husband. She returned to Balham on 13 March. Two days later Charles, delayed in London on a case and still staying with his family, wrote this curious note in which, on the one hand he sought to heal his marital wounds with a balm of sickly endearments and, on the other, rubbed a large cake of parental salt into them:

As you make sunshine wherever you go, your presence here is much needed, for we have rain, snow and sleet . . . Father Joseph has promised to give us the barouche on condition we put down the cobs. By giving up the cobs and Mrs Cox we can save £400 a year and be as comfortable. But I only want your love, and without your love, riches and honours will be as nothing . . .

By giving up the cobs *and Mrs Cox*! Could anything be as deliberately calculated to distress Florence as this tactless suggestion from Palace Green? And if Mrs Cox got to hear of it, could this scarcely veiled threat of dismissal not furnish her with a more urgent and valid motive for murder?

By mid-March Florence Bravo, bride of three months, was confused and exhausted. She miscarried again early in April, causing her spirits and her general constitution to ebb lower still. This was her third miscarriage (her second with Charles but remember the abortion at the hands of Dr Gully in Germany) and she was deeply depressed at the prospect of a fourth or fifth. It was at this point that she asked Charles to quit the marital bed. This had two effects: she was able to invite the ever-solicitous Mrs Cox to share her room and to nurse her; more crucially, Florence was able to stave off – for the time being at least – the prospect of a further abortive pregnancy. Florence sleeping alone was Florence sleeping in safety.

This arrangement, whereby Charles Bravo slept miserably by himself in a small bedroom adjacent to the marital bedchamber while Mrs Cox took his place alongside Florence, was clearly unsatisfactory to Charles, who possessed all the natural urges, instincts and desires of a recently married man of thirty. Sensing that Charles planned to reclaim his conjugal rights, did Florence – appalled at the possible consequences – seek to quench his ardour? Or did she seek some altogether deadlier remedy?

We have arrived back at Charles Bravo's washstand, and his customary bottle of water. It is time to theorize, to speculate.

Although contraceptive methods had been devised and developed by the 1870s, they were by no means generally known or widely practised as a means of family planning. A woman wanting to avoid pregnancy often slipped a strong emetic into her husband's drink. This had the almost instant effect of making the man wretchedly sick. And a man in the throes of vomiting is a man with neither the time nor the stomach for love-making. Of course, as historian Elizabeth Jenkins pointed out to me, 'it was only a temporary respite, but at least it kept the man off the woman for the time being. And that is what I, for one, believe Florence Bravo was trying to do. She had already had two miscarriages since her wedding. She was only just recovering from the second when Charles Bravo showed signs of wanting to come back and share her bed.'[1]

On the night of Charles's fatal seizure, Florence had sat through dinner convinced that he planned to seek her favours that very night. It was this alarming thought that caused her to hit the sherry bottle in an effort to steady her

nerves. Seeing that her husband had regained his composure after his nightmarish gallop aboard the runaway horse
Cremorne, and was eating and drinking heartily enough,
she realized that her only defence lay in administering to
Charles a hefty dose of emetic. This she did when she
tottered upstairs after dinner alone. It would have taken
less than a minute to scurry into the neighbouring room
and to drop a handful of poisonous crystals of antimony
into the water bottle; she could bank on Charles taking his
customary massive swig before slipping down the landing
to her room. And that, I surmise, is exactly what happened.
Florence Bravo did not intend to murder her husband,
merely to cool his ardour. But in her tipsiness, she overdid
the poison, and instead of a grain and a half – the emetic
dose – she fouled the water bottle with a massive, murderous dose of something like thirty grains. This explains
Florence's subsequent behaviour – which was absolutely
consistent with innocence – and Charles's apparently inexplicable refusal (or rather inability) to tell the doctors what
he had taken, other than the laudanum for his neuralgia.

As for Mrs Cox, she may have connived at a contraceptive dose of poison, but she had no compelling reason to
want to be rid of Charles Bravo. Even had she got wind of
the economies proposed at Palace Green, there was no
reason to suppose that Charles Bravo intended to
implement her suggested dismissal; on the contrary, only
weeks before he died he was telling dinner guests at The
Priory that he had no intention of sacking her. In any case,
even had he done so, Mrs Cox was planning an extended
trip to Jamaica to visit a dying aunt, so what difference
would it have made?

'We find that Mr Charles Delaunay Turner Bravo did
not commit suicide; that he did not meet his death by
misadventure; that he was wilfully murdered by the administration of tartar emetic; but there is not sufficient evidence to fix the guilt upon any person or persons.'

The verdict of the jury at the second, shameful inquest cut through the packed and steaming billiards room of the Bedford Hotel like sheet lightning. Wilfully murdered! The crowd in the pit had their verdict, but they had no victim, for no killer had been named. Florence walked free, the prisoner only of suspicion, leaving the last word to the press. 'It is hardly too much to say,' snorted a writer in the *Saturday Review*, 'that the inquiry as to the death of Mr Bravo is, in every way, one of the most disgusting public exhibitions which have been witnessed in this generation.'

The contraceptive theory is only a theory, and the Bravo case is thick with theories. Whole books have been written to prove either that Florence murdered not only Charles Bravo but her first husband, Alexander Ricardo, as well (see *Suddenly At The Priory* by John Williams[2]), or that Charles died accidentally by his own hand, mistaking tartar emetic for a bedtime draught of Epsom salts (see *How Charles Bravo Died* by Yseult Bridges).[3]

The case ruined reputations and shattered lives. Dr James Manby Gully, exposed as the unscrupulous seducer of a wealthy young woman, was ruined socially and professionally, expelled from every medical society to which he belonged, finally to die in ignominy six years later. Mrs Jane Cannon Cox evidently returned to Jamaica as she had planned to do, and died penniless and in obscurity.

Florence Bravo herself became a recluse. The Priory, with its ghosts, became an intolerable prison, and within a year she had terminated the lease and auctioned every last stick of furniture in it. She changed her name to Mrs Turner, sought solitude in Southsea where she leased a villa and, like her first husband, drank herself to death in September 1878. 'I can't breathe, I can't breathe, save me!' she cried at the last, spewing up a mixture of brandy and blood. She was buried at Buscot churchyard, leaving over £60,000 in her will. Apart from minor bequests, the money was left in trust to her brother for his descendants. Mrs Jane Cannon Cox, one-time trusted friend, confidante and chaperon, received nothing.

The room in which Charles Bravo died more than a century ago is now Ian Pringle's one-bedroom flat. The view over Tooting Bec Common is much the same, but the side window through which Charles vomited on the night he was poisoned has gone.

'This,' said Norma downstairs, 'was Mrs Bravo's dining room, and it is now my studio flat. It's the only room in the house to retain the original height of the ceiling. In the centre of the room would have been the dining table. And, as master of the house, Charles Bravo would have sat at the head of the table which is actually where my sofa is now. And he'd have probably looked out through my french windows on to the garden when they were having their evening meal. The Bravos had a massive, heavy sideboard, and that would have been where my kitchenette and bathroom are now.'

I asked Norma if living alone in the Bravos' dining room didn't give her the creeps. 'No, not at all,' she said. 'I know that the house has had a lot of tragedy connected with it, but I've always been very happy here.' We looked out through the magnificent french windows that stretch from floor to ceiling. It was dark outside. Norma's cat was moving somewhere on the patio where Florence would have tended her roses. A train ran through the cutting beyond the boundary wall, heading for Victoria, but there was no smell of steam to mask the spectral aroma of whiting, roast lamb, eggs and bloater paste.

6

Providence House, Peasenhall, Suffolk

Dora Pepper is the oldest inhabitant of Peasenhall. She is ninety-six, so old that she can clearly remember the day Rose Harsent was found murdered at Providence House. Rose was what they called a fast girl. She had more than one lover. For this reason, decent lads in the village ignored her.

Dora was only ten, but her sister, Nell, was five years older. 'We were getting to the age when we wondered why Mum hid all the newspapers. One day she went out shopping, and Nell and I found the *News of the World* hidden under the couch. And I said to Nell: "Let's have a look!" (We were scared stiff that Mum would come back at any minute.) And of course it contained all this murder business. All this trial. Everything!'

Peasenhall is by no means the prettiest village in Suffolk. It has only one street, called (depressingly) The Street. If you drive in from Stowmarket on the A1120 you are in the middle of the village before you know it. On the left is a row of pastel-washed cottages, some with added-on shop fronts, most with thatched roofs. There is a pub called The Swan, and a sub-post office. Across the street is a tiny stream running parallel with the road, crossed here and there by little bridges. This is known as The Causeway. The houses on The Causeway side of the street are bigger, with names like Plane Tree House, Pine View, Wisteria Cottage, The Thatched House and Gooseberry Cottage. If you drive on, you will be in Yoxford in ten minutes, and you can pick up the A12 and rejoin the rest of the twentieth century. Peasenhall, however, has become trapped between

Victorian and Edwardian England. There is an unsettling stillness here. 'The uncanny thing,' said Bartholomew Hodgkiss as we stood in his back garden, 'is if you look at photographs of the village at the turn of the century, and if you stand in the village street at the same spot as the photographer, it's not just the view that's the same. So are the people. A few more cars, a few less bicycles, the clothes are different, but the people are there. The postures are the same. They're standing in groups talking exactly the same as if it were a photograph taken eighty years ago.'

Barty Hodgkiss is right. Perhaps it takes incomers like us to see it.

'It's a delightful place to live in, self-contained, a finite village. Most people live and work in and around it. I'm unusual. I travel to and from London regularly. That's unusual for Peasenhall, but not so unusual in the surrounding villages like Westleton, where more people have holiday homes, who live there at weekends and commute to and from London, leaving a smaller proportion of local people.'

We walked up the garden, away from the house.

'I think partly it's to do with the way the land surrounding the village is owned by one man, John Levett Scrivener. The family has been here since the sixteenth century. They own quite a few houses in the village, and much of the farmland surrounding it. I think their presence has formed Peasenhall, giving it a sort of continuity.'

Dora Pepper lives in the tiniest cottage in Peasenhall, at the end of a terrace overlooking The Causeway. It used to be a lovely village, but oh, she said, it isn't a bit like it was. She lives alone, long widowed, and never answers the door unless she's expecting visitors. She is so old that strangers have to make an appointment to see her. This can be done at Mr Wright's sub-post office. Dora is very deaf. 'On the road out to Sibton,' she recalled, 'there was all them country cottages. All their windowsills and gardens were lovely in summer. Sex? Well you see they never talked about those sort of things in my time at all. I mean all my young life, until I went into service in London, did I ever hear such a word mentioned. And no boys in the village ever mentioned such a thing. So different to now!'

Barty Hodgkiss owns the grandest house in Peasenhall. It is The Ancient House, set at the end of The Causeway, but screened from the road by a wall and discreet rhododendrons. It is next door to Providence House. We walked into the lane which separates the two. 'The point about this murder which absolutely intrigues me is that it's alive today as it clearly was eighty years ago. For one thing, the people living in the village have been here a long time. They've actually stayed put. Also, they're so old! So they re-live the drama in the pub, in the shop, and for them it's so real. Of course, they have loyalties, either to Rose Harsent or to Willie Gardiner. And they feel that when you're talking about this murder their loyalties are being challenged. For me, coming here as an incomer, that is absolutely fascinating.'

We had walked down to the point where the lane between The Ancient House and Providence House meets the main road. Opposite, two women were gossiping outside Emmett's the grocer's. I asked Barty Hodgkiss how long the murder house had been for sale. 'Ages,' he said. 'Poor bloke just doesn't seem able to sell it. Probably people get to hear about what went on there and get frightened.'

The late spring of 1901 coincided with the dawn of Edwardian England. Among the 700 villagers of Peasenhall lived William Gardiner, his wife and their six[1] children. Gardiner was not deeply loved in the village, but folk respected his devout religious convictions and his dislike of strong drink. He was generally thought of as a model family man. For some years, Gardiner had worked for Smyth and Sons, a local firm making farm equipment, where he had been promoted to foreman in the carpentry department. Smyth's was a prosperous company, thanks largely to the success of its mechanical seed drill. A few years earlier, the firm had sent Gardiner to represent them at an exhibition in Paris. Since few inhabitants of Peasenhall had ever been further than Ipswich, this marked Gardiner out as a person of some importance and sophistication. However, his employers tempered their esteem for their carpenters' foreman with a grasping disregard for his creature comforts; they paid him a pittance of just twenty-six shillings (£1.30) a week. So William Gardiner owned only two shirts and lived in a small cottage on the main street.

William Gardiner was in his mid-thirties, a dark, swarthy-complexioned character. He was heavily built, and sported a jet-black beard. Some fancied this made him look like a Spanish pirate; others, especially the village children, thought he looked like a Russian spy and ran away when Gardiner strode through Peasenhall to his office at the drill works. An old man still living in the village remembers being afraid of Gardiner. 'People said at the time there was a lot of Russians about here with big black beards, and he was a big, strong man with a black beard. If I saw him, my brother and I runned home. We were afraid of anybody with a big black beard.'

Gardiner was a leading figure in the Primitive Methodist community at Sibton, a nearby hamlet just across the parish boundary from Peasenhall. He was superintendent, treasurer, and trustee of the Sunday school, assistant society steward, and choirmaster. It was his link with the choir that was to prove his undoing, for among the choristers was a girl named Rose Anne Harsent. Gardiner had known Rose for many years, watching her bloom from a winsome teenager into a desirable woman. Rose was friendly with Gardiner, and with his wife, Georgina.

In May 1901 Rose was twenty-two, and working as a domestic servant to a local Baptist elder, Deacon Crisp. He and his wife were elderly people, living quietly at Providence House. The Crisps had taken Rose on to replace a servant who had become pregnant three years earlier in somewhat embarrassing circumstances. The layout of Providence House was such that the maid's bedroom was directly above the kitchen and could be reached only by a separate staircase. The Crisps were not only old, they were rather deaf, and evidently knew nothing of what went on under their own roof late at night. It was an arrangement that suited Rose Harsent admirably.

She was a girl with an exceptional appetite for sex. A flirtatious attachment seems to have existed between her and the lad living next door, Fred Davis, but whether she entertained him in her room at Providence House is unclear. She had a reputation in Peasenhall as a girl of easy virtue. She relished the company of men, and primped herself up to attract their attention. She may have been genuinely pretty, or even beautiful. She may have been just tarty. No pictures of Rose survive to explain her allure, but she was, in the recollection of old Billy Roe 'a bit warm'. Everyone agreed on this, whatever else may be doubtful in the case. Surely, though, not everyone would go along with the criminologist William Henderson's ungallant assessment[2] that 'living as she did in a part of England not notably celebrated for a particularly high standard of moral purity, she was probably a fair specimen of the girlhood of her district'.

Rose Harsent was no ordinary country girl; she possessed an earthy and ultimately fatal guile. She was thrilled by dirty talk. She revelled in the pornographic jokes and songs bandied around Peasenhall by the village lads. She had even asked Fred Davis to write some of them down; he did so, and Rose kept them in a drawer in her room; it seems harmless enough today but nearly ninety years ago most young girls would have been shocked at such depravity. She also knew some of the cruder passages in the Old Testament, the result, perhaps, of whiling away too many hours in the choirstall during boring sermons. But whatever people muttered about her behind her back, it seems that Rose Harsent relished her role as village belle. She had charms, and she flaunted them. Respectable young men in the district did not consider Rose a suitable prospect for marriage. She was certainly not the type of girl the villagers expected to find in the company of such an upright man as William Gardiner.

But suddenly, that spring, came a breath of scandal as hot and heavy as anything the folk of Peasenhall could remember.

On the evening of 1 May 1901, as Georgina Gardiner lay at home in the final stages of her eighth pregnancy, Rose was seen making her way along a path which led to a small, thatched building known as the Doctor's Chapel. This was where old Deacon Crisp worshipped, and Rose was responsible for cleaning it as part of her domestic chores. It was just across the road from Providence House and directly opposite the drill works where Gardiner was employed. Rose was spotted by two young men who also worked there. One of them, George Wright (known in the village as 'Bill'), actually worked under William Gardiner; his friend, Alphonso Skinner (known as 'Fonzo'), worked for another foreman. They might have thought nothing of seeing Rose and, after a little ribald sniggering, might have passed on. But they were amazed when, moments later, Gardiner appeared from the direction of the drill works and followed Rose down the path into the Doctor's Chapel. Intrigued, Wright and Skinner crept up outside the chapel, straining to hear what was going on inside. Village gossip had already linked the names of choirmaster and chorister; but here was firm evidence of the juiciest scandal the village had ever enjoyed. The two listened breathlessly.

What happened between Rose and William Gardiner in the chapel that night has been hotly disputed ever since. According to the eavesdropping Wright and Skinner, Rose and Gardiner could clearly be heard enjoying sexual inter-course, climaxing with Rose's shouts of 'Oh! Oh!' Then came a rustling sound as though clothing was being replaced, followed by peals of girlish giggles. At this point Wright seems to have lost his nerve and left, leaving the older man, Skinner, listening alone. Rose, so he said, then asked Gardiner if he had noticed her reading her Bible on the previous Sunday; Gardiner asked her what she had been reading about, to which Rose replied: 'I was reading about what we have been doing here tonight. I'll tell you where it is. Thirty-eighth chapter of Genesis.' (This chapter concerns the adventures of the widow Tamar at the hands of her brother-in-law, Onan and father-in-law, Judah. The actual verse allegedly mentioned by Rose was never specified.)

George Wright returned after about twenty minutes. He and Skinner then heard Rose say she would be out tomor-row at nine o'clock, adding: 'I must go now.' She then came out of the chapel, followed some time later by Gardiner.

The Doctor's Chapel still stands at the bottom of the large garden behind The Ancient House. Barty Hodgkiss retraced Gardiner's footsteps. 'He'd have walked through this lovely little pathway between these steep banks. He too would have been brushing aside the beech leaves and the bracken, as you've just done. I think you'd describe it as slipping away to the chapel. Of course that's just the feel of it. Under these trees, great tall chestnut trees, and in through the door here.'

The chapel is built of wood, and the roof is thatched. It is not large, but long and narrow, perhaps sixteen yards long and only three or four yards wide. It was known as the Doctor's Chapel because in Gardiner's day a doctor lived at The Ancient House. Some older residents of Peasenhall knew it as the Weavers' Chapel, because it is thought to have been built in the sixteenth century by the Huguenots who used it as a place of worship. It is no longer consecrated, and the building is used to store garden furniture and hay for the Hodgkiss's horses. There is a small fireplace at the back, and oak beams holding up the roof. The feeling inside is a confined one, and cramped for a congregation of any size.

'The floor's the same, and if you look at the picture published in the Ipswich paper at the time of the case, the whole of the inside of the chapel is virtually identical to the way it is today. I think there was an oil lamp hanging from the middle of the roof, that's gone, and there were a few chairs and a harmonium in one corner. Otherwise,' said Barty Hodgkiss, 'it's unbelievably the same.'

No one is quite sure exactly where Wright and Skinner did their eavesdropping. There are a couple of ventilation shafts, which were probably open on a warm May evening. If you experiment and stand beneath these openings, you can clearly hear what's being said inside the chapel. It's likely that the two men were listening on the blind side of the building, out of sight of the doctor's house. Had they been disturbed they could have made their escape across open farmland, which stretches away to the south of Peasenhall towards Saxmundham.

It's important to remember that Gardiner never denied being in the Doctor's Chapel with Rose. But he angrily rejected charges of impropriety. There had, he said, been no debauchery, and no conversation about Biblical fornication. According to Gardiner, Rose had called him over to attend to a troublesome door that had stuck. Their conversation, such as it was, concerned hymns for a forthcoming Primitive Methodist anniversary.

Wright and Skinner watched William Gardiner leave the Chapel and waited until the coast was clear. Then they dashed back into the village to spread the tale. It was only a matter of days before the scandal reached the ears of Gardiner himself. On 8 May he sent for Wright and Skinner at the drill works. 'What's this you have set afloat about me?' he rasped. The two young men repeated their story. Gardiner was furious and demanded a written apology. Wright and Skinner refused, saying they had told only the truth.

Gardiner then wrote to Rose:

Dear Rose,
I was very much surprised this morning to hear that there's some scandal going the round about you and me going into the Doctor's Chapel for immoral Purposes so that I shall put it into other hands at once as I have found out who it was that started it. Bill Wright and Skinner say they saw us there but I shall summons them for defamation of character unless they withdraw what they have said and give me a written apology. I shall see Bob' tonight and we will come and see you together if possible. I shall at the same time see your father and tell him.
Yours &c.,

William Gardiner

By now Gardiner urgently needed a written retraction from Wright and Skinner. Everyone in Peasenhall had become aware of the scandal. Local Primitive Methodists had been dismayed to hear the rumours, and felt it reflected on the good name of their chapel and its members. So they decided to hold an inquiry into the affair. It took place at Sibton on 11 May. Wright and Skinner agreed to appear (though neither was a Methodist), but Rose Harsent did not go. Instead she was interviewed separately, and hotly denied the story. Once again, so did Gardiner.

The inquiry decided that a case had not been made out against William Gardiner. The assembled elders evidently preferred the word of one member of their sect to that of two outsiders. Even so, Gardiner resigned all his offices. (This turned out to be something of an empty gesture, since a month later he was solemnly re-elected to them all.) The inquiry chairman had a quiet word with Rose, and warned Gardiner against getting too friendly with female choristers. For his part, Gardiner conceded that in the past he had been indiscreet.

On the day of the inquiry, Gardiner wrote again to Rose:

Dear Rose,
I have broke the news to Mrs Gardiner this morning, she is awfully upset but she say she know it is wrong for I was at home from ½ past 9 o'clock *so I could not possibly be with you an hour* so she wont believe anything about it. I have asked Mr Burgess to ask those too (sic) Chaps to come to Chapel tonight and have it out there however they stand by such a tale I don't know but I dont think God will forsake me now and if we put our trust in Him it will end right but its awfully hard work to have to face people when they are all suspicious of you but by God's help whether they believe me or not I shall try to live it down and prove by my future conduct that its all false, I only wish I could take it to Court but I dont see a shadow of a chance to get the case as *I dont think you would be strong enough to face a trial.* Trusting that God will direct us and make the way clear, I remains
   Yours in trouble,

                                             W Gardiner

Although Gardiner was pessimistic about his chances of forcing Wright and Skinner to retract their story he went through the motions nevertheless. He consulted a solicitor in Halesworth, who duly wrote to them threatening legal action unless they gave a written apology. But they were not intimidated by this; they never apologized, and no writ was ever issued against them. The matter was officially dropped. In time, it might have been forgotten entirely, had events turned out differently.

Gardiner had been warned. He knew that the gossip was common currency in Peasenhall. If he was, indeed, conducting a love affair with Rose, he was going to have to be highly discreet. But even if their friendship was perfectly innocent he realized that it was open to misinterpretation. Whatever the truth of the matter it would be impossible, in the normal course of events, to avoid being seen together, if only at the weekly choir practice and Sunday services.

But there is evidence that the couple were up to something.

Nine months after the incident in the Doctor's Chapel a meddlesome man called Henry Rouse, one of the Sibton elders, spotted Gardiner and Rose walking down a lane at nine o'clock at night. He wished them goodnight, but neither said a word in reply. A few days later Rouse called Gardiner aside after a prayer meeting and warned him about continuing an association which could only 'do the chapel a great deal of harm'. According to Rouse, Gardiner asked that his wife should not be told. Rouse promised to keep silent, in return for which Gardiner undertook to stop seeing Rose at night. Again, Gardiner later denied that this encounter ever took place.

A second incident, also denied by Gardiner, was reported a few weeks later. The redoubtable Rouse was ranting in the pulpit when he glanced behind him to see Gardiner reclining in the choirstall with his feet up on Rose's lap. 'You gentlemen,' said Rouse later in court, 'know what I mean by the lap of a person. I ceased to speak, with the intention of telling one of them to walk out of the chapel but something seemed to speak to me not to expose them there.' In the event, Rouse did not speak to Gardiner at all; instead, on 14 April 1902, he dictated a letter to his wife which he then sent anonymously to Gardiner, assuming (correctly) that her writing would not be recognized. Gardiner kept this letter, and it was read at the trial:

Mr Gardiner,
I write to warn you of your conduct with that girl Rose, as I find when she come into the chapel she must place herself next to you, which keep the people's minds still in the belief that you are a guilty man, and in that case you will drive many from the chapel, and those that will join the cause are kept away through it. We are told to shun the least appearance of evil. I do not wish you to leave God's house, but there must be a difference before God's cause can prosper, which I will hope you will see to be right as people cannot hear when the enemy of souls bring this before them. I write to you as one that love your soul, and I hope you will *have her sit in some other place* and remove such feeling which for sake she will do (sic).

If all this tittle-tattle were true, it must have been perfectly obvious to anyone who was interested that Gardiner was still carrying on with Rose, although whether he was the father of her child, conceived the previous November, is far from certain; Rose as we have seen, was that kind of girl. By now she was having trouble concealing her condition from the world; she borrowed a book on abortion from Fred Davis next door (it seems he had no end of uses) but she was still carrying the child in mid-May when she was taxed with her condition by her mistress, Mrs Crisp. Although nearly six months pregnant, Rose denied it. She knew, however, that the time was coming when she would inevitably follow her predecessor into early retirement. What could she do? Who was there to turn to? Like

Mrs Crisp, Rose's mother was suspicious and disapproving. Her only hope was to appeal for help to the father of the child. We must assume that this man, whoever he was, already had a wife, since local opinion (if not natural chivalry) would have driven him to the altar had he been in a position to marry. But Rose remained singularly single, and singularly pregnant. So we must assume, too, that at the end of May 1902 a married man from Peasenhall was facing the unpleasant prospect of being exposed as an unscrupulous seducer of young girls.

The morning of Sunday 1 June dawned bright and clear following a violent thunderstorm overnight. At twenty past eight Rose Harsent's father called at Providence House to deliver his daughter's laundry. The back door was open. William Harsent went into the kitchen and found his daughter dead on the floor. Her throat had been cut, twice, severing the windpipe. Blood was everywhere.

Rose lay on her back, still wearing her nightdress and stockings. Her head lay close to the stairs leading up to her bedroom, and underneath was a copy of the *East Anglian Daily Times*. Part of this newspaper was charred, but Rose's hair had not been burnt. The lower part of her nightdress was also charred, but the part covering her chest and throat was intact. William Harsent found part of a paraffin lamp lying on the floor close to his daughter's body; he moved this out of the way and covered Rose with a rug. The rest of the lamp was scattered elsewhere on the kitchen floor.

As William Harsent surveyed this appalling scene James Crisp, the brother of Rose's employer, came to the door. He set off at once to raise the alarm, returning within minutes with the local constable, Eli Nunn, and Dr Charles Lay, a surgeon with a practice in Peasenhall. The elderly Crisps had now been called from their bed, and the little kitchen was crammed with people grouped around Rose's body. A candlestick with a burnt-out candle stood on the floor nearby, together with the shattered remains of a medicine bottle. The neck of this bottle lay near the fireplace, the cork still firmly fixed inside. Dr Lay picked up the fragment of glass bearing the label and saw it was marked *For Mrs Gardiner's chdn.* He put this in his pocket for safe keeping.

Constable Nunn went upstairs to search Rose's bedroom. The bed had not been slept in. He found a number of letters, including the two from William Gardiner concerning the scandal over the Doctor's Chapel, and a third, unsigned, letter of assignation:

D. R.
I will try to see you tonight at 12 o'clock at your Place if you Put a light in your window at 10 o'clock for about 10 minutes then you can take it out again. Dont have a light in your Room at 12 as I will come round to the back.

There were more unsigned letters, all containing references to sex.

And what of William Gardiner? On that sunny June morning, he had left home at nine-thirty to take his children to Sunday school, and it was mid-morning when he was told of Rose's murder. His reaction was curious. He had known the girl for nearly ten years, and had met her frequently for choral and other purposes each week for the previous four, yet he scarcely seemed surprised or upset. It seems curious, too, that the police allowed a full twenty-four hours to go by before interviewing Gardiner about the killing; they knew (as did everyone in Peasenhall) about the gossip linking Gardiner and Rose, and they had found two letters signed by Gardiner in the dead girl's room. But it was Monday morning before Superintendent George Staunton called on Gardiner at the drill works. Staunton questioned him about the unsigned letter of assignation. Gardiner denied writing it, but conceded that the writing was remarkably like his own.

The police paid several visits to Mrs Gardiner that day, but at this stage they neither searched the house nor examined any of Gardiner's clothes. They simply asked her to account for her husband's movements between the time he left work on the Saturday until eight o'clock on Sunday morning. Late on Monday afternoon the police called on Mrs Gardiner again to ask about the medicine bottle found near the body. Mrs Gardiner recalled Rose suffering from a cold, and giving her some camphorated oil. 'I may have put it in that bottle,' said Mrs Gardiner, 'I am not sure whether she took it away.'

Meanwhile a new piece of information had come to light. A local carpenter, Harry Burgess, remembered chatting with Gardiner at about ten o'clock on Saturday night. This conversation had taken place as Gardiner stood at his front door watching the storm blowing up. Burgess said that on leaving Gardiner he had walked up the street past the Swan. As he did so, he had noticed a light in a bedroom window of Providence House.

Superintendent Staunton re-read the mysterious letter of assignation. The implication of Harry Burgess's evidence was unmistakable: Gardiner had written the letter and was standing at his front door watching for Rose's signal. At seven-thirty the following evening, Tuesday 3 June, William Gardiner was arrested at his home and driven away in a horsecart. The police took with them some of Gardiner's clothes: a coat, undervest, a dirty shirt and a pair of trousers. In Gardiner's pocket they found a two-bladed pocket knife. This was sent away for forensic tests. When charged with Rose Harsent's murder William Gardiner replied: 'I am not guilty.'

On the day Gardiner was arrested the local coroner opened the inquest into Rose Harsent's death. The hearing took place at the Swan, where the accommodation was hopelessly inadequate. The resumed hearing at the end of June took place in the more commodious surroundings of the Peasenhall Assembly Rooms, almost opposite Providence House. By now, police inquiries had uncovered a number of important new witnesses. Gardiner's next-door neighbour, Mrs Rosanna Dickenson, for example, said she saw Rose Harsent call at Gardiner's back door at 9 P.M. on the night of the thunderstorm. But she received no reply; Gardiner had driven over to Kelsale on business and his wife had gone out to the village shop that stayed open late on Saturday nights.

James Morriss, a gamekeeper with a highly developed talent for detection, testified that in the early hours of Sunday he had seen two sets of footprints leading to and from Gardiner's cottage to Providence House. These had been made by rubber-soled shoes with bars across the treads. Although no such footwear had been found when the police seized the contents of Gardiner's wardrobe his wife had produced a pair of indiarubber-soled shoes which, she said, had been given her by her brother a week before the murder. These had bars across the soles, as described by Morriss. But Gardiner's solicitor, Mr Leighton, was not impressed. Wouldn't any footprints on a hard, macadamed road have been washed out by the heavy rain? he asked. 'Not at all,' was the emphatic reply. 'What makes you say so?' asked Mr Leighton. 'Because,' said Morriss, 'I saw them.'

The findings of the forensic experts who examined Gardiner's knife were just as inconclusive. They were certain that the knife could have inflicted Rose's fatal wounds, and it appeared from the condition of the blade and traces of oil that it had been newly sharpened. The knife had also been meticulously cleaned (it had even been scraped inside the haft) but a tiny trace of mammalian blood remained between the metal and bone of the handle. Gardiner explained this by claiming he had been hulking (gutting) a rabbit. But, as every countryman knows, rabbits are only fit for the pot between October and February because their meat, when 'struck', produces intestinal disorders. Gardiner would later concede that the rabbit was inedible and had to be buried.

The inquest jury returned a unanimous verdict of murder, naming William Gardiner. This was not surprising; criminal proceedings against Gardiner had already started at Saxmundham. The prosecuting solicitor outlined the police case: Gardiner had been unable to keep the appointment with Rose Harsent at midnight as arranged because of the fierce thunderstorm. Instead he went to bed with his wife, slipping out of the house to meet Rose some time in the early hours. He stole down the street to Providence House wearing indiarubber shoes and carrying a medicine bottle filled with paraffin. Rose, in her night-dress, met Gardiner in the kitchen. He attacked her, probably from behind, and stabbed her in the neck with his pocket knife. There may have been a scuffle, which would explain why a bracket behind the kitchen door was broken. Rose fell to the ground and Gardiner cut her throat twice. He meant to set fire to her body by pouring the paraffin over it, but the cork was jammed so tightly into the neck of the bottle that he could not get it out. He tried to unscrew the lamp but failed. So Gardiner had to break the bottle, pour what paraffin he could over the body and set light to it.

Against this brutal scenario the prosecution called its witnesses. A leading handwriting expert from London, Thomas Gurrin, said the famous letter of assignation had not, in his opinion, been written in a disguised hand. A Home Office analyst told the magistrates that the clothes seized from Gardiner's house on the day he was arrested were totally free of either blood or paraffin. A tiny piece of bloodstained cloth, three-sixteenths of an inch across, found on a broken piece of glass was of a different sort from the cloth of Gardiner's clothes; there was no hole in either his jacket or trousers from which this cloth could have come. The analyst reported that although there were traces of blood on Gardiner's pocket knife, he could not say how old it was, or whether – for certain – it was human blood.

The magistrates sent William Gardiner for trial at the Ipswich Assizes. Before being driven to prison Gardiner and his wife were allowed a few minutes together in an anteroom. Both were in tears. In public, however, Gardiner bore up bravely. 'At the railway station,' reported the *East Anglian Daily Times* 'he sat in the stationmaster's office until the 4.59 train came in, and by it he was taken back to Ipswich Prison.'

The police had managed to make out a prima-facie case against Gardiner, but they knew it was riddled with holes. For one thing, there was no firm evidence about the exact time Rose Harsent had met her death. Dr Lay, who was no expert on these matters, judged from the progression of rigor mortis that death had occurred between half-past twelve and half-past six, with the probabilities in favour of half-past four. But the police were not impressed with this, preferring to link the killing with the time proposed in the letter of assignation: midnight. The violent thunderstorm during the night had disturbed the Crisps; Mrs Crisp had gone downstairs to check that rain wasn't leaking through the windows. They were roused again later by a scream and a thud, but Deacon Crisp had told his wife not to bother with it, since Rose had been invited into their bedroom if ever she was nervous. Mrs Crisp had told the coroner that the scream had occurred between one and two o'clock, but it turned out later that this was a pure guess:

she had not checked the time by the clock. What was certain was this: Rose expected her lover at midnight, by which time a storm was raging outside and continued to rage for at least another hour and a half. The rain had stopped by four o'clock. Rose evidently expected her lover, since her bed had not been slept in, but it seems unlikely that she anticipated any sexual activity. She is more likely to have planned a discussion about her future as an unmarried mother, now that Mrs Crisp had begun asking awkward questions.

From the crucial question of timing, the police turned to the matter of the letters. They were encouraged by the findings of Gurrin, the handwriting expert, and delighted to find that the buff envelope containing the unsigned assignation note was identical to the ones used at the drill works. But the real breakthrough came shortly before the opening of Gardiner's trial. Herbert Stammers, whose house overlooked Gardiner's back yard, came forward with a damaging story. He claimed that at half-past seven on the Sunday morning, nearly an hour before Rose's body was found, Gardiner had gone to his wash house and had lit a large fire. The police were convinced that Gardiner had done this to burn his bloodstained clothing.

Gardiner's trial – the first of two, as it turned out – opened at Ipswich on 6 November 1902 and lasted four days. It was not an edifying affair. The judge was the irascible Mr Justice Grantham, a foxhunting squire with a habit of making up his mind early in a case and refusing to have his initial opinion swayed by the evidence. In a case where almost every piece of evidence against the accused was circumstantial this was scarcely satisfactory. Henry Dickens KC, a son of the novelist Charles Dickens, led for the Crown. For the defence, Gardiner's solicitors briefed a young barrister called Ernest Wild.[4] The trial was lengthy and, even by Edwardian standards, lurid. Rose Harsent's twenty-year-old neighbour, Fred Davis, admitted being the author of the indecent verses found in Rose's bedroom, and also of this letter, which was read in open court by the clerk:

Rose, My innermost yearnings have made me write down on paper a few lines about her who has enraptured my whole heart, a Rose among the many thorns that reside in our midst. Her shapely form and wavy hair makes her the very ideal that I worship. She means to me my very existence. You may smile, fair reader, at my nonsense, but since she crossed my path the very moments spent in her company are like a breath from paradise. The time may come when she may leave me to woo some other man, but Heaven only knows the pain that will gnaw at my heart. Life will not be worth living; but should I win her heart for my very own it would seem like Heaven upon earth. A glimpse of her at any time can cheer me through the day . . .

With her loving charms she has won my very soul, and when I at night sleepless lie, I think I see her face smiling at me as only those in love can know. I dare not think of her as being out of my reach; she has engraved her image upon my heart, and I pray that she will soon return my love. If not, Heaven only knows the consequences. Burn this.

But Rose had not burned it. It had been found by PC Nunn, carefully preserved by Rose along with a bundle of Fred Davis's dirty ditties. Examples of these were not given in evidence, but were passed to the jury during a lunch break. The jury foreman said they were glad this smut had not been read out in open court; the thrill-seekers in the public gallery must have been disappointed. Davis, in evidence, said he had sent Rose these verses at her request. 'Her request!' exclaimed Wild. 'You say that of a dead woman, that she requested you to give her this filth?' 'Yes,' said Davis, adding later: 'I done it for fun. It was only a sportive flirtation.'

Ernest Wild gave Davis a tough time. He had no evidence that Davis was the murderer – indeed, Davis's father was in court and prepared, if necessary, to support his son's alibi that he had been asleep in bed for the whole of the murder night – but Wild did suggest that Davis was the father of Rose's unborn child. Davis denied this indignantly: he and Rose had never had sexual relations. Despite the protestations in his lovelorn letter Davis claimed that it was Rose who had made the first move.

'She was the seducer?' asked Wild sceptically.

'That's about the truth of it,' Davis replied.

'What a gallant, chivalrous young man!' remarked Wild. The sour old judge, too, was unimpressed. 'I do not know,' he said sternly, when Davis had finished his evidence, 'what you are doing for yourself now; but I hope that all that has come out will be a caution to you, and remind you how abominably you have behaved. It is a disgrace to humanity – a young fellow like you!'

Mr Justice Grantham summed up vehemently against the prisoner before turning the case over to the jury. They could not agree on a verdict (in those days, a unanimous verdict was required) and the judge discharged them. It quickly emerged that only one juror had held out for Gardiner's acquittal, the other eleven finding him guilty. Gardiner had to be tried again.

In the meantime, Mrs Georgina Gardiner wrote to *The Times*:

I am the wife of William Gardiner, accused of the Peasenhall murder. I have six children. My husband has been in prison for more than five months, and during that time my children and I have received parish relief. What little money I could get together went to pay for my husband's defence, and I am now penniless and heart-broken. I know that my husband is innocent, and I cannot allow him to go undefended, if it can be avoided, at his next trial. Would you help me, and ask the public to also help me? PS: The editor of the *East Anglian Times*, Ipswich, has been so good as to promise to acknowledge contributions.

Gardiner had waited more than five months for his first trial; his second began on 21 January 1903. The same court, same dock, same lawyers – for several hundred pounds had poured in as a result of Mrs Gardiner's press appeal. The money was enough to re-engage young Ernest Wild, who had made a good fist of the defence at the first trial. The prosecution remained in the hands of the older and vastly more experienced Henry Dickens KC. There was, however, a different judge. This time, the case was tried by Mr Justice Lawrance, a towering figure of six foot six inches, known in legal circles as 'Long Lawrance'. People who had attended the first trial now thought Gardiner looked thinner and paler, but the reporter from the *East Anglian Times* considered that the prisoner still cut a dash in spite of his ordeal: 'He is a man of striking and rather intelligent appearance. His forehead is very broad and moderately high; his eyes are black and piercing; nose large and slightly aquiline; the hair and complexion so intensely dark as to suggest the Spaniard rather than the Englishman.'

Opening the case for the second time, Henry Dickens recited the familiar sequence of events leading up to the discovery of Rose Harsent's body at Providence House. He told the jury that the encounter between Rose and Gardiner in the Doctor's Chapel in 1901 was the key to the case; 'Fonzo' Skinner could not have invented such a tale. Dickens outlined the prosecution's theory concerning the oil lamp and the broken bottle found on the kitchen floor: Rose's killer had brought the bottle of paraffin to start a fire, but had corked it too well and could not get it open; he had then taken the oil lamp apart, but had been unable to get at any oil, and had finally smashed the bottle, forgetting that his wife's name was written on the label. This and all the other evidence, said Dickens, pointed to Gardiner as the culprit.

There was little that was new in the prosecution evidence. The facts by now were depressingly familiar. So were most of the witnesses. Ernest Wild opened the defence with a mild concession. Gardiner, he said, was 'perhaps not too popular owing to the fact that he is a teetotaller, and that he is a man professing religion' but he was certainly no scoundrel. Gardiner could not have murdered Rose Harsent without getting scratched or getting his clothing stained, and there was no suggestion this had happened. As for Wright and Skinner and their tale of debauchery at the Doctor's Chapel, they were nothing more than 'lewd louts with lewd minds' who belonged to 'that most contemptible class of humanity – people who lurk about, searching to see what filth and dirt they can possibly discover'. Their whole story, said Wild, was a malicious invention to bolster up scandalous rumours that they were already repeating in Peasenhall. Not only was the case against Gardiner not proven: he was entitled to a verdict of not guilty on this 'unjust' charge brought against him.

The second trial proved an ordeal for Mrs Georgina Gardiner. She fainted in the witness box. Accordingly her cross-examination had to be postponed, and William Gardiner himself then gave evidence. Basically he simply denied everything. Wright and Skinner were liars; old busybody Rouse was a liar and so was his neighbour Stammers with his story about the early-morning fire. Morriss, with his statement about the footprints in the street, was in all probability mistaken. Gardiner agreed that his writing looked like the writing on the letter of assignation, but all the same he had not written it; two subsequent witnesses, an accountant and a bank clerk, both said they did not believe Gardiner was the writer. Two experts, an architect and a quantity surveyor, said they had made tests at the Doctor's Chapel: it was not possible, they said, to hear from the outside what was going on inside.

The Reverend John Guy, superintendent of the Wangford Methodist circuit, who had presided at the inconclusive investigation at Sibton, made it clear that he had never been satisfied of Gardiner's innocence in the Doctor's Chapel affair. And although he admitted making a mistake in saying that Rose Harsent had been questioned by the inquiring elders he scornfully denied that his memory was defective. He also denied ever describing the chapel incident as a trumped-up affair. However, a succession of elders of the Primitive Methodist connection followed each other into the witness box to swear to their faith in Gardiner and to contradict the evidence of Mr Guy. Brother Goddard was quite clear: Guy had indeed called the accusation of impropriety a fabrication and a trumped-up affair. Brother Cripp agreed, and Brother Noah Etheridge agreed with Brother Cripp. Brother Goddard said that Guy had described Gardiner as being 'in the clear' and this was backed up by Brother Fiddler.

Mrs Gardiner, meanwhile, was not listening to this part of the case. She was lying on a table in the court waiting room in a state of collapse. The next day, on her way to court, she threw a fit of hysterics. A doctor was called and calmed her down. Eventually she made her way into the witness box to face the questioning of Henry Dickens. She was pale and distraught, but unwavering in her belief that her husband was an innocent man. Their married life had been happy, she said, and Gardiner had been a good husband and father. She had been aware of the scandalous talk concerning the Doctor's Chapel affair, but the gossip had not affected her relationship with her husband as she was convinced he was blameless in the matter. Mrs Gardiner said she had been on friendly terms with the murdered girl. Rose Harsent had been a frequent visitor to their house, even after the scandal of May 1901.

Dickens now moved on to the morning after the murder. Was it true that Gardiner had lit a fire in the wash house? Mrs Gardiner agreed that he had, but said the fire was for the purpose of boiling a kettle for Sunday morning tea. Her husband had taken the children to Sunday school at half-past nine. She had not heard of Rose's death until her next-door neighbour broke the news on her way to church. According to another passer-by, Rose had committed suicide. Mrs Gardiner also recalled the various police visits to the house and the clothes they had taken away. Confronted with the letter of assignation Mrs Gardiner had insisted to Superintendent Staunton that the handwriting was not her husband's.

Ernest Wild, in his closing speech to the jury, played on Mrs Gardiner's unhappy state of mind and body. 'Shall it go forth to the world,' he asked, 'that this poor country girl, who has staggered from her illness in order to go through the ordeal of cross-examination, is the wife of a murderer; and are these poor, helpless children to be branded for all time as the children of a man who has committed such a dastardly crime as that which you are investigating here today?' Wild ended on an impassioned plea, asking the jury to find that the case against Gardiner was not proven and that the accused was, in England, therefore entitled to an acquittal.

Dickens, who had the last word to the jury on behalf of the prosecution, pointed out that murder had been committed, and that everything pointed to Gardiner as the guilty man. Mr Justice Lawrance summed up, and instructed the jury to consider their verdict. They were out for just over two hours.

'Are you agreed upon your verdict?' asked the clerk.

'No, sir,' was the foreman's reply.

There was the inevitable sensation in court. Even the judge was surprised. 'You are not agreed?' he asked. 'Is there any chance of your agreeing?'

'No, sir,' said the foreman.

'None whatever?'

'I am afraid not.'[5]

So ended the second and final trial of William Gardiner. Five days later the Crown decided not to proceed with a third trial, and Gardiner was released. But he could not face returning to Peasenhall, where he remained the prisoner of suspicion. So he shaved off his beard and travelled to London in search of obscurity. He was never heard of again, except for a single sighting by a villager from Peasenhall during a visit to South London some years later. Walking into a grocer's shop to buy some items of food, the villager was astonished to see Gardiner, clean-shaven and clad in white coat and apron, serving behind the counter. The visitor did not let Gardiner see that he had been spotted, but returned to Peasenhall to tell his story.

Providence House is now known as Stewart House. The present owner, a melancholy man called Don Hammond, lives there with his son, but with eleven rooms it is too big for them. Don Hammond has been trying to sell for some years, but something about the house seems to put people off. 'The men seem quite keen,' he told me, 'it's the women. When they hear the history of the place they tend to say: "Well, no way will we move there." We had a barrister live in the village until recently and when he moved down to Peasenhall from London he wanted to live here, but his wife wouldn't. A doctor wanted to move in, but his wife wouldn't.'

He showed me the stone kitchen floor where William Harsent had found the body of his daughter nearly ninety years before. 'Well,' he said gloomily, 'it looks like the original floor.'

Rose Harsent's bedroom, where she had set a candle in the window on the night she died, is now a disused attic. You can no longer see the window from the front door of William Gardiner's cottage because the trees obscure the view.

I said I supposed that in a place the size of Peasenhall it's impossible to conceal the story.

'Well,' said Don Hammond, 'everybody tends to live on it, as if it happened yesterday. That's the problem. Still. There's always another year. Lots of people in the village tend to re-live the whole thing as if it happened last year or last week.'

Billy Roe and Reggie Friend are in their nineties now. They still discuss the case when they meet in the public bar at the Swan. Reggie's uncle put Rose in her coffin. Gardiner murdered her, Reggie is certain. 'Of course he did. But with him being a Sunday-school teacher, you see, the jury disagreed. They said: "Would a man like that go and do a thing like that?"' Billy Roe agrees. 'That were chapel people who got him off who were on the jury.'

Then Billy Roe said: 'I tell you ... they didn't say she was murdered, not till Monday. And I saw about four policemen come and arrest him about half-past seven Tuesday night. I'd come down to the butcher's with my father and I see him sat in the front in the cart. Two police behind and two police in the front, and he sat in the middle. And of course I asked my father where they were going to take him. And my father said: "Just for a ride, that's all."'

On the back of an unsolved mystery ride the inevitable legends. One tells of a greying man seen walking through Peasenhall in the 1920s who bore a startling resemblance to William Gardiner. This man walked along the main street to Providence House and stopped to look up at the gable window that had once been lighted. Another, more lurid, legend has it that every seven years a thunderstorm breaks out over Peasenhall affecting that village alone, exactly on the anniversary of the night of Rose Harsent's death. But this is where fact ends and fancy begins. Certainly on a summer's evening there is a sense of brooding in the vast East Anglian sky where it falls behind the hill on Bruisyard Road. If you walk up the hill out of Peasenhall you come to the gate of the old cemetery. A few yards off the main path, in a tangle of thorns and weeds, stands a dilapidated stone cross. The inscription is the epitaph to this story: In affectionate remembrance of Rose Anne Harsent, whose life was cruelly taken on the 1st of June 1902.

7

63 Tollington Park, North London

It is not what it was. At the time of the case Tollington Park, a long, straight road on the northernmost fringe of Islington, bore the stamp of Edwardian bourgeois respectability. 'Its houses suggest not what houses of a similar capacity in other districts so often suggest, a decayed and fallen gentility, but rather a crescent and gratified prosperity,' wrote one journalist. 'You feel that the people who live there have come not from a better neighbourhood, but from one not so good, and that they are proud to live in Tollington Park.'[1] Another writer, half a century later, speaks of its 'early-Victorian drabness . . . In half a century Tollington Park has perhaps declined a little in the social scale, but with its church, its colonnaded chapel, and its avenue of trees it still preserves its air of respectability.'[2] Today, as you travel along Stroud Green Road from Finsbury Park underground station, you might be in any flyblown part of north London, a dusty urban desert of cheap restaurants, launderettes, and Asian-run tobacconists. Crescent and gratified prosperity has yielded to decayed and fallen gentility once more, and Tollington Park itself awaits the attention of the gentrifiers with their builders' skips and entryphones. The houses are big and desirable, dating from the late-Victorian age and designed to meet the pretensions of the clerking lower-middle classes. They run in short terraces, the end houses in each being naturally slightly more desirable than those in the middle. One of these end houses, number 63, has already been spruced up, and is one of the finest in the street. It is undoubtedly the most infamous, for in the year 1910 it was the home of one of the cruellest, most calculating poisoners in British criminal history, Frederick Henry Seddon.

Fred Seddon was a Lancashire man with a hard-headed, unsentimental approach to life. He was forty years old and balding, but he compensated for this by cultivating a fashionable and luxuriant waxed moustache and affecting unnecessarily formal dress: top hat and frock coat. He probably liked strangers to think he was a banker or a stockbroker, but in fact he was merely an insurance superintendent, earning £5 6s (£5.30) a week plus commission. This was a fair wage in those days but in addition to the upkeep of the house in Tollington Park, Seddon also supported his wife, their five children and his elderly father. Seddon also employed a servant-girl and a charwoman. He supplemented his wages by speculating in property, an endeavour which he enjoyed hugely, for Fred Seddon worshipped money and in particular profit. He would do anything to turn a profit, however small, however paltry. In the evening he would hustle for walk-on parts at local music halls for half-a-crown (12½p) a time; he bought and sold old clothes, set his wife up in a small business of her own selling wardrobes, and even charged his own teenage sons six shillings (30p) each a week for board and lodging. Finding the house too big for his needs, he let the basement to his employers, the London and Manchester Industrial Assurance Company, for five shillings (25p) a week (Seddon used this basement room as an office) and rented the top floor as unfurnished lodgings for 12s 6d (62½p) a week. A contemporary writer summed him up thus: 'He appears to have been a man who wished to turn if possible every transaction of his daily life into a means of making money; pleasure meant singularly little to him; so far as one knows, his chief passion was the passion to be the possessor of property . . . He was one of those people for whom the word business has an almost sacred significance, and there can be no doubt that money was his god.'

We need to look through the grimy net curtains of 63 Tollington Park a little more closely to get to know the motley band of occupants in the long, fiendishly hot summer of 1911. Fred and Margaret Seddon slept in the first-floor front bedroom, along with their newly arrived baby daughter, Lily. On the same floor was a room shared by their two eldest daughters, Margaret and Ada, and the servant, Mary Chater. In order to maximize the amount of spare room in the house, Seddon had partitioned this room into two; on the other side of the partition slept his two sons, William and Freddie, and his old father, William. Cramming his growing family and the servant into two rooms was deeply satisfying to Fred Seddon, as it meant that the entire second floor could be rented off at a profit. So if we climb the stairs to the upper landing we find the room occupied by Seddon's lodger, a disagreeable old maid called Eliza Mary Barrow.

Miss Barrow, at the age of forty-nine, was unmarried, eccentric, exceedingly deaf, squalid and dirty in her personal habits and hygiene, a heavy drinker, sallow, cantankerous, suspicious and – like her landlord – grasping and mean with money. Although singularly unattractive in almost every respect she was undeniably a woman of some substance in the flitting, twilight world of North London lodgings. She owned capital of some £4,000, mainly in the form of £1,600 India 3½ per cent stock, and had the lease of a pub in Camden High Street called the Buck's Head, together with that of a barber's shop next door. She kept most of her money in gold and banknotes stashed in a cash-box in her room; almost daily it was her delight to gloat over her hoard of wealth. Miss Barrow's small circle of relatives (she seems to have had no friends whatsoever) tolerated her solely on account of her money; indeed, they sought to ingratiate themselves with her in the hope that one day they would inherit at least some of it. But Eliza Barrow was no fool, and although she cordially disliked most of them she knew that their expectations would guarantee cheap board and lodging for herself and her cash-box for the rest of her life. Between 1902 and 1908 she had lived on this basis with some relations called Grant in Hampstead, but when Mrs Grant died (two years after her husband) she moved in with another set of relatives, the Vonderahes, in North London. She took with her the Grants' seven-year-old son, Ernie, for whom the drab old spinster had developed an apparently genuine affection. This strange couple lived uneasily with the Vonderahes for some fifteen months before the quarrelsome Miss Barrow gave notice in a fit of pique, spat in the face of Mrs Vonderahe, and ordered her furniture and other belongings to be loaded into a horsedrawn cart. She had heard of rooms to let in a large house in nearby Tollington Park, and, she announced indignantly to the Vonderahes, she proposed taking them without delay.

When she arrived on Frederick Seddon's doorstep at 63 Tollington Park on that hot afternoon in July 1910, Eliza Barrow was not alone. Standing there with her were little Ernie and his uncle and aunt, a young, newlywed couple called Mr and Mrs Robert Hook, who were also looking for accommodation. Seddon was delighted. His top floor was empty, and there was ample room for all four lodgers. The weekly rent would be twelve shillings (60p). The arrangement was that Miss Barrow paid the rent for all four, with Mrs Hook acting as maid and cook in return for free board and lodging for herself and her husband. The deal was neat but did not endure. Within a week Miss Barrow had fallen out with the Hooks (she was miffed that the newlyweds had taken young Ernie out for the day without her) and was begging Seddon, as landlord, to turn

them out of the house, claiming she was afraid of them.
Seddon, having feasted his eyes on the contents of the old
maid's bulging cash-box, obliged at once, giving the Hooks
just a day's notice, which he nailed to their locked door in
the middle of the night. 'I suppose it's her money you're
after,' said Robert Hook ruefully to Seddon the following
morning.

With the Hooks out of the way Frederick Seddon
proceeded to court favour with Miss Barrow, to the point
where he offered the services of his own daughter, Maggie,
as her maid for a weekly wage of seven shillings (35p).
Seddon learned that Miss Barrow was anxious about her
financial affairs, and in particular the effect that Lloyd
George's Budget might have on the fortunes of her pub,
the Buck's Head. She explained that the barber's shop next
door depended on the pub for its customers; fewer drinkers
at the Buck's Head would mean fewer clients for the
barber. Worse still, the value of her India Stock had started
to fall. Seddon listened attentively. He and Miss Barrow
were birds of a feather; both were terrified by the prospect
of poverty. So Seddon made Miss Barrow a proposition:
he would guarantee her an annuity of £10 a month and
waive her rent in exchange for her India Stock and the
titles to the pub and the barber's shop. Eliza Barrow
agreed, and signed the necessary papers. Seddon paid her
the first monthly instalment on the annuity in January
1911. At the same time he sold the stock and used the
money to buy some cheap houses on a mortgage. Miss
Barrow seems to have been satisfied with the deal, but
insisted on Seddon making his monthly payments in gold.
This she stashed in her cash-box, together with £216, also
in gold, which she withdrew from her bank.

Miss Barrow's hoard of gold continued to grow throughout the early part of 1911 as Seddon continued to make his
monthly annuity payments. The arrangement seems to

have endeared Seddon and his wife to Miss Barrow and
young Ernie Grant, who, in turn, were encouraged by
Seddon to feel more like part of the family than lodgers.
Indeed, in early August, the entire household (including
Seddon's elderly father) went on holiday together to South-
end, leaving the maid, Mary Chater, to look after the
house. It was around this time that Eliza Barrow's health
faltered. She paid several visits to a nearby doctor during
August, but on 1 September she took a turn for the worse,
and took to her bed with a bilious attack, accompanied by
fits of vomiting and diarrhoea. The Seddons sent for their
own physician, Dr Henry Sworn, who examined the
patient, declared she was the victim of a local epidemic of
diarrhoea and prescribed a mixture of bismuth and morphia.
Finding no improvement, Dr Sworn tried an effervescing
mixture of citrate of potash and bicarbonate of soda, telling
his recalcitrant patient that unless she swallowed the prescribed dose, he would have to send her into hospital. Miss
Barrow, characteristically, said she wouldn't go. Dr Sworn
continued to visit her, but by Monday 11 September Miss
Barrow had grown weaker. He told Mrs Seddon to dose
her with brandy and Valentine's meat juice.

In the afternoon of that same Monday, Miss Barrow
called Seddon up to her room. 'I don't feel well,' she told
him, 'and I'd like to see if anything happened to me that
Ernie and Hilda (his sister) get what belonged to their
mother and father.' Seddon (according to his own account)
demurred, and suggested calling in a solicitor to draw up a
proper will. But Miss Barrow was adamant. 'No, you can
do it for me,' she snapped. That evening Seddon sat down
at his desk and scribbled out a makeshift will, which he
took upstairs to show Miss Barrow. She called for her
glasses and checked it over, asking Seddon where she
should sign it. Seddon, calling his wife and father to the
bedside as witnesses, propped the old woman up on her

pillows and showed her. Miss Barrow signed. The witnesses signed. 'Thank God,' said Miss Barrow, sinking back, 'that will do.'

When the doctor saw her again on the following Wednesday he found her still weak but in no immediate danger. He did warn Mrs Seddon, however, that as Miss Barrow was a heavy woman, an asthmatic whose exhausted state made her susceptible to heart failure, she should not be allowed out of bed. It is not clear whether Dr Sworn also warned Mrs Seddon about the filthy state of Miss Barrow's sickroom. The patient's chronic diarrhoea and her dirty personal habits had made it scarcely habitable. Dr Sworn said later he had never seen so many flies. It was these flies that finally drove the patient from her own room to the room next door occupied by Ernie Grant. There was only one bed, and despite the squalid and distressing circumstances, it had to be shared by the fresh-faced, unquestioning boy and the stricken, malodorous Miss Barrow. After a couple of days, she was finally persuaded back to her own room, flies and all. Protesting bitterly that the room was too hot and plagued by flies, Miss Barrow sought relief by bidding young Ernie Grant constantly to fan her.

At midnight that Wednesday she cried out suddenly, 'I'm dying!'

Seddon did not hear these words, for he was still at the music hall where he had spent the evening – working, of course, and arguing with the manager about his appearance fee for a walk-on part. (Seddon claimed he had been promised half-a-crown (12½p) but had received only a florin (10p); the difference of sixpence (2½p) kept him at the theatre until nearly midnight.) When he finally arrived home at half-past twelve, however, Miss Barrow was still alive. Mrs Seddon sat at her bedside for most of the night. Seddon himself also kept a vigil of sorts, sitting on a chair outside the patient's door, smoking and reading the newspaper.

Dr Sworn was still in bed when, at seven o'clock the next morning, Thursday 14 September, Frederick Seddon knocked at his door to announce that Eliza Barrow had died an hour earlier. Seddon said that he and his wife had been up with Miss Barrow all night; she had been in considerable pain, had sunk into a coma and finally died. Surprised but unsuspecting, Dr Sworn wrote Seddon a death certificate, giving Miss Barrow's cause of death as epidemic diarrhoea.

From his house of mourning, Seddon next paid a visit to a local undertaker, William Nodes, in Stroud Green Road. Seddon explained that there had been a death in his house and that he wanted to make arrangements for 'an inexpensive funeral'. It needed to be cheap, Seddon added, because he had found only £4 10s (£4.50) in the old girl's room, and this would have to cover not only the funeral expenses but the doctor's fees as well. Mr Nodes suggested an inclusive funeral costing £4, but explained that such a cheap affair would mean burying Miss Barrow in a public grave. Seddon didn't seem to mind this, but pointed out that the remaining ten shillings (50p) would not cover the medical fees, at which the obliging Mr Nodes knocked another 12s 6d (62½p) off his price, bringing it down to an extremely cheap £3 7s 6d (£3.37½p). This satisfied skinflinty Seddon, who accepted Mr Nodes' offer of a lift back to Tollington Park in his trap where the undertaker measured the body.

'When can the funeral be?' asked Seddon.

'Whenever you like.'

'Saturday?'

'If you wish,' said Mr Nodes, thinking that a quick funeral would be no bad thing, given the state of the body, the infernally hot weather, and an unlined coffin. Moreover, the presence of a ten-year-old lad still living in the same room (which stank of diarrhoea) made it even more desirable to move the body out as quickly as possible. This was done the same evening, and Miss Barrow's funeral took place at Islington Cemetery, East Finchley, the following Saturday. It was a triumph for Frederick Seddon: not only did he now have control over most of her money and property, he had also managed to give her the meanest send-off it was possible to devise, and in the shortest possible time. To cap it all, he arranged with undertaker Nodes that although, as agreed, the funeral would be priced at £3 7s 6d, the receipt would be for £4, so that Seddon could pocket the difference by way of 'a little bit of commission, like'.

The passing of Miss Eliza Mary Barrow, and the penny-pinching funeral that followed, were low-key affairs and news of her death was slow to spread. So much so that she had been in her grave several days before word reached the ears of her relatives, the Vonderahes, who were still living round the corner from Tollington Park. They went immediately to see Seddon, who brazenly inquired why they had not attended the funeral. He produced a carbon copy of a letter which, he said, he had sent them immediately after Miss Barrow's death. The Vonderahes protested that they had never received the letter, which had been addressed to their old house and not the one they now occupied in Corbyn Street, off Tollington Park.

The letter was addressed to Mr Frank Vonderahe.

'Dear Sir,' it began:

I sincerely regret to have to inform you of the death of your Cousin, Miss Eliza Mary Barrow, at 6 A.M. this morning, from epidemic diarrhoea. The funeral will take place on Saturday next about 1 to 2 P.M.

Please inform Albert Edward and Emma Marion Vonderahe of her decease, and let me know if you or they wish to attend the funeral.

I must also inform you that she made a 'will' on the 11th instant leaving what she died possessed of to Hilda and Ernest Grant, and appointed myself as sole Executor under the 'will'.

Yours respectfully,

F. H. Seddon

(If this letter was ever sent, it was neither forwarded nor traced.)

Seddon also handed the Vonderahes three documents. The first was another letter, signed by Seddon, and addressed to the relatives of Miss Barrow. It stated that she had died leaving everything to Hilda and Ernest Grant, and had appointed himself as sole executor to hold her property in trust until they came of age. The Vonderahes read on in amazement:

She (Miss Barrow) stated in writing that she did not wish any of her relatives to receive any benefit at her death, and during her last illness declined to have any relations called in to see her, stating they had treated her badly and had not considered her, and she would not consider them.

The second document was a copy of Miss Barrow's will, dated three days before her death, signed by her and witnessed by Seddon's wife and father. It did indeed name the Grant children as her heirs, and Seddon as sole executor.

The third and final document was much smaller than the others, and was edged in black, being a memorial card 'In ever loving memory of Eliza Mary Barrow' and inscribed with this poetic sentiment:

A dear one is missing and with us no more,
That voice so much loved we hear not again,
Yet we think of you now, the same as of yore,
And know you are free from trouble and pain.

The Vonderahes looked at each other and then at Mr and Mrs Seddon. The visitors were under no illusions: they had been swindled out of their inheritance. What, they asked, had happened to the Buck's Head pub, and the barber's shop next door? Seddon blithely told them that these, like Miss Barrow's investments, had passed to him. 'Yes,' he added with scarcely concealed satisfaction, 'everything.' One of the Vonderahe women shot Seddon a suspecting glance. 'Well,' she said acidly, 'whoever persuaded Miss Barrow to do that was a remarkably clever person.' And what about the funeral? Why a public grave? Should she not have been buried in the family vault at Highgate? Mrs Seddon smiled weakly. 'Oh, we had a very nice funeral,' she said. 'We did everything very nicely.'

But the Vonderahes were far from satisfied. After a family conference, they told the police of their suspicions. Miss Barrow's body was exhumed from the grave and a post-mortem performed by a young pathologist from St Mary's Hospital, Paddington, Dr Bernard Henry Spilsbury, fresh from his triumph at the trial of Dr Crippen at the Old Bailey. It didn't take long for Spilsbury to reach a conclusion: Miss Barrow's body was riddled with arsenic. Characteristically, the arsenic had also had the effect of preserving the body; 'extremely well preserved', as Spilsbury noted on one of his famous case cards, adding: 'No disease apparent.'

A week after the exhumation of Miss Barrow's body, an inquest was opened into her death. The senior scientific analyst from the Home Office, Dr William Willcox, gave it as his opinion that Miss Barrow had died of acute arsenical poisoning. On 4 December Seddon was arrested. His reaction was characteristic. 'Absurd! What a terrible charge, wilful murder! Are you going to arrest my wife as well?'

A curious incident occurred two days later. Through his

lawyer, Seddon sent his daughter, Maggie, to buy some flypapers. He explained that he was trying to test a theory put forward by his wife that the arsenic in Miss Barrow's body may have come from some arsenic-impregnated flypapers which had been used in the dying woman's sickroom to keep down the flies. Seddon wanted similar flypapers analysed to support this theory. Whatever his true motives were, Seddon's ruse proved disastrous, for it gave the police their first positive clue as to how Miss Barrow had met her death. They recalled, no doubt, the celebrated case of Florence Maybrick, convicted in 1889 of murdering her husband by poisoning him with arsenic supposedly extracted from sheets of flypaper by soaking them in water. But this, the detectives decided, had been a joint venture, and in January they arrested Seddon's wife, charging the couple jointly with the wilful murder of Miss Barrow. Their trial opened at the Old Bailey on 4 March. In keeping with the tradition in Old Bailey poisoning trials the Attorney-General himself, Sir Rufus Isaacs (later Lord Reading), led for the Crown. Isaacs had not been long in the job, and this was his first capital case. For the defence, Seddon's solicitors briefed the greatest advocate of the day, the famous Edward Marshall Hall KC. The man known throughout all Britain as the Great Defender was, at the age of fifty-three, at the height of his powers. Since taking silk in 1898 he had appeared in a succession of controversial and highly publicized cases, including many trials for murder, but curiously this was his first case involving a client accused of murder by poisoning. Hall would, in all probability, have defended Dr Harvey Hawley Crippen on such a charge in 1910 but, in his absence on holiday, his senior clerk had rejected the brief because of a disagreement with Crippen's solicitor over fees. Now, at last, Hall was presented with a major poison defence brief. It was an opportunity he seized with relish, in spite of his misgivings about Seddon as a man. 'This,' he announced after the initial consultation with Seddon's solicitors, 'is the blackest case I've ever been in.' Marshall Hall's pessimism and lack of faith in Seddon is explained by his biographer, Edward Marjoribanks, who wrote that Hall went into the case 'without that passionate personal belief in his man's innocence which had carried him through so many of his trials. But this did not affect his devotion to the great task before him. He returned all other work, and could think of nothing but the Seddon case. In the many anxious consultations, he repeated again and again: "Remember, two people's lives depend on us" . . . He went into training like an athlete for a race and a student for a fellowship examination, going to bed early and saturating his mind with works on the scientific questions involved in the case.'[3]

The case was followed with intense interest throughout the country. It was after all, an all-star affair: the Attorney-General versus the Great Defender, a myriad of minor mysteries to be unravelled or left unexplained, and the joint defendants, prosperous, middle-class people from a respectable, almost genteel, London suburb. The public gallery was packed throughout the ten-day trial, all eyes fixed on the well-dressed insurance man and his wife seated on chairs in the dock – 'two singularly calm and attentive figures,' as one reporter observed, 'more like those of people assisting at an academic discussion than prisoners on trial for their lives.' In the absence of any direct evidence implicating the Seddons in the death of Miss Barrow, the prosecution assembled an intricate chain of damaging circumstantial evidence. This hinged largely on the strange series of financial transactions between Seddon and his lady lodger, the identification of bank notes from Miss Barrow's hoard which had been found in the Seddons' possession, and the medical evidence of Drs Willcox and

Spilsbury. The Attorney-General, in his opening speech, told the jury how Seddon was seen, on the day Miss Barrow died, with at least two hundred gold sovereigns plundered from the dead woman's cash-box. The following day, Seddon had gone to a jeweller with a ring and a watch belonging to Miss Barrow, asking him to enlarge the ring to fit his own finger, and to erase the name Eliza Jane Barrow (Miss Barrow's mother) from the watch and fit a new dial.

On the morning of the sixth day of the trial, Frederick Seddon himself stepped into the witness box to do battle with the Attorney-General. And yet if he found the occasion overaweing he did not show it. He remained, as Filson Young wrote, unshaken and unperturbed. 'He appeared to be as calm and collected as if he had been in his own office. It was quite evident that his demeanour and coldness told against him with the jury – one could almost see it happening before one's eyes.' The Attorney-General described the deathbed scene to the jury, the sparsely furnished room at the top of Seddon's house, lit by a single flickering gaslight above the mantelpiece.

'Did you like her?'

'Did I *like* her?' echoed Seddon, evidently surprised at the simplicity of the question.

'Yes,' said the Attorney-General, 'that is the question.'

Seddon paused for a moment. 'She was not a woman that you could be in love with,' he said slowly, 'but I deeply sympathized with her.'

'Was she a woman about eight or nine years older than yourself?'

'She was nine years older than myself.'

The Attorney-General sniffed. 'You talked of her as 'an old lady' when you went to the undertaker.'

'I always addressed her as "an old lady",' said Seddon.

The jury had already heard from little Ernie Grant, the

adenoidal orphan, about the night Miss Barrow died, and how she had heaved herself out of bed and sat on the floor, saying 'I am going.' Now Seddon himself amplified the details, describing how the lad had called out to Mrs Seddon that 'Chickie' (Ernie's pet name for Miss Barrow) was out of bed. Miss Barrow had complained of pains, and had asked for hot flannels and brandy. 'There was a shocking smell in Miss Barrow's room that night,' said Seddon. 'I couldn't bear to be in the room, as I have a delicate stomach.' So Mrs Seddon sat with the patient in a wicker chair by the bed and Seddon stationed himself outside the open door, smoking his pipe and reading the paper. As Miss Barrow lay dying she was snoring, and breathing noisily through her mouth. 'I was smoking and reading,' said Seddon, 'and my wife was dozing, when this snoring didn't seem quite so heavy, and all of a sudden it stopped.

'I said: "Good God, she's stopped breathing. She's dead!"'

Later Seddon explained his extraordinary conversation with the undertaker, in which he had arranged for the cheapest possible funeral and a public grave. Seddon claimed that the commission of 12s 6d (62½p) had been the undertaker's idea, and said that he had been affronted by the undertaker's initial suggestion that in the absence of any close relatives at the funeral the Seddons should hire a 'composite carriage' which would have carried three or four people to the cemetery with the coffin covered by a pall and stashed out of sight under the seat. 'I don't want the coffin exhibited like that,' Seddon had protested.

'It isn't seen,' the undertaker assured him. 'It is quite a respectable turnout.'

Seddon described in detail how, that same afternoon, he had sat down at his typewriter and, taking his last two sheets of black-edged typing paper, had written to the

Vonderahes telling them of Miss Barrow's death. He had made a carbon copy of the letter, and had handed the top copy to his daughter for posting, urging her to be sure to catch the 5 P.M. post ('I want them to get it tonight.').

The Attorney-General needed to show the jury that Seddon was a man motivated solely by profit, a man whose motive for murder might be found in his acquisitive, mercenary nature. Sir Rufus took as his starting point Seddon's innate ability as a seller of insurance, a man paid to make a professional judgement in the business of risk-taking. 'You said something just now,' said the Attorney-General, 'about your not thinking she was a good life [risk, for insurance purposes]?'

'I did not,' Seddon agreed. 'From my observations I thought she was an indifferent life.'

'Did you form that opinion at the time you were negotiating with her for the annuity?'

'I might have done.'

'You would have done?'

'Yes, I might have done. I looked upon her as an indifferent life.'

'That,' said Sir Rufus, 'is an element which you would take into account in determining whether or not you would enter into the annuity transaction?'

'Her average expectation of life in any case was only twenty or twenty-one years, and I calculated if she lived out that term how my financial position would be. It would increase year by year.'

The Attorney-General shot a glance at the listening jury. 'Your view was that she would not live over that term?'

'I did not feel she would,' said Seddon.

'And according to your view, you thought she would live less than that term?'

'Yes. I didn't expect her to live her average expectation of life – a woman in her indifferent state of health.'

'And you have told us you would not expect her to live twenty-one years?'

'Yes. She would not be a life that I could recommend to an insurance company to accept.'

The Attorney-General had won the point; now he pressed home. 'I should like to understand, if the ordinary expectation of her life was twenty-one years – the life of a woman of that age (49) – and you thought, as you told us, it was going to be less than that, what sort of a view did you form in your own mind about it?'

Seddon realized, too late, that he had walked into a trap. 'I couldn't say,' he mumbled. 'I couldn't tell how long the woman was going to live.'

'But some years less?' The question dangled in the dusty courtroom for what must have seemed an age.

Finally Seddon spoke. 'I have known people in consumption outlive healthy people,' he said. 'As the old saying is: "A creaky gate hangs a long time."'

The Attorney-General's relentless cross-examination of Seddon continued for two full days. Only towards the end did the prisoner show any evident discomfiture, when Sir Rufus spoke of Seddon counting Miss Barrow's gold in his basement office the day after her death, in the presence of two of his insurance collectors. These two men had testified that this was the £200 missing from the dead woman's cash-box, but Seddon angrily denied this, maintaining that 'it was the company's money and my own. It's not feasible a man is going to do a thing like that.'

'What do you mean?'

'The prosecution are suggesting that I am dealing with the deceased woman's gold; that I should bring it down from the top of the house to the bottom, into the office, in the presence of my assistants, and count it up? Is it feasible?'

Once again, Sir Rufus eyed the jury before turning to Seddon. 'I do not want to argue with you,' he said urbanely, 'but you know that sometimes people do very foolish things?'

'Well, I am not a degenerate,' cried Seddon. 'That would make it out that I was a greedy, inhuman monster!'

Sir Rufus blinked. 'What?'

'That I am a greedy, inhuman monster, or something with a very degenerate mind, to commit a vile crime such as the prosecution suggest, and then bringing the dead woman's money down and counting it in the presence of my two assistants and flouting it like that. The suggestion is scandalous! I would have all day to count the money.'

When Marshall Hall rose on the ninth morning of the trial to begin his marathon closing speech in defence of Frederick Seddon, he made much of the absence of conclusive proof. There was absolutely no proof that Seddon ever handled arsenic, or that he administered any, or that he knew that flypapers contained arsenic. And Hall submitted that there was no evidence to show that Miss Barrow had, in fact, died of arsenical poisoning.

Marshall Hall was feeling the strain. Looking tired and haggard, he nevertheless reviewed with painstaking care the details of the scientific evidence against Seddon and the financial position of Miss Barrow at the time of her death. He told the jury that under the terms of the annuity Seddon only benefited by her death to the tune of £1 8s 0d (£1.40p) a week. 'People,' said Hall, 'do not commit murders for £1 8s 0d a week.'

The defence theory was clear: somehow, arsenic had got into Miss Barrow's body, not in sufficient quantity to cause her death but enough to prevent her recovery from the illness with which she was suffering in her last days.

Finally, Marshall Hall came to his peroration: 'Gentlemen, I have practically done. I have attempted no high flights of forensic eloquence. I have attempted to deal with this as a business proposition, addressing twelve businessmen. I have only dealt with the evidence before you – the evidence against my client. I submit that that evidence is entirely unsatisfactory. The presumption of innocence has never been removed; the prisoner is entitled as of right to your verdict of acquittal, and you must say he is not guilty because he has not been proved to be guilty.

'Gentlemen, I often think when I look at the great figure of Justice which towers over all our judicial proceedings, that it is possible that the bandage over the eyes of Justice has a two-fold purpose. Not only is it put there so that the cause of justice should not be warped by prejudice or undue influence one way or the other; but sometimes I think it is put there so that those who gaze should not see the look of infinite pity in the eyes behind that bandage, the look of infinite mercy which must always temper justice in a just man . . .

'Gentlemen, the great scientists who have been here have told us of the many marvels of science and of the deductions that can be made therefrom. There is one thing the scientists have never yet been able to discover, with all their research and all their study, and that is how to replace the little vital spark that we call Life. Upon your verdict here depends so far as I am concerned the life of this man. If your verdict is against him, that vital spark will be extinguished, and no science known to the world can ever replace it. As far as I am concerned, my responsibility is ended. To the best of such abilities as I possess I have put this man's case strongly and forcibly before you. I have endeavoured to put it in the fairest light that I can from his point of view; but yours is the responsibility. Not that you are to be afraid of it. If your oaths constrain you to find a verdict of guilty, let no consideration of the consequences hinder you. In the name of Society find that verdict, if you are constrained to find it. But, gentlemen, regarding the consequences of your verdict I must remind you that they are irrevocable. I invite you to say, on all this evidence, having heard it all and listened to it all and weighed it all, that you are constrained to come to one verdict and one verdict only – that the Crown has not proved the case against Frederick Henry Seddon and that, therefore, your verdict must be a verdict of not guilty.'

Marshall Hall's brilliant, impassioned speech had lasted just over four hours. It had run to nearly 40,000 words. Now he sank, exhausted, into his seat. The last word was with the Crown. The Attorney-General rose. He, too, addressed the jury for some four hours, a sledgehammer speech in which he drove home every last point that might tell with the jury against the accused. Only in his closing remarks did Sir Rufus Isaacs suggest that there might be enough doubt in the case of Mrs Seddon to warrant a verdict of not guilty.

Mr Justice Bucknill launched into his summing up by describing the death of Miss Barrow as a murder, not of passion, not of hatred, not done in a moment of heat or anger, but a murder designed to get the woman's money. The judge seemed uneasy, almost restrained, as he reviewed the evidence, and towards the end made it clear that Mrs Seddon was entitled to an acquittal. But then, turning to Seddon himself, the judge said something that struck many in court as rather strange. 'It matters not what religion a man belongs to,' he said, 'what nationality he is, *what sect or brotherhood or anything else he may belong to* (author's italics), he who lives under the protection of the laws of the country in which he abides must keep them, and if he breaks them he must pay the penalty, even although the penalty be his life.' What 'sect or brotherhood' was the judge speaking of? None other than the brotherhood of Freemasons, to which he – and Frederick Seddon – both belonged.

The jury was out for exactly an hour before bringing in its verdict. Seddon was guilty of wilful murder. His wife was not guilty. Seddon turned and kissed his wife, who broke down sobbing before being led away from the dock to be discharged. Seddon, strangely unmoved, turned again to face the bench, and to hear the time-honoured words of the clerk of arraigns: 'Frederick Henry Seddon, you stand convicted of wilful murder. Have you anything to say for yourself why the court should not give you judgement of death according to law?'

Few men, at that awful moment, would have responded. But Seddon, cool and composed, was ready. Taking a piece of paper from his pocket, he made a lengthy statement in a voice untrammelled by any dread sense of occasion, pointing out errors in the judge's summing up and offering a careful explanation of various financial transactions that had been mentioned in evidence. Seddon ended his remarks with the single most dramatic gesture of the entire ten-day trial. He raised his right hand in a masonic salute. 'I declare before the Great Architect of the Universe, I am not guilty, my lord.'

Mr Justice Bucknill, facing the prisoner across the well of the court, was totally unnerved by Seddon's gesture. It was a heart-bursting moment for the judge. He knew he had no alternative but to condemn Seddon to death; the law prescribed it. And yet the judge also knew, as a Freemason, that he was bound by the masonic code to protect a brother Mason. The chaplain had placed the black cap over his wig, and the court usher was proclaiming the traditional warning to 'all persons to keep silence while sentence of death is passing on the prisoner at the bar, upon pain of imprisonment'. Bucknill was speechless. He sat, silent, for a full minute in the hushed court, trying to compose himself. Finally he spoke:

'Frederick Henry Seddon, you have been found guilty of the wilful murder of Eliza Mary Barrow. With that verdict I am bound to say I agree. I should be more than terribly pained if you thought that I, in my charge to the jury, had stated anything against you that was not supported by the evidence. But even if what you say is strictly correct, there is still in my opinion ample evidence to show that you had the opportunity of putting poison into her food or in her medicine.

'You have a motive for this crime. That motive was greed of gold. Whether it was that you wanted to put an end to the annuities or not, I know not. You only can know. Whether it was to get the gold that was or was not – but which you thought was – in the cash-box, I do not know. But I think I do know this: that you wanted to make a great pecuniary profit by felonious means.

'This murder has been described by yourself in the box as one which, if made out against you, was a barbarous one; a murder of design, a cruel murder. It is not for me to harrow your feelings,' added the judge, although it was he, and not the prisoner, who by now was visibly shaking. Seddon looked on impassively, 'the most peaceful man in the court', according to Filson Young.

'It does not affect me,' said Seddon, butting in. 'I have a clear conscience.'

The judge's voice cracked and dropped to a whisper as the dread moment approached. 'I, as minister of the law, have now to pass upon you that sentence which the law demands has to be passed, which is that you have forfeited your life in consequence of your great crime. Try and make peace with your Maker.'

Seddon, still unflinching, replied: 'I am at peace.'

Bucknill could scarcely speak for the emotion now

welling up inside him. He was on the verge of breaking down completely. 'From what you have said, you and I know we both belong to one Brotherhood, and it is all the more painful to me to have to say what I am saying. But our Brotherhood does not encourage crime. On the contrary, it condemns it. I pray you again to make your peace with the Great Architect of the Universe. Mercy – pray for it, ask for it . . .'

By now, the judge was totally distracted. He had to stop and brace himself to utter the words of the death sentence. Tears filled his eyes as he faced Seddon across the court. 'The sentence of the court is that you be taken from hence to a lawful prison, and from thence to a place of execution, and that you be there hanged by the neck until you are dead. And that your body be buried within the precincts of the prison in which you shall have been confined after your conviction. And may the Lord have mercy on your soul.'

At these last words, Bucknill broke into tears. Behind him, the black-robed chaplain murmured, 'Amen.'

Filson Young, watching from the reporters' bench, looked in vain for any emotion from the condemned man in the dock. 'But Seddon,' he wrote later, 'was calm, and when it was all over, and while the Judge, wiping his eyes, was excusing the jury from attending for ten years, he hitched his overcoat about him with his old gesture and took a drink of water, and made ready to descend the stairs that would take him away from the world of men for ever. As he turned to go down he looked through the glass at the people at the back of the Court, where his own friends were, and where his own little girl had been sitting earlier in the afternoon – a bleak wintry look – and then he was gone.'[4]

Seddon's appeal failed, and he was hanged at Pentonville on 18 April 1912.

He went to the gallows protesting his innocence to the end. He made no confession of any kind, but the question of his guilt remains problematical. Several months after the case his wife published a signed article in the *Weekly Dispatch* claiming that she saw Seddon give poison to Miss Barrow on the night of her death. He had ensured his wife's silence by threatening her with a revolver. Inquiries by a rival publication, *John Bull*, however, showed that Mrs Seddon's story was false; she had made it to earn some money, and to stifle gossip among her neighbours in Tollington Park who, despite her acquittal, still spoke of her as a murderess.

Even in the condemned cell Seddon's thoughts centred on his precious money. On the day before his execution, he sent for his solicitor. His concern was not for last-ditch legal help, but for news of how much his furniture had fetched at auction. On learning the smallness of the amount, he struck the table in resigned anger, shouting 'That's done it!'

Seddon was a tightfisted, tightminded skinflint – but was he a murderer? The prosecution case was full of holes, and based wholly on circumstantial evidence. How Seddon administered poison to Miss Barrow, if, indeed, he did, remains unclear. Was the flypaper story in fact concocted by Seddon to confuse the police and to set them on a false trail? Dr Willcox, the chief medical witness for the Crown, claimed after the case that although he believed in Seddon's guilt he doubted whether he had obtained the arsenic from flypapers. Indeed, to this day no one seems to have any clear idea how the hapless Miss Barrow got arsenic into her system. It has been suggested that Seddon cunningly devised the flypaper theory as a blind, and that the poisoning of Miss Barrow was actually accomplished using some form of rat poison or even weedkiller. Faced with the many ambiguities in the case the jury may well have based its verdicts on personal impressions of the Seddons in court rather than clear and compelling evidence linking them with the administration of poison. In particular, Seddon's hard-headed demeanour in the witness box may have told against him as much as his curious behaviour before and after the death of Miss Barrow. As Lord Birkenhead, later Lord Chancellor of England, puts it: 'The jury may have concluded from his coolness that he was indeed capable, as the prosecution declared, of consummating a wicked and premeditated poisoning, with two doctors in attendance and a party of relatives taking "pot-luck" in the house, in order to satisfy that greed of gain to which he was enslaved.'

8

Trenhorne House, Lewannick, Cornwall

As with wine, so with murder. The year 1931 produced cases of the very finest vintage. In Liverpool the death of Mrs Julia Wallace in the front parlour of her home triggered the nonpareil of all mysteries; in Long Beach, New York, showgirl Starr Faithfull was found suffocated on the shore, and her strange death remains unsolved. The month of January alone saw not only the murder of Mrs Wallace but the trial of salesman Alfred Arthur Rouse for the Blazing Car Murder in Northamptonshire, and the disturbing case of Evelyn Foster, found dying on a bleak moor in Northumberland in the wreckage of her burned-out taxi.

But in the West Country in January 1931 the talk was of a mystery as perplexing and intractable as any of these. It concerned the death of a farmer's wife, Alice Thomas, and the sudden disappearance of her neighbour, Annie Hearn. There was talk of illicit passion, and of poison. The case excited divided consternation in the tiny Cornish village of Lewannick, near Launceston. It still does.

Trenhorne House sounds grand enough, but in the autumn of 1930, when this story starts, it was actually split into two separate wings. Annie Hearn lived alone in one of these, eking out a threadbare existence by selling home-made cakes and pastries which she displayed in her front window. A lifetime of care had left its marks on her faded cheeks. She was forty-five, but looked older. Slight and round-shouldered, she gazed at the world through sad, lined eyes, and when she smiled it was to reveal imperfect teeth and an almost studied shyness. She was originally from Yorkshire, and a widow – or so she claimed. Her life had been a series of bitter disappointments: her husband had left her a week after their marriage, and her sister had died in the summer of 1930 after a long and painful illness. Annie Hearn's plight had aroused the sympathy of her neighbours, William and Alice Thomas, who lived along the road at Trenhorne Farm. The Thomases had known Mrs Hearn since she had moved to Lewannick from the north of England in 1921 with her sick aunt and elder sister. They admired Mrs Hearn's selfless devotion to her ailing Aunt Mary, and had grieved with her when the old lady died in 1926. Then her sister Minnie had taken ill, and again Annie Hearn had nursed her until Minnie's death in the summer of 1930 at the age of only fifty-two.

Alone in the world, Annie Hearn was grateful for the friendship of William and Alice Thomas, and Alice's occasional small gifts of homemade junket and clotted cream. She was also grateful for the occasional small loan from William Thomas. Over a period, these loans had amounted to the sum of £38, but Mr Thomas was in no hurry to have the money repaid; he was comfortably off, and could well afford to cancel the debts if necessary. He and his wife agreed that it was more important to see Annie Hearn settled and happy after her dark years of loneliness and heartbreak.

It was in this spirit that, one bright October day in 1930, the Thomases invited Annie Hearn to go with them on a trip to the coast. Annie was delighted, and shortly after lunch on Saturday 18 October, the three left Lewannick in William Thomas's motor car to drive twenty miles to Bude, a small resort on the north Cornish coast. At Littlejohn's Café (now demolished) on Bellevue Hill they ordered tea and sat down. Annie produced a packet of tinned salmon sandwiches which she had prepared herself with some homemade salad cream as her contribution to the outing. (This seems an odd thing to do by modern standards, but these were the days of the slump, and pennies counted, especially to the canny Cornish.) The sandwiches, on white bread, were set out on two plates and eaten with relish. Afterwards, Annie Hearn and Alice Thomas went for a stroll in the town while William Thomas went for a walk on his own. Feeling a little queasy, he stopped at a pub for a couple of whiskies, which revived him. When he met up with the ladies at the car his wife complained of 'a sweety taste' in her mouth, and sent him into a shop to buy some bananas to take the taste away.

On the drive home, however, Alice Thomas was violently ill. The car stopped several times along the way so that she could be sick. By the time they arrived back at Lewannick Mrs Thomas was suffering from severe stomach pains and diarrhoea. Her husband ordered her straight to bed and called the doctor out. He diagnosed nothing more serious than food poisoning and recommended a simple diet of fish and water. Now it was Annie Hearn's turn to be the good neighbour and, having collected a few things from Trenhorne House, she returned to the Thomas's farm to nurse Alice. At first the patient rallied, and there seemed to be no cause for alarm. Alice stayed in bed for a fortnight, by which time she was feeling sufficiently strong to go downstairs for a traditional Sunday lunch (prepared by Annie) of roast mutton, sprouts and potatoes. By now, the doctor had ceased to call every day, and Alice's mother had moved in to help Annie with the nursing duties and household chores. Alice ate her meal, and stayed downstairs until mid-evening when her husband carried her back to bed, having given her an aspirin from a bottle supplied by Annie Hearn.

That night Alice's condition deteriorated dramatically. The following morning William Thomas sent again for the doctor. When he arrived, he was so shocked at the change in his patient that he called in a consultant. By now Alice was delirious, partially paralysed, and unable to move her legs. The two medical men consulted anxiously and agreed that she appeared to be suffering the classic symptoms of arsenical poisoning. There was no time to lose. An ambulance was called to rush Alice to hospital in Plymouth. She was admitted shortly before midnight on Monday 3 November. Alice Thomas sank gradually during the night. At 9.30 the next morning she died.

A post-mortem examination ordered by the suspicious doctors revealed 0.85 grains of white arsenic in Alice's body. The arsenic was found to be of a type often found in garden weedkiller. At this stage, the findings of the analyst should have been kept secret, but somehow they were leaked to William Thomas as he grieved for his wife at Trenhorne Farm. In the circumstances his response was curious. He at once confronted Annie Hearn and warned her that one of them was likely to be blamed for Alice's death. There would be police inquiries, and possibly an inquest. William Thomas made it plain that he considered Annie responsible for the death of his wife. By the time the funeral was held the following Saturday, the whole village was rife with rumour that Annie Hearn had poisoned her friend and neighbour, Alice Thomas.

Annie herself faced the accusation with a mixture of bewilderment and stoic defiance. She attended Alice's funeral in spite of the festering whispers, and joined the Thomas family when they gathered after the service at Trenhorne Farm. It was a deeply unpleasant occasion for everyone. In the dining room Annie was confronted by the dead woman's brother, Percy Parsons, whom she had never met. Parsons fixed her with a hostile stare. He did not mince his words. 'I've heard about those salmon sandwiches,' he hissed. 'What else was in them? That's what I'd like to know. It needs clearing up, and you've not heard the last of this.'

To other guests at the gathering Percy Parsons was even less guarded. ''Tis that woman!' he told them, pointing accusingly at Annie. Running home in floods of tears, Annie blurted out to her neighbour at Trenhorne House: 'They seem to think I have poisoned Mrs Thomas with the sandwiches. They think down there all tinned food is poisoned!'

The behaviour of William Thomas, meanwhile, is worth considering. Why, having all but accused Annie Hearn of poisoning his wife, did he brook her presence at the funeral? And why, a couple of days later, did he relent, to the point of inviting Annie back to Trenhorne Farm to stay? Furthermore, why did he demand a receipt for the £38 he had loaned her over a two-year period? Were these the confused reactions of a man overcome with grief at his sudden loss? Or were they those of a man who had something to hide and who now regretted his initial and rash efforts to divert suspicion from himself? Annie Hearn was as confused as he was, for although she agreed to return, temporarily, to the farm, she refused to share his table. Finally, on 10 November, she could stand it no longer and stormed out of the house, leaving Thomas a tormented letter:

Goodbye. I am going out if I can. I cannot forget that awful man (Parsons) and the things he said. I am *innocent, innocent*. She is dead and it was my lunch she ate. I cannot bear it. When I am dead they will be sure I am guilty, and you at least will be clear. May your dear wife's presence guard and comfort you still.

Yours,

A. H.

My life is not a great thing anyhow, now dear Minnie's gone. I should be glad if you send my love to Bessie (Annie's surviving sister) and tell her not to worry about me. I will be all right. My conscience is clear, so I am not afraid of the afterwards. I am giving instructions to Webb about selling the things, and hope you will be paid in full. It is all I can do now.

By the time William Thomas read this letter Annie Hearn had disappeared.

Reading the letter over, it was clear to Thomas that Annie was intent on taking her own life. In spite of her protestations ('I am *innocent, innocent*'), her outpourings could have amounted to an implicit admission of guilt ('She is dead and it was my lunch she ate'), or even an attempt to protect the reputation of Thomas himself ('. . . you at least will be clear'). On the other hand, the letter might even have been a bluff, a calculated ploy by an evil, scheming poisoner.

Annie's movements on leaving Trenhorne House at Lewannick were easy to trace. After posting the letter at nearby Congdon's Corner, she had hired the subpostmaster to drive her down to Looe some twenty miles away on the south Cornish coast. The fare had been eighteen shillings (90p), and he had dropped her off at the bridge. But then the trail went cold. A few days later, police found Annie's black and white check coat near the edge of some cliffs. Nearby, they found her hat and a shoe. The implication was obvious: Annie Hearn had committed suicide by jumping from the clifftop. The discovery of her clothes would have ended the story neatly, but local fishermen pointed out to the police that had Annie jumped from the spot suggested, her body would have plunged directly on to rocks below where it would have remained. Had she been swept out by the tide her body would have been washed up within hours because of the prevailing winds. This, the police decided, was no suicide. It was a fake.

The search for Annie intensified when an inquest jury at Plymouth returned a verdict that Alice Thomas had been murdered by arsenical poisoning 'by some person or persons unknown'. The coroner had probed deeply in his search for a motive.

'Had you any rat poison?' he asked William Thomas.

'Yes, locked in my desk.'

'Did your wife ever object to Mrs Hearn coming to the house?'

'Never.'

'You and Mrs Thomas were friendly with Mrs Hearn's sister?'

'Yes.'

'Did you ever give your wife any cause to be jealous of Mrs Hearn?'

'Never,' William Thomas insisted.

Police now issued a photograph of Annie Hearn, with a detailed description: 'Mrs Hearn is aged 45; 5' 2" or 3" in height, with grey eyes, brown, shingled hair, of sallow complexion, and medium build. There is a noticeable defect in one of the front teeth. She walks briskly, carries her head slightly to the left, and when in conversation she has the habit of looking away from the person she is addressing. She is well-spoken but has a north country accent. She is of rather reserved disposition.'

While this description was being circulated, the Cornish police were making inquiries in Lewannick about Annie Hearn and her shrinking circle of relations. They discovered that five years earlier, Annie had shared her half of Trenhorne House with no fewer than three other women: an old Cornish woman called Mrs Aunger, who had since died; Annie's Aunt Mary, whom she had nursed until the old lady's death in 1926; and her invalid sister Minnie (Lydia was her real name) who had also died after being nursed over a period by luckless Annie. Village gossip had it that Aunt Mary had left everything she owned to her niece, but this, a final, grateful gesture from an ailing woman of seventy-six, seemed scarcely remarkable. As for poor Minnie, she had suffered for years from gastric troubles, and her death in July 1930 seemed nothing more than a blessed relief to the villagers who had known her. The Home Office, however, thought differently, and since the symptoms of their illnesses were also consistent with those of arsenical poisoning they ordered that the bodies of both Minnie and Aunt Mary be exhumed from where they lay in Lewannick churchyard.

Public interest in the case of Annie Hearn reached a sudden shattering crescendo on the day the bodies were exhumed. It was a windswept Tuesday, 9 December, and the village was lashed by a snowstorm. Police officers battled against the icy wind to erect tarpaulin screens around the freshly opened graves and to block the view from the road. Old people in Lewannick today still recall the scene vividly, for although the view from the road was indeed blocked, the police had forgotten the houses overlooking the churchyard at the back, from where the view of the macabre exhumations was uninterrupted in spite of the weather. The coffins were raised and opened; men in thick overcoats hunched over the bodies wielding their instruments and removing vital organs, which they placed in large glass jars.

On the same day, Fleet Street had smelled a story. The *Daily Mail*, locked in a fierce circulation war with its arch rival, the *Daily Express*, had splashed the case on its main news page, under the banner headline 'Cornish Arsenic Drama'. In a spectacular move the *Mail* offered a huge reward of £500 'for the discovery of Mrs Annie Hearn, the missing witness'. The headlines thundered the questions the length and breadth of the nation: WHERE IS MRS HEARN? IS SHE STILL ALIVE? 'What will be the result of the pending exhumation of bodies?' asked the *Mail*. 'What are the chemical reagents of the analysts likely to reveal?' The answer came a day or two later when the organs removed from the bodies at Lewannick were examined by the Home Office analyst, Dr Gerald Roche Lynch. In the remains of both bodies Dr Lynch reported finding 'distinct quantities of arsenic'.

So Annie Hearn was now wanted for questioning about three possible murders. But in spite of the general hue and cry, the police hunt and the exertions of the Press, there remained no word of her. So was she dead? Had she, after all, taken her own life on the cliffs at Looe, and her body swept out to sea by a freak current? The answer on both counts was no.

When Annie Hearn stepped out of the car that had taken her from Congdon's Corner to Looe she had apparently taken the path along the clifftop where she had abandoned her coat and faked her own suicide. Then she had hurried to the railway station and caught a train to Torquay, where she checked into a hotel under a false name. Using yet another alias, she moved the next day to smaller, cheaper lodgings, explaining to the landlady that her husband was ill in the local hospital. She had some calling cards printed in the name of Mrs Faithful, and answered an advertisement for a cook-housekeeper placed in the local paper by an architect, Cecil Powell. She made a favourable impression with her new employer, although he confessed later to having been puzzled by her occasional air of preoccupation. When the *Daily Mail* published her picture in its splash story about the reward Mr Powell seemed to recognize it 'in a vague sort of way', but he was the quiet type who shunned publicity. And in any case he was reluctant to upset his wife, who was in delicate health. So, for the time being, Mr Powell did nothing.

Christmas 1930 came and went. On New Year's Day 1931 Annie Hearn treated herself to a day at the sales in Torquay, and bought a new coat to replace the one she had left on the cliffs at Looe. The coat was too long, so she left it at the shop to be shortened, leaving a deposit in the name of Mrs Dennis. A week or so later the shortened coat was duly delivered by an errand boy. The door was opened by Mr Powell's son, who said that there must have been a mistake since no one called Mrs Dennis lived there. In the confusion, Annie confessed to having ordered the coat, but her explanation about a false name failed to convince the already suspicious Mr Powell, who consulted his friend, the mayor of Torquay. The mayor, in turn, informed the police at Launceston.

Mrs Hearn was arrested on 12 January. The police had set a trap, telling Mr Powell to send her out on a bogus errand. As she left the house, a policeman waiting in the shadows across the street stepped forward.

'Mrs Hearn?'

'Yes?'

'I think I know you. I think you know Lewannick.'

'Yes,' she replied, 'I have been there.'

The officer placed a hand on her arm. 'Then I must ask you to come to the police station.'

That evening Mrs Hearn was charged with the murder of Alice Thomas. Just after midnight she made a statement to the police: 'On the Sunday before Mrs Thomas was taken away, I prepared roast mutton for dinner. I have read in the newspapers that I might have carved Mrs Thomas's portion. I did not carve it, and I did not help with the gravy or anything. I remember Mrs Thomas complaining that a junket that Mrs Parsons (her mother) made was too sweet. She did not complain of the meals I prepared. Mr Thomas appeared to be very grateful to me for my help up to the time when he returned from Plymouth after Mrs Thomas's death. He then appeared more abrupt in his manner towards me. On one occasion he said to me: "They are going to send some organs to be analysed. They will find out what it is. They will blame one of us. The blame will come heavier on you than on me ..." It appeared as if somebody was going to be charged with murder ... sooner than that I thought I would go my own way and take my life. I did go to Looe with that intention but later found that I could not do what I thought of doing.'

Cecil Powell, the architect who had delivered her into the arms of the police, offered Annie the lifeline she needed, at the point in her life when her fortunes were at their lowest ebb. He claimed the reward from the *Daily Mail* and donated the £500 towards the cost of her defence. He handed the money to a solicitor he knew, with instructions to brief the best barrister he could find. The solicitor immediately contacted Norman Birkett KC, one of the ablest counsels of his day, who had just successfully prosecuted Alfred Arthur Rouse, the Blazing Car Murderer, at Northampton Assizes.

Norman Birkett studied the brief with his customary care. He read reports of the evidence from the police court, and realized the overwhelming prejudice boiling up locally against Annie Hearn. Indeed, so strongly was local feeling running against Mrs Hearn that the jury at her trial in Bodmin had to be empanelled from the far side of Cornwall. She was indicted on two separate counts, concerning her sister and Alice Thomas respectively, but the Crown elected to proceed only on the second count, the murder of Mrs Thomas. Mrs Hearn pleaded not guilty when the trial opened at Bodmin Assizes on 15 June 1931.

The chief witness in the early stages of the trial was William Thomas, who described the outing to Bude, the eating of the salmon sandwiches and the subsequent illness of his wife. Mr Thomas agreed that his wife had been very fond of Mrs Hearn; indeed, it was she who had suggested asking Mrs Hearn along on the trip. They had been on picnics together before; sometimes Mrs Thomas had brought the food, sometimes Mrs Hearn, and sometimes both of them. Mr Thomas, cross-examined by Norman Birkett, recalled the tea at Bude in great detail. The sandwiches had been placed on the table in two piles, each containing three sandwiches. He agreed with Birkett that once the sandwiches had been set on the table no one had juggled with them. He could not say who took the first sandwich, but agreed that all three took one and ate it.

'Did your wife take the second sandwich?' asked Birkett.

'I don't remember,' Thomas replied.

'But you knew what was in the sandwiches – you had eaten one?'

'Yes, but I didn't know what kind of fish it was.'

'Did you tell the doctor what your wife had had for her midday dinner?'

'I can't remember.'

'Do you remember what you did have?'

'No.'

Mr Thomas said it was quite unexpectedly that Mrs Hearn was asked to go to Bude. In the same way, she was asked to stay at his house. She appeared to him to do her very best for his wife.

'If,' said Birkett, 'after the death of your wife, you had said to a woman: "The blame will come heavier on you than me", is that a thing you would be likely to forget?'

'There was no blame to come on me,' said Thomas hurriedly.

'In her letter to you, Mrs Hearn wrote: "I am going out if I can." I suggest you said to that woman that people were talking?'

'I may have said so.'

'Did you tell her that people were talking about you both?'

'I might have said people were talking about the sandwiches and that my wife had died from poisoned sandwiches.'

'Might you have said: "The blame will come heavier on you than me"?'

'I may have. I don't remember. It was Mrs Hearn's sandwiches my wife took.'

'Did you say: "A detective might be here at any time"?'

'I said someone might come to make inquiries. I may have said "detective" but I don't remember.'

'Did you say: "Whatever there is they will find it out"?'

'Yes.'

'Were you referring to food poisoning?'

'Yes.'

'Did Mrs Hearn say: "If people think like that I had better go to my own house"?'

'Yes.'

Birkett paused. 'It is true, then, that she said people were blaming her?'

'I might have said people were talking about the poison in the sandwiches.'

Birkett pounced. '*Poison*, sir! Did you use the word "poison" to her?'

'No.'

'When Mrs Hearn wrote to you: "Goodbye. I am going out if I can" did you think that she meant she was going to take her own life if she could screw her courage to the sticking point? Is that how you read it?'

'Yes.'

'Then, when Mrs Hearn wrote: "I cannot forget that awful man and the things he said", did you know she meant Parsons?'

'Yes.'

'Did he say: "It is that woman, Mrs Hearn"? Did you know that had been said about her?'

'I knew Mr Parsons had said things. I don't know exactly what he had said.'

Birkett reached for Annie Hearn's letter threatening

suicide, and read from it. "I am *innocent, innocent*." Were those two words underlined?'

'Yes,' Thomas replied.

'You knew people were talking about the sandwiches?'

'Yes.'

'Do you think that was the letter of a distraught woman, of a woman very upset and very grieved?'

'I took it that she was upset.'

Birkett looked again at the letter. '"My conscience is clear and I am not afraid of afterwards." You knew she was referring to the great hereafter?'

Thomas nodded and said, 'Yes.'

William Thomas remained in the witness box for most of the second day of the trial. Both sides had completed their questioning, and Thomas was just stepping down when Mr Justice Roche motioned him to stand firm. 'It is said,' the judge murmured, 'that your wife died from arsenical poisoning. It was not for you to express an opinion on that at all. You have been asked questions about food given to your wife on 2 November, and you have said that you gave her tea and brandy, and possibly medicine. Did you, from first to last, ever yourself give your wife any arsenic?'

Thomas flushed angrily. 'No sir, never in all my life,' he barked.

The judge blinked. 'Are you sure?'

'I've never had arsenic in my possession,' said Thomas with some indignation, 'except sheep dip and tablets which are things any farmer might have.'

Various relatives of Mrs Thomas trooped in and out of the witness box, including Percy Parsons, Mrs Thomas's brother, who related the conversation with Annie Hearn at his sister's funeral. The talk had turned to the food eaten on the trip to Bude, and someone had asked where the sandwiches had come from. Mrs Hearn had said something to the effect that 'we brought them with us'. At this point, Parsons' mother had piped up: 'Mrs Hearn made those sandwiches and brought them with her.' Parsons had then remarked: 'This looks serious and will have to be seen into.' Cross-examined by Norman Birkett, Percy Parsons agreed that he had not been on visiting terms with the Thomases, but had been on speaking terms with his sister.

'Were you on speaking terms with Mr Thomas?' asked Birkett.

'I suppose we were not,' Parsons admitted. 'There was a disturbance years ago and we never spoke.'

'Have you been harbouring resentment all these years?'

'No.'

'It is a fact that you haven't spoken to him for years?'

'I have given him the time of day,' said Parsons, with characteristic charity.

'You did not speak on the day of the funeral?'

'Yes,' said Parsons. 'We shook hands then.'

Birkett moved on. 'Have you seen the letter in which Mrs Hearn wrote: "I cannot forget that horrid man and the things he said"? You know the "horrid man" was you?'

'Yes.'

'You had spoken to her bitterly that day, had you not?'

'No.'

'Did you say: "This is serious and has to be seen into"?'

'That I did say.'

'Do you think you were horrid that day?'

'No.'

Police Sergeant Trebilcock of Lewannick described how he arrested Mrs Hearn in the street in Torquay. At first she had claimed her name was Dennis. While Superintendent Pill was writing down her statement Mrs Hearn said to him in a low voice: 'Mr Thomas used to come to our house every day with a paper. Of course, that was only a blind.'

Norman Birkett sought to cast doubt on that apparently damaging statement. He rose to cross-examine.

'Have you ever found a sentence of yours not properly caught by the hearer?'

'Yes,' said Sergeant Trebilcock, 'at times.'

'Your voice is not too clear. It is possible to make a mistake about what you said?'

'I thought I spoke very plainly,' said Sergeant Trebilcock, in a Cornish accent so rich that it drew laughter in the court.

Birkett smiled. 'But this statement of Mrs Hearn's. Do you not think that it was a misunderstanding of what she said?'

'I made no mistake about that.'

'Well,' Birkett continued, 'listen to this: "Mr Thomas used to bring a paper. He was *very kind*." "Mr Thomas used to bring a paper. It was only *a blind*." Don't you think you could have made a mistake?'

'No.'

Birkett tried again. 'Do you suggest in this serious case that while your superintendent was taking the statement down Mrs Hearn turned and whispered confidentially to you this statement you have told us?'

'I will not say that she whispered.'

'She spoke in a low voice that the superintendent couldn't hear?'

'That's what I'm telling you,' said Trebilcock.

'I suggest Mrs Hearn never said anything of the kind about it being a blind,' said Birkett.

'I say she did.'

But Birkett fared rather better with other Crown witnesses, extracting a series of admissions that poor Minnie Everard might have died of natural causes. This had the effect of weakening the charge relating to the death of Mrs Thomas, and Norman Birkett determined to exploit this to the full. 'If,' Herbert du Parcq KC for the Crown, had told the jury in his opening speech, 'you are satisfied that there was arsenic in the sandwiches and that it might have been put there by somebody other than Mrs Hearn, you are entitled to consider the circumstances of the death of Miss Everard. Mrs Hearn was the person in contact with both of these. In each case arsenic was the cause of death, and you will have to consider whether this does not take the case far beyond the region of suspicion.'

The defence team disagreed. 'It seemed to me more likely to have the opposite effect,' Sir Sydney Smith, then professor of forensic medicine at Edinburgh University, recalled in his memoirs.[1] 'The medical evidence was definitely weaker in the case of Miss Everard; if this charge could be destroyed the charge in respect of Mrs Thomas would be badly shaken.' Professor Smith was hired by the defence to advise Norman Birkett throughout the trial. 'While he was cross-examining I passed notes to him from time to time, drawing his attention to particular points arising from the witness's replies, and he made full use of them.'

Sydney Smith was not called to give evidence on Annie Hearn's behalf, but it was he, more than anyone else, who was responsible for the verdict. Smith was in no doubt that Alice Thomas had died from arsenical poisoning. But it was 'highly improbable', in his view, that there was any arsenic in the sandwiches eaten by the day-tripping party at Bude on 18 October. Mrs Thomas's illness on the return journey to Lewannick was, he argued, a simple case of food-poisoning. The fatal dose of arsenic was administered much nearer the day she died. The case of Annie's sister, Minnie, was even more ambiguous, lacking most of the classic symptoms of arsenical poisoning.

Professor Smith's opinion was that Minnie Everard died a natural death.

And he drew Norman Birkett's attention to a singularly curious fact to support this opinion.

The professor did not doubt that the Home Office analyst, Dr Gerald Roche Lynch, had found arsenic in Minnie's muscles, nails and hair. In most cases, Professor Smith would have agreed that such traces would have pointed to arsenical poisoning.

But this was a particular case. A case that was set in Cornwall. Minnie Everard had been buried in Cornwall. In Cornish soil. That was the curious fact that persuaded him of the innocence of Annie Hearn.

'Cornwall is famous for its tin,' wrote Smith, 'and where there is tin in the ground there is usually arsenic too. In Cornish soil the arsenic content is exceptionally high. In Lewannick – in that particular churchyard – the soil was fairly impregnated with it.'

Armed with this information Birkett made short work of Dr Eric Wordley, the pathologist who conducted the exhumation of Minnie Everard's body at Lewannick churchyard. Dr Wordley was forced to admit that minute particles of arsenic from the contaminated soil around the coffin would have got into the unstoppered jars containing the organs as he performed the post-mortem at the grave-side. 'Am I right in saying,' asked Birkett finally, 'that a piece of soil, so small that you could hold it between your fingers, dropped on to this body would make every single calculation wrong?'

'Yes,' said Dr Wordley.

Professor Sydney Smith was sitting behind Norman Birkett at Bodmin Assizes on the fifth day of Annie Hearn's trial when Birkett rose to put his first – and deadliest – question to the Crown analyst, Dr Lynch.

'Have you ever,' he asked, 'examined a living patient suffering from arsenical poisoning?'

'No,' Dr Lynch replied.

'With soil so heavily impregnated as the soil of the Lewannick churchyard, if that impregnation is at all widespread in Cornwall there is some chance of arsenic being found in the drinking water?'

'Traces,' said the unhappy analyst, 'I have no doubt.'

'Were you surprised to find so much arsenic in the soil?'

'Had I known I was going to find arsenic in the soil, I should certainly have had many other things done.'

Birkett pressed home. 'It was, then, a matter of surprise to find arsenic in the soil?'

'Yes,' said Dr Lynch, 'it was.'

'I make the plain suggestion to you that the possibility of contamination of the hair and organs by diffusion from the surface of Lewannick churchyard cannot be excluded,' said Birkett, sternly.

Dr Lynch gave one final wriggle. 'I agree it cannot be excluded,' he said, 'but it is extremely unlikely.'

The prosecution had proved that Annie Hearn had bought a tin of weedkiller four years earlier, and implied that this had been the source of the arsenic which had killed Alice Thomas. According to the Crown, Annie had added the weedkiller to the tinned salmon as she prepared the sandwiches before setting off in the car to Bude with the Thomases. This was a fine theory, but it was flawed in one critical respect.

All weedkillers containing arsenic are coloured with a purple dye.

Once again Birkett had turned to Professor Smith for help. When the court rose at the end of the first day of the trial, the professor hurried back to his hotel to make some experiments. He used the same brands of weedkiller and tinned salmon as Annie Hearn had bought, and mixed 14.3 grains of weedkiller with the salmon. He prepared a round of sandwiches using the poisoned fish, then sat back and waited.

Within thirty minutes the white bread that he – and Annie Hearn – had used was stained a most unappetizing shade of bluish-purple.

Norman Birkett had been hugely impressed with Smith's experiment, and decided to use the results to confound the sandwich theory of Dr Roche Lynch.

'You say that in your opinion the weedkiller was used in solid form?' asked Birkett.

'I suggest so,' replied the doctor.

'Have you taken a sandwich and put 14.3 grains on it?'

'No,' said Lynch, failing to mask his surprise.

'You have shown that arsenic put in Benger's Food discolours the white food?'

'It changes the colour.'

'That is with two grains?'

'Yes.'

'Seven times as much would greatly discolour it?'

'Yes, it would.'

Birkett glanced at Smith's experiment notes and peered at Dr Lynch over the rim of his spectacles. 'If you put fourteen grains of blue weedkiller on a sandwich and carried it for hours, I suggest it would be blue?'

'I haven't tried it,' replied Dr Lynch. 'but my opinion, for what it's worth, is that it would not be.'

'But,' said Birkett, 'you have not tried it. On the theory of the prosecution, it was a most terrible risk to run?'

'Personally I don't think so,' said Dr Lynch.

Birkett now sought to illustrate the point to the jury. 'If you have sandwiches in two piles of three each – assume for the moment that the topmost sandwich of one of those piles alone contains arsenic – am I right in assuming that the sandwich with the blue weedkiller would stain downwards?'

'Yes.'

'The white bread, like the white Benger's Food, would make the stains instantly discernible?'

'I agree, and the white bread being more localized, the blue would come through in spots or stains.'

'I am much obliged,' said Birkett, shooting a triumphant glance towards the jury. 'And would not the stains also go upwards?'

'Yes,' said Dr Lynch.

No one in the crowded courtroom could have been left in any doubt. The suspect sandwiches were suspect no more. No one could have tampered with them without risking detection through the telltale dye.

The jury had clearly been impressed. Now it remained for Birkett to make a bigger impression still, this time through the slight, bespectacled figure who had followed the evidence from her seat in the dock. After making an unsuccessful submission to the judge that, in the case of Alice Thomas, there was no evidence to go to a jury, Birkett turned and said softly: 'I call Sarah Ann Hearn.'

Rustling and coughing died away as Annie Hearn took the oath and sat down in the witness box. Birkett's first questions concerned her early life. Mrs Hearn said she was not quite certain about her age, but she was just over forty (in fact she was forty-five). She was a farmer's daughter from Lincolnshire, and regarded herself as a widow, having neither seen nor heard from her husband since he left her in 1919.

'Mrs Hearn, have you ever at any time or in any form given arsenic to Mrs Thomas?'

'No, sir.'

'Have you at any time or in any form given arsenic to your dead sister, Minnie?'

'No, sir.'

She made an excellent witness, giving her evidence in a clear, firm voice and never faltering. Her sister Minnie, she explained, was about nine years older than she. At the age of about twenty, Minnie went to Sutton-on-Sea to help a

Mrs Poskitt with her dressmaking business. Annie herself had left home at about the age of nineteen to live with an aunt in Harrogate who ran a cookery school there. Both Minnie and another sister, Mabel, had been sickly, and it had fallen to Annie to nurse them. When Mabel died, Minnie and Annie moved south to Cornwall for the sake of Minnie's health, but during their first winter there Minnie grew worse and was very ill with inflammations of the bowels and stomach, coupled with eye trouble and neuritis in her feet. This made it very painful for her to walk. With her nose and throat, Minnie also had what the doctors called dry catarrh, and by the time they moved into Trenhorne House in 1925 Minnie was so weak that she couldn't even sit up in bed. In 1926 their aunt died, and the two sisters returned to Harrogate and stayed about a year. Towards the end of 1927 they moved back down to Trenhorne House, but the mild Cornish climate still seemed to have little effect on Minnie's health.

Norman Birkett put to her the evidence of a doctor who had spoken of Minnie complaining about being poisoned. 'What my sister said was: "I think the medicine is too strong. I feel that I have been poisoned",' said Mrs Hearn. 'I said in reply: "Oh, Minnie!" The doctor said something about taking half a dose. I showed the doctor the medicine I had given Minnie; it was the doctor's medicine on his own orders.'

'Did you ever give Minnie any medicine or any Benger's Food or anything else with arsenic in it?'

'I never did,' said Annie Hearn emphatically.

She explained her disappearance after the death of Alice Thomas by agreeing with Norman Birkett that she intended to commit suicide, but adding that she had been unable to go through with it. She agreed, too, that she had lived in Torquay under false names as she didn't want to be found or have her true identity established.

It was Herbert du Parcq, during his lengthy cross-examination, who first raised the question of Annie Hearn's relationship with her neighbour and benefactor, William Thomas. 'Have you heard any suggestion which would impute any motive to you getting rid of Mrs Thomas?' he asked.

'No.'

'Did it occur to you then that people might be saying: "Here is a husband and here is another woman, and between them they had wanted to get rid of the wife"?'

'No.'

Now Norman Birkett was on his feet, complaining to the judge about du Parcq's questioning. In his opening speech, Birkett pointed out, du Parcq had said nothing about motive.

'I do not understand Mr du Parcq to be suggesting that there was anything between Mr Thomas and Mrs Hearn implicating Mr Thomas,' said the judge. Du Parcq said he had tried to frame his questions so that there would be no such suggestion.

'I do not know that Mr du Parcq would object or that any harm would be done if I inferred the motive,' the judge continued. 'It is that this woman had conceived a desire to marry Mr Thomas if he were free and was under the impression that Mr Thomas was not unwilling.'

It was left to Birkett to repair the damage during his re-examination of Mrs Hearn. She said that until that very moment no one in the world had suggested that she wanted to marry Mr Thomas. There was never at any time in her mind, she insisted, the thought that she might marry him.

Birkett spoke bluntly. 'I want you to understand that it is now suggested that you killed Mrs Thomas in order to do that. Is there a word of truth in that?'

'Not an atom.'

'Did you ever conceive a passion, guilty or otherwise, for Mr Thomas?'

'No.'

'It is suggested that on 18 October you gave Mrs Thomas a poisoned sandwich in order to marry Mr Thomas. Is there a shadow of truth in that?'

'Not a shadow of truth.'

'From first to last in this matter, have you administered or given in any shape or form arsenic, either to Mrs Thomas or your sister?'

'No, I have not, ever.'

'That,' said Birkett finally, 'is the case for the defence.'

The seventh day of the trial was taken up with the closing speeches from both sides. Because Norman Birkett had called no defence witnesses other than Annie Hearn herself, he was entitled to the last word to the jury. Accordingly, it was Herbert du Parcq KC who rose first to address the court on behalf of the Crown. He had not been on his feet for long when he faltered, his face turned pale, and he slumped back into his seat. He left the court supported by Birkett and du Parcq's junior, Patrick Devlin (later Lord Devlin), and was taken to an anteroom where he fainted. Birkett administered some smelling salts, and Mr du Parcq was attended by Dr Roche Lynch. Meanwhile the judge adjourned the sitting for an hour and a half. On the resumption, du Parcq was allowed to continue his speech sitting down. The judge explained to the jury: 'It is as well not to make a mystery of these things. Mr du Parcq's indisposition was perfectly simple of explanation. When the brain is working, blood flows to the head, and, speaking quickly after a meal, blood is thus transferred from the stomach, and digestion is interfered with. This causes pressure by the intestines upon the heart, causing this faintness.' The judge added that it had happened to him once early in his own career, and, amid laughter, observed: 'I am still here, and older than Mr du Parcq.'

The spell had been broken, and the jury distracted by the unfortunate indisposition of Mr du Parcq. He must have been dismayed, too, at the judge's comment about feeling faint after food, since this must have prompted the jury to think of Mrs Thomas's illness after eating Annie Hearn's sandwiches at Bude. Mr du Parcq rallied valiantly towards the end of his speech, urging the jury to consider Mrs Hearn's behaviour following the death of her friend, Mrs Thomas. He submitted that they could say with the utmost confidence that Mrs Hearn had not a clear conscience, but a knowledge of guilt. She had never had the slightest intention of committing suicide when she left Trenhorne House. She was running away to avoid justice and detection; it was, he said, a carefully prepared scheme.

Referring to Mrs Hearn's letter to Mr Thomas, Mr du Parcq said: 'When it is a hypocritical thing – a person using sentiment and emotion for her own ends – it becomes a nauseating document.' And on the question of motive he invited the jury to ponder the words allegedly used by Annie Hearn about Mr Thomas's daily visits to Trenhorne House being 'only a blind'. 'If she did use these words,' said Mr du Parcq, 'it indicates that, innocent as Mr Thomas is, the idea occurred to Mrs Hearn that he was paying attention to her. If she thought that, she might well feel that in this small place she had an attraction for him, and she might also well have thought that if Mr Thomas were some day a widower, she might be the second Mrs Thomas.'

Du Parcq closed his speech with a few words about the death of Mrs Hearn's sister, Minnie. Mrs Hearn had not only ample opportunity but every opportunity, he said, to administer arsenic. She was a woman quite capable of telling and inventing ingenious lies. The jury should take the view that not only Mrs Thomas but Minnie Everard had met her death at the hands of Mrs Hearn.

Birkett, in his four-hour closing speech, reminded the jury that Mrs Hearn was charged on one indictment only, that relating to Mrs Thomas, although the Crown had made use of the second indictment referring to her sister Minnie. The jury had to decide it was satisfied beyond all reasonable doubt that Mrs Hearn had murdered Mrs Thomas. 'At twenty minutes past four,' said Birkett, pointing at the clock, 'for the first time in the case, the Crown on Saturday suggested that there might be a motive – a motive, I suggest, fanciful and fantastic – that Mrs Hearn had conceived some kind of idea that if Mrs Thomas were not there, Mr Thomas would marry her.' And yet, said Birkett, Thomas himself had never once been asked whether by word or gesture or in any way, if Mrs Hearn had shown that she was fond of him. Then there was the evidence of the Home Office man, Dr Gerald Roche Lynch. 'Dr Roche Lynch has never attended one person suffering from arsenical poisoning; yet he spoke of symptoms with exactly the same confidence as he spoke of other matters. Let the cobbler stick to his last,' commented Birkett. The fact that arsenic had been found in Alice Thomas's body did not prove she died from arsenical poisoning. Even if the Crown had proved Mrs Thomas had died from arsenical poisoning, was it proved that Mrs Hearn was responsible?

'Suspicion will not do, or speculation. The Crown must prove it.'

Norman Birkett was a craftsman, and he had spent some time considering how best to end his closing speech in defence of Annie Hearn. His original idea had been to base his peroration on a quotation from the fourteenth chapter of St John's Gospel which, the jury had heard in evidence, a kindly neighbour had been in the habit of reading to the dying Minnie Everard: 'Let not your heart be troubled, neither let it be afraid.' But he dropped this Biblical approach on being told that the jury on the previous Sunday had opted for a drive in the country in preference to attending church. Instead, Birkett – in a brilliant stroke – seized on the shafts of bright sunlight streaming in through the windows of the court on that June afternoon. 'For five months,' he told the listening jury, 'this woman has lived in Exeter Gaol during the darkness and dreariness of winter. She is now here before you in the sunshine of summer, but she is still walking in the valley of a great shadow. It is you, and you alone, that can lead her back again to the road of sunshine, your voice alone that can speak the word of deliverance. I ask you to speak that word to her, to stretch forth that hand that will help her back into the sunlight away from the shadows which have haunted her so long. That is my last appeal to you all.'

The following day the jury took less than an hour to find Annie Hearn not guilty of the murder of Alice Thomas. On the judge's instructions, the jury formally returned a similar verdict in the case of her sister Minnie. Finally, Mr Justice Roche turned and addressed the weeping prisoner in the dock. 'Sarah Ann Hearn,' he said simply, 'you are discharged.'

Annie Hearn, supported on one side by a nurse and on the other by a prison wardress, turned and walked out of the court. After switching clothes with her surviving sister in an anteroom Mrs Hearn was driven away in an open car, unrecognized by most of the crowd waiting outside. A couple of days later she left Cornwall for ever and travelled to Yorkshire to stay with her sister. Three weeks after the trial ended, Professor Sydney Smith, received a letter from her:

Doncaster
July 15th, 1931

Dear Sir,

I have only just got your address, and I want to thank you so much for all you have done for me, but for you I dare not think what the end might have been. I had no idea all those long lonely months, how much, how very much was being done for me. Mr West (her solicitor) has told me how you put aside important engagements to come to Bodmin and help to save a life, my life.

I am convinced no one else could have done what you did there, it was wonderful. I feel that I owe my life to you, and I do want to thank you, but it feels too big a thing to put into words, but please accept my heartfelt gratitude and sincere thanks – I shall never forget.

Yours very sincerely,

ANNIE HEARN

Every student of the Annie Hearn case seems to agree that poor Alice Thomas was murdered – but not by Annie Hearn. As Mr Justice Roche put it to the jury in the course of his summing up: 'The issue is now down to two people – Mrs Hearn and Mr Thomas. It is no use beating about the bush.' One theory circulating even today in Lewannick holds that William Thomas did indeed poison his wife, but not in order to marry Annie Hearn. He was content to let suspicion fall upon her, however, while he turned his attention to yet another woman. We will never know the truth of it. William Thomas died a few days before Christmas 1949 on a remote farm at Broadoak in Cornwall where he had lived a lonely, blighted existence since the trial eighteen years earlier. Annie Hearn herself never returned to Cornwall or Trenhorne House, and sought oblivion and anonymity in the north of England. Whether she salvaged anything from her ruined life we do not know. Almost certainly she ended her days a bitter and wronged old woman, turning the past over and over and perhaps speculating herself on the mystery of how Alice Thomas really died.

9

Villa Madeira, 5 Manor Road, Bournemouth

Mrs Antonia Landstein, small and neat, served afternoon tea in the sitting room at the Villa Madeira, and recalled in hesitant Central European accented English the day she saw the house for the first time. It was 1940. She and her husband had fled to England from war-torn Europe a few months before. The couple wanted a house in the south of England for the sake of Dr Landstein's health. They motored to Bournemouth and walked down Manor Road. It was the loveliest road that Mrs Landstein had ever seen. It was April, and all the rhododendrons were in flower. They particularly liked the little white house peeping out from behind the pine trees. One day, they thought, they would settle there.

They returned to London, where Dr Landstein was engaged in war work, and although fifteen years were to pass they never forgot the little house in Bournemouth. In 1955 they returned to the town in search of a retirement home. 'We drove along Manor Road,' said Mrs Landstein, 'and we saw our little house. It looked very sad and neglected, but it was for sale. So of course we bought it.'

The estate agent was less than candid. 'He was anxious not to mention the murder. He knew that people objected to things like that,' said Mrs Landstein. 'The first time I heard about it was from the electrician who was doing the rewiring. He said he hoped they had mopped up all the blood. I was afraid that someone had had an accident, but he said: "No, don't you know about this house? There was a terrible crime here." And that was the very first time I heard about it.'

Twenty years earlier, few people in Britain had not heard of the murder at the Villa Madeira. In the early jubilee summer of 1935 a beautiful Canadian woman, Alma Rattenbury, stood trial at the Old Bailey accused of bludgeoning her husband to death in that same sitting room with a carpenter's mallet. With her in the dock was Alma's lover, a teenage boy half her age called George Stoner. As the novelist and criminologist Miss Fryn Tennyson Jesse, who sat through the trial, wrote later: 'There was probably no one in England, and no one in court when the trial opened, who didn't think Mrs Rattenbury was guilty of the crime of murder. In everyone's mind, including mine, there was a picture of Mrs Rattenbury as a coarse, brawling, drunken and callous woman. But life is not as simple as that ... And the woman, who at first seemed so guilty, was seen to be undoubtedly innocent.'[1]

So how did Alma Victoria Rattenbury come by her reputation for razzle and raffishness? She was born around the turn of the century, the daughter of a German gold prospector in the Canadian Rockies. Alma's mother was English and said to be one of the most beautiful women on the Pacific coast. Her daughter inherited her pouting good looks. The child was apparently christened Ethel but her mother changed this to Alma when the child proved musically talented. (It would sound better, she reasoned, when the girl became famous.) Alma was playing the piano in public from the age of eight, encouraged, cajoled and finally forced by her mother who used to beat her if she refused to practice her scales. Alma's accomplishments on both the piano and violin meant that her fame as a child prodigy spread throughout western Canada; a dazzling career as a professional musician seemed to beckon. But she was still a teenager when she met an Irishman named Caledon Dolling and eloped with him, settling in Vancouver as man and wife. When war broke out in Europe

Dolling sailed for England to enlist. Alma, still infatuated, travelled with him to London and took a job at the War Office. Dolling was wounded in France in 1916 and awarded the Military Cross for conspicuous gallantry. He was wounded again on the Somme. Discharged from hospital, Dolling returned at once to his regiment. He was killed at Mametz Wood by an exploding shell. Devastated by his death, Alma became a nurse, working just behind the British lines in France, tending the wounded and doubling as a stretcher-bearer. She was wounded twice, and was awarded the Croix de Guerre with star and palm. At about this time she took up with a dashing officer in the Coldstream Guards, Captain Thomas Compton Pakenham, a member of the family that holds the Earldom of Longford, and who shared Alma's love of music. When the war ended they decided to make a match of it, and married in 1921. After the birth of their son, Christopher, the couple emigrated to the United States where Pakenham took a prestigious but poorly paid job as a music critic for the *New York Times*. Alma supplemented the family income by giving piano lessons, but they remained short of money. Finally Alma left Pakenham and fled with baby Christopher back to Canada. It was there, in Victoria, the handsome capital of British Columbia, that she met and captivated a distinguished architect twice her age, Francis Mawson Rattenbury.

In contrast to Alma's mercurial career as musical prodigy, impulsive lover and ministering angel, Rattenbury had led a life of almost leaden gravity. He was a Yorkshireman in declining middle age, who had left school in Leeds to join his uncle's firm of architects, Mawson and Mawson[2], in Bradford. The firm designed many of Bradford's grandest public buildings, including the town hall and covered market, and had been commissioned by the great Yorkshire industrialist, Sir Titus Salt, to design his purpose-built mill town of Saltaire. But in 1892, at the age of only twenty-five, Francis Rattenbury left England and sailed for British Columbia where he entered a competition to design a new legislative building in Victoria. To everyone's amazement, including his own, Rattenbury won. His fee was a staggering $40,826.07. The official opening of what the *Victoria Times* called 'a marble palace' took place in 1898, accompanied by military parades, choirs and a firework display. 'The beauty of the structure,' said the *Victoria Times* reporter, 'calls forth the admiration of everyone.' For Rattenbury, it was a personal and professional triumph. Other important commissions followed, including the design of Victoria's elegant Empress Hotel. He became chief architect for the Canadian Pacific Railway, designing château-like hotels for the CPR in the Rockies, Vancouver and Victoria. He married an extremely plain woman called Florence and settled at Oak Bay near Victoria in a small mansion he designed himself and which he named 'Iechinihl'[3], an Indian word meaning 'The place where a good thing happened'. With the exception of his courtship of Alma these must have been the happiest years of Rattenbury's life. Filled with the confidence and zest of the imperial age, Rattenbury embarked on one venture after another, including several land speculations, and founded a company running steamships up the Yukon river to the newly discovered goldfields in the Klondike. Sadly, in this, as in many of his entrepreneurial schemes, Rattenbury displayed an abysmal grasp of simple business principles, and by the early 1920s he had lost much of his money, his land company was bankrupt, and his marriage to the now even uglier Florence was on the brink of collapse. Life was indeed at a pretty low ebb for Francis Rattenbury when, a few days before Christmas 1923, he chanced to attend a dance in Victoria. The evening was to transform his life, and ultimately to bring it prematurely to an end.

'Last night I was out to a Dance,' he wrote to his sister, Kate, 'and danced every dance, until two in the morning and enjoyed every minute. The Lieutenant-Governor remarked: "You have simply renewed your youth".' This sudden rejuvenation was brought about by the presence at the dance of the beautiful fugitive pianist Alma Pakenham, 'a young married woman about 26, the belle of the ball and a marvellous musician. She knocked me out by saying: "Do you know that you have a lovely face?" "Great Scott," said I, "have I? I am going right home to have a look at it. I've never thought it worth looking at yet." "I'm not joking," she said. "You have almost the kindest face I ever saw."'

Rattenbury's chance encounter with Alma coincided with a dramatic upturn in his professional fortunes, and shortly after their first meeting he was able to tell her of two major commissions he had received worth nearly $100,000. The first was for a steamship terminal building in Victoria and the second an amusement centre for the same city in the style of the Crystal Palace. Consequent upon this excellent news their courtship blossomed, and both Rattenbury and Alma were divorced from their respective partners in 1925. Two months later they married quietly in the United States. Rattenbury wrote ecstatically to his sister that he had 'struck oil'. In an extravagant description, he said his new bride looked 'like a fragile Madonna, rather sad, but really full of fun', and continued, in his characteristically hyphenated style:

Musicians say that she is a divine player – that there is none who can surpass her – quit her music at twenty – & volunteered to go to France as a VAD – was stretcher-bearer in the trenches – wounded several times – married a Captain Pakenham – son of Admiral Pakenham – has one son – who will be Lord Longford⁴ – I'm becoming quite appreciative of music – and beginning to understand – In short a very interesting – most lovable – human soul – and best of all – simply adored by all her girl friends –

including those who lived with her in France – and by all elderly people as well – I can't tell why she linked up with me – at her age it seems unreasonable – for she had the world at her feet – perhaps the restful life appealed – and she seems to find all kinds of qualities in me – that she likes – and that I never knew of. *However* – It looks like some years of happiness and interest instead of the loneliness I see so much around – I look years younger . . .[5]

Rattenbury's rapture was of the introspective kind that refuses to be trammelled by the soured reproaches of the wider world; he either didn't know about, or refused to acknowledge, the whispering campaign against him that had been triggered by his marriage to the delicious Alma. It had its roots among Rattenbury's own family; his son Frank, in particular, was especially spiteful, and seems to have done his utmost to fuel resentment within Victoria society circles by putting it about that Alma was reckless with her new husband's money and little more than a glorified lush. This smear campaign, coupled with the running sore of an interminable legal suit with the government, finally forced the Rattenburys to quit Canada for good. By now the family was a foursome (their son John was born in 1927) and it seemed as good a time as any for the increasingly irritated and unpopular Rattenbury to return to England.

And so they came to Bournemouth, renting the pretty little white house known as the Villa Madeira in Manor Road. It is a salubrious spot, a town likened by Thomas Hardy to a fairy palace 'suddenly created at the stroke of a wand, and allowed to get a little dusty'.[6] The Rattenburys would have recognized that description; they would have doubtless concurred with the opinion of Godfrey Smith, writing half a century later, that seven miles of sand and two thousand acres of scented pines had lent Bournemouth 'a luxuriant, balmy, feminine torpor'.[7] It was this lethargic and ever so slightly faded gentility that commended Bournemouth to Francis Rattenbury, exhausted and emotionally bruised from his failing years in British Columbia; the town's own symphony orchestra and excellent rail link to London appealed to Alma's musical and social propensities.

As Rattenbury's career as an eminent architect faded, and his mental faculties deteriorated (he was now over sixty), Alma's musical career suddenly re-ignited. This renaissance had nothing to do with the concert platform of her younger years; it was to do with the brasher and infinitely more bankable world of Tin Pan Alley. She began composing popular songs, chiefly sentimental ballads, some of which Rattenbury persuaded the Keith Prowse company to publish, broadcast and record. Under the pseudonym Lozanne, she rattled off a series of numbers with such whimsical titles as 'Avelette', 'Zanita', 'By Naples Water', 'Sheldermene', 'You Brought My Heart The Sunshine', and 'Dark-Haired Marie'. Top popular singers of the day hurried to record Alma's songs, among them the tenor Frank Titterton and Peter Dawson, whose baritone rendition of Dark-Haired Marie gave her the biggest hit of her songwriting career.

The royalties rolled in, and life at the Villa Madeira was extremely comfortable: young John became a weekly boarder at a nearby prep school, and school holidays were filled with happy family outings to the New Forest or the beach; there was money aplenty to fill Francis Rattenbury's nightly whisky tumbler and to indulge Alma's unstinted passion for expensive clothes, her Daimler car, and (although she never touched drink) her cocktail-circuit lifestyle. Then a series of disconnected events occurred which, in their different ways, were to cast a shadow over Alma's happiness. First, her husband sank into a state of deep depression, worrying about money and afflicted with an old ailment that rendered him morose, lethargic, and permanently chilly. He became withdrawn, taking less and less interest in his wife's continued success. Whisky, followed by more whisky, was Rattenbury's self-prescribed remedy, although one of his few friends, Dr William O'Donnell, did his best to wean Rattenbury on to something more efficacious.

Then, in the summer of 1932, Alma herself fell ill, and pulmonary tuberculosis was diagnosed. The one lasting effect of this was that Alma began to drink heavily. Her feelings for Rattenbury seemed to wane, and the couple began to bicker, then quarrel, over money. Rattenbury became increasingly irritated over his young wife's extravagance, for despite the hefty royalty cheques from London she was for ever wheedling money out of him. He paid Alma an annual allowance of £1,000 (a very large sum in the Depression years of the early Thirties), but she often pleaded poverty on the basis that this money had to cover all the household expenses, clothes for the family, and John's school fees.

Alma's allowance also had to pay the wages of her housekeeper-cum-companion at the Villa Madeira, a dreary-looking woman called Irene Riggs. She was about the same age as Alma, and the two became more like friends than mistress and servant. She lived in, and accompanied Alma on many of her shopping sprees in London.

Francis Rattenbury, staying at home at the Villa Madeira, was becoming more depressed than ever over the state of his finances. Half-ruined in Canada, he now fretted over his losses on the London Stock market, and seems to have convinced himself that he was heading for total ruin. Native Yorkshire thrift had always made him careful with money: now he was becoming distinctly tight. He took a dim view of Alma's capricious way with money, especially money she had extracted from him on what he judged to

be frivolous pretexts. Alma knew this, and took to inventing excuses for asking for more, always timing her requests
to coincide with her husband's nightly appointment with
the whisky decanter. On one occasion she persuaded him
to part with £250 for a trip to London, pretending that she
needed the money for an operation and brushing aside her
husband's mumbled complaint that it was all getting very
expensive. At her trial a few years later, Alma was asked
why she resorted to lies. Her answer was simple. 'It saved
rows,' she explained.

She may have been thinking back to a night in July 1934
when Francis Rattenbury was in one of his deeper fits of
morbid depression, talking of suicide and of putting his
head in the gas oven; on and on he rambled, becoming
gloomier and gloomier, until finally Alma could stand it
no longer and blurted out that it was a pity he didn't do it
instead of just harping on about it. In a flash, Rattenbury
started from his apathy, jumped out of his chair and hit her
hard across the face. Alma fought back, biting his arm, and
Rattenbury stormed out of the front door. He went
missing for several hours, returning finally in the early
hours to find his wife sound asleep in bed. Dr O'Donnell
had called, treated her for a black eye, and given her an
injection of morphia.

But the one event that set in motion the tragedy that was
to overtake the Villa Madeira was the arrival in September
1934 of a new member of staff: a likeable, open-faced lad
of nearly eighteen called George Percy Stoner. He had
answered Mrs Rattenbury's advertisement in the *Bournemouth Daily Echo* for 'Daily willing lad, 14–18, for
housework. Scout-trained preferred.' Stoner was paid a
wage of £1 a week to drive the car, take the boy John to
and from school, keep the garden trim, and do odd jobs
around the house. He was an easy-going sort, who fitted
in well. Even choleric old Francis Rattenbury took a shine

to him, and shared his cigars and his business problems with him in long talks over whisky in the sitting room. Alma liked George Stoner even more, and on 22 November, three days after his eighteenth birthday, she seduced him.

The mousey Irene Riggs had watched the events of a few short weeks since Stoner's arrival with dismay. Since coming to the Villa Madeira in 1931 she had gradually been accepted by Alma as part of the family, earning the trust and then the friendship of a woman she admired and respected. Now, in a matter of days, this ignorant youth, the son of a bricklayer from the wrong side of town, had bulldozed his way into her mistress's house, her affections, and now her bed. For Alma kept nothing back from Irene, and had told her, with some brazenness, that she and George Stoner had become lovers.

The seduction had a profound effect on Stoner. He was a simple soul (his father later admitted that he had been backward as a child) and clearly was unable to handle the situation into which he had unwittingly stumbled. The once-unassuming, happy-go-lucky lad was now transformed into an overbearing, selfish, strutting tyrant, the possessor of a sophisticated and still-beautiful woman twice his age who began to lavish upon her youthful lover all her most ardent attentions. At her invitation, Stoner moved out of his parents' home in Redhill Drive and into his own room next to Alma's bedroom. That Francis Rattenbury slept alone in his own bedroom downstairs made illicit intercourse a good deal easier; that young John Rattenbury slept in his mother's room on his weekends at home from school was regarded by Alma as a minor problem. John, she claimed later, was a very sound sleeper.

Did Francis Rattenbury know what was going on between his wife and their junior servant behind his back (or rather, over his head) in his own house? Alma claimed that he had long ago told her to make her own arrangements in the matter of sex; he had ceased to care, and had come to terms with his own failing drive. But opinion in the household after the case was that Rattenbury was unaware that Alma had taken Stoner – of all people – as a lover. When Miss Tennyson Jesse visited the Villa Madeira shortly after the trial she found this hard to believe. 'It is so small as to be remarkable,' she wrote,[8] 'small as the witch's cottage in *Hansel and Gretel.* On the ground floor are the kitchen, drawing room, and a room that Mr Rattenbury used as a bedroom, and which opened off the drawing room. Is it possible that a man, in a house as small as Madeira Villa, would not hear the footsteps over his head whenever Stoner came into Mrs Rattenbury's room, and that he would not hear the occasionally loud quarrels which took place between them? Looking at Villa Madeira, the answer would seem to be that it would be quite impossible.'

Having enjoyed a guided tour of the house myself, led by Mrs Antonia Landstein, I am inclined to agree with Miss Tennyson Jesse. The house is small, not so small as to be cramped, but small enough for four resident adults to know more or less exactly where anyone is at any one time. There are four bedrooms upstairs; one has now been converted into a kitchen. The two bedrooms at the back of the house face south. The larger of these was Alma's. It has French windows which open out on to a small balcony, where she and the children could sit and enjoy the sun. It is directly over the downstairs sitting room, and although Rattenbury was somewhat deaf it seems impossible that he would not have caught the sounds of lovemaking from overhead as he sat reading at night in his favourite armchair. Adjoining Alma's room (but not connected by a door) is the small room occupied by George Stoner. This, too, has a balcony and enjoys a pleasant view over the back garden. Half way along the landing is what used to be the children's room, now a kitchen. And at the front of the house, overlooking the front garden and Manor Road, is what was in fact the principal bedroom, occupied by Irene Riggs.

As the affair between Alma and her young chauffeur-handyman progressed, she responded to the assertive change in Stoner's personality and warmed to it. Whether she realized it or not, she was falling in love. Stoner, mastering the situation, ordered her to stop drinking: she complied at once. Alma was completely dominated, submissive, deriving intense satisfaction from the manner in which her thrusting young lover had suddenly taken control of her life and given it purpose, meaning, direction. She found a delicious thrill in their tiny tiffs, and when they had their first serious quarrel Alma revelled in a sort of masochistic ecstasy when Stoner drew a knife and threatened to kill her. This row, according to Alma's evidence at the trial, blew up because she had discovered that Stoner, whom she had thought to be aged twenty-two (and therefore in his majority) was in fact only eighteen. She had inwardly blushed at this, and sought, rather half-heartedly it seems, to end the affair on the grounds of age difference. Stoner would hear none of it. Early in 1935, apparently to impress his worldly-wise mistress, Stoner announced that he was taking drugs. Her reaction was to panic. She sent for Dr O'Donnell, confessed her relationship with Stoner, and begged him to speak to the boy about his increasingly violent behaviour towards her and his self-confessed drug habit. The doctor confronted Stoner, who admitted taking cocaine, but although O'Donnell offered to help him with his problem Stoner curtly told him to mind his own business.

In March 1935 Alma proposed to Stoner that she take him up to London for a short holiday. This greatly upset the faithful Irene Riggs, who was told she would be left behind at the Villa Madeira as Stoner would find her presence at the hotel inhibiting. Alma explained this trip to town to Rattenbury by her familiar subterfuge of claiming to need another minor operation. The weary Rattenbury shrugged, and wrote her a cheque for £250 to cover the trip. In London Alma and Stoner stayed at the Royal Palace Hotel in Kensington, registering as brother and sister and occupying rooms across the corridor from each other. Stoner must have thought it was Christmas: the staff called him 'Sir', and for three hectic days Alma led him on a shopping spree of cornucopian proportions. At Harrods alone, Alma lavished over forty pounds' worth of clothing on him, including two pairs of shoes, three pairs of crêpe-de-Chine pyjamas (at £3 a pair), three shirts, three ties, a dozen linen handkerchiefs, two silk handkerchiefs, three pairs of socks, two pairs of gloves, two sets of underwear, two off-the-peg suits and a mackintosh. Alma also gave Stoner some money; with this he visited a jeweller's in Old Bond Street and bought her a diamond ring costing over £15. The couple spent their evenings at the theatre or the cinema, and their nights in bed together. But for the fact that the trip covered Tuesday to Friday, it might have been an archetypal dirty weekend. The judge at the trial referred to the London visit as 'an orgy'. But as Miss Tennyson Jesse put it later: 'The private coming together of a pair of lovers and their normal physical ecstasies, however reprehensible these may be morally, do not seem well described by the word "orgy". Even shopping at Harrods does not quite come under this heading ... The fact, nevertheless, remains that Stoner's trip to London must have thoroughly unsettled him. He was happy enough at Villa Madeira where the social regime was easy and pleasant for such as he.'[9]

The lovers arrived back in Bournemouth late on the Friday night. Rattenbury was already asleep in bed, but the following day found him in one of his blacker moods. He was miserable, depressed, and so distracted that he failed to inquire, even politely, about the London trip or the success or otherwise of Alma's imaginary operation. He spent most of the day complaining to anyone who would listen about his involvement in a scheme to build a block of flats. Rattenbury was to be the architect, but the scheme was being held up because of the financial depression and he was worried about his fee. On the Sunday morning, 24 March, Alma suggested a drive, but when the outing failed to revive Rattenbury's spirits, she paced up and down the sitting room trying to snap her husband out of his mood. Rattenbury, however, had buried his head in a book. At last, Alma hit on an idea. She suggested that she ring up her husband's old friend William Jenks, who lived in a large house at Bridport, and invite themselves over the next day. This idea perked Rattenbury up at once, because Jenks, a retired barrister, was a wealthy man, and might be interested in financing Rattenbury's proposed block of flats. Alma made the call, and Mr Jenks said he would be pleased to see them; not only should they come for the day on Monday, they would be welcome to spend the night as well. Alma said they would be delighted to stay the night, a remark overheard by George Stoner as he cleared away the afternoon tea things in the sitting room. His reaction was precipitate and frightening. Rushing upstairs to his room, Stoner snatched up an air pistol he kept in a drawer and ran back down to where Alma was still making polite conversation on the telephone to Mr Jenks. She hurriedly terminated the call when Stoner appeared in the doorway and began threatening her with what she thought was a revolver. Stoner, as Alma explained at her trial, was beside himself with rage, and said he would kill her if she went to Bridport. Stoner began ranting, accusing Alma of having had sex with her husband that afternoon with the bedroom door closed.

'What did you say to him about that?' Alma's counsel asked at the trial.

'I assured him that I had not, and he must put that revolver away and not make an ass of himself.'

'What did he then say?'

'He told me I must never have that bedroom door closed again, and that if I went to Bridport he would not drive. He was very annoyed at my going to Bridport.'

'Did he say why he did not want you to go with Mr Rattenbury to Bridport?'

'He was very jealous of Mr Rattenbury – unnecessarily so . . . He thought I would have to share the same bedroom there.'

'When he said that, did you say anything to him about what the arrangements were to be?'

'I assured him that I would have a separate bedroom.'

Stoner, however, did not accept Alma's assurance, and spent the rest of the afternoon brooding moodily over the prospect of his mistress sharing the same bed as her husband. At about 8 P.M. he turned up at the home of his grandparents and spent some time chatting with them about family matters before asking them, perfectly openly, if he could borrow their carpenter's mallet. He explained he wanted to drive in some pegs for the Rattenburys' canvas sunshelter. Armed with the mallet, he returned to the Villa Madeira.

It was Irene Riggs's evening off, and Alma and her husband had spent the evening alone, playing cards in the sitting room. Irene let herself in with her own key at about 10.15 P.M. and went straight up to her room. By now Alma was also upstairs, having kissed Rattenbury goodnight, and was sorting out some clothes to take with her the next day on the trip to Bridport. Presently, Irene tiptoed downstairs to fix herself a snack in the kitchen. Passing along the hall, she heard the sound of heavy breathing coming from the sitting room. Assuming that Rattenbury had fallen asleep in his chair, as he often did, she passed on. A few minutes later, walking along the landing to visit the bathroom, she found Stoner leaning over the bannister at the head of the stairs. She asked him what was the matter. 'Nothing,' Stoner replied, 'I was looking to see if the lights were out.'

At about 10.45 P.M., Irene had a visitor in her room. It was Alma, now packed, who wanted to tell her about the following day's trip to Bridport. The two women chatted briefly, then said goodnight. Alma walked silently down the landing to her own room. Here, some ten minutes later, she was joined in bed by George Stoner, who was wearing pyjamas. Alma knew something was wrong; Stoner seemed agitated.

'What's the matter, darling?'

Stoner was barely coherent, muttering that something was wrong but he could not tell her what it was. Alma pressed him, thinking that Stoner was involved in some minor family trouble. Finally she dragged it out of him. 'He told me that I wasn't going to Bridport the next day as he had hurt Ratz (the family's pet name for Francis Rattenbury). It didn't penetrate my head what he did say to me at all until I heard Ratz groan, and then my brain became alive and I jumped out of bed.

'He said he had hit him over the head with a mallet.'

Alma hurtled downstairs in her nightdress and bare feet. In the sitting room she found Rattenbury sitting in the chair where she had left him. He appeared to be asleep, and looked quite normal apart from a black eye (the effect of *contrecoup* when a blow is delivered to the back of the head). She knelt and tried to rub his hands; they were cold. She tried taking his pulse, and shook him to try to make him speak. But Rattenbury had lost consciousness and remained, slumped and silent, in his chair. Alma rose and looked helplessly around the room. 'Then I saw this blood, and I went round the table, and I trod on his false teeth, and that made me hysterical, and I yelled – I can't remember, only vaguely . . .'

In fact she was yelling for Irene, who quickly appeared downstairs in her nightclothes. She found Alma gulping down a glass of neat whisky. 'Fetch the doctor,' she screamed. 'Hurry!' Irene did so, as Alma went raving about the house, vomiting from the effect of the whisky, crying and shouting repeatedly: 'Oh! Poor Ratz! Poor Ratz! Can't someone do something?'

By the time Dr O'Donnell arrived it was nearly midnight and Alma Rattenbury was already very drunk. He and Irene managed to drag the injured Rattenbury from his chair to his adjoining bedroom where they laid him on the bed. Dr O'Donnell then telephoned a surgeon he knew called Alfred Rooke who lived a few minutes' drive away in Boscombe. Rooke arrived shortly after midnight, and the two men agreed that with Alma in the state she was in, the only proper place for her husband was the nearby Strathallan Nursing Home. When they got him there they shaved his head and discovered three serious wounds to the back of the skull. Dr O'Donnell telephoned the police and told them what had happened, adding that the wounds were the result of external violence and that Rattenbury would almost certainly not survive them.

Back at the Villa Madeira the scene was one of complete chaos. Irene Riggs had done her best to mop up the blood on the carpet, but Alma Rattenbury was even more drunk than before. Every light in the house was on, the front door was wide open and the radio-gramophone was blaring out music. Four police officers were wandering around the house. Only when Dr O'Donnell and a police inspector returned from the nursing home at 3.30 A.M. was any sort of order restored. Dr O'Donnell, extremely shocked, marched straight over to the radio-gramophone and switched it off. He tried to explain to Alma that her husband's condition was extremely grave, but she did not seem to be able to take it in. Inspector Mills tried to spell it out to her: 'Your husband has been seriously injured, and is now in the nursing home.' Mrs Rattenbury's drunken response was: 'Will that be against me?' Cautioned, Alma told the listening inspector: 'I did it. He has lived too long. I will tell you in the morning where the mallet is. Have you told the coroner yet? I'll make a better job of it next time. Irene doesn't know. I've made a proper muddle of it. I thought I was strong enough.'

Dr O'Donnell was also listening to all this, and intervened, pointing out to the inspector that Alma was blind drunk and in no fit state either to answer questions or to know what she was saying. He took her upstairs and put her to bed, giving her a large dose of morphia to make her sleep. But a few minutes later he was amazed to find that Alma had staggered back downstairs and was talking again to the police inspector. Dr O'Donnell remonstrated with the officer. 'Look at her condition,' he shouted. 'She's full of whisky, and I've just given her a large dose of morphia. She's in no condition to make any statement.' So saying, he took Alma's arm and helped her back upstairs. It was now after 4 A.M., and Dr O'Donnell was ready for his own bed. Had he stayed, he may have been able to prevent another police officer, Inspector Carter, marching into Alma's room at 6 A.M. and ordering Irene Riggs to make her mistress some coffee. Alma was in an appalling state, having had less than two hours' sleep after a four-hour drinking binge and a hefty shot of morphia. Yet, on the evidence of Inspector Carter, she was in a fit state by 8.15 A.M. to make a statement, which he duly recorded in his notebook. 'About 9 P.M. on 24 March,' Alma allegedly told him, 'I was playing cards with my husband when he dared me to kill him, as he wanted to die. I picked up a mallet and he then said: "You have not got the guts to do it!" I then hit him with the mallet. I hid the mallet outside. I would have shot him if I had had a gun.'

Alma was taken to Bournemouth police station to be charged with attempted murder. Before leaving the Villa Madeira she managed to snatch a few words with Irene Riggs, telling her to 'get Stoner to give me the mallet'. Formally charged, Alma replied: 'That's right. I did it deliberately and would do it again.' But she remembered nothing of this or of anything else for that matter, until she emerged from her drugged stupor three days later to find that she was lying alone in a cell at Holloway Gaol in London.

Meanwhile, what of George Stoner? We have not heard of him since leaving him gibbering in his crêpe-de-Chine pyjamas in Alma's bed. He evidently dressed and made himself useful in the mêlée that ensued when the police arrived, and it was he who chauffeured Dr O'Donnell to and from the Strathallan Nursing Home down the road from the Villa Madeira. (During O'Donnell's initial examination of the injured Rattenbury, Stoner had stayed outside in the car, sleeping peacefully.) Once Alma had been arrested and taken away, he and Irene Riggs were left alone in the house. Irene had noted Alma's whispered request to 'get Stoner to give me the mallet', and had indeed mentioned this to Stoner, but she knew that the police had already found a mallet hidden behind some bushes in the garden on the night of the attack, so there seemed little point in worrying about it now. The atmosphere in the house as Alma languished in jail accused of trying to murder the dying Rattenbury must have been unbearable. To lighten the mood Stoner suggested a drive in the country, and on the Tuesday the couple motored over to

Wimborne Minster. On the return drive, Stoner casually mentioned borrowing the mallet from his grandparents, but added that there would be no fingerprints on it since he had been careful to wear gloves. With considerable courage, given the tense circumstances, Irene turned to Stoner and asked him why he had done it. Stoner explained that he had discovered Alma and Rattenbury making love on the Sunday afternoon. He had decided that Rattenbury had to go.

This was Irene's chance to save her mistress, but she did not hasten to the police with Stoner's confession straight away. Instead, next day, she persuaded her mother to move in with her at the Villa Madeira, and consulted a priest about the wisest course of action to take. Returning to the house late that night she learned that Stoner – a lifelong teetotaller – had got himself extremely drunk and had spent much of the evening running up and down Manor Road shouting: 'Mrs Rattenbury is in jail, and I put her there!' Irene confronted Stoner, who promised that he would give himself up to the police the next day. But first, he said, he was going to London to see Alma.

It must have been with a thick head that Stoner woke early the following morning, Thursday, and caught the first train to London. Quite what he did in the capital that day is unclear, but he certainly did not manage to see Alma at Holloway. Whatever he did, he spent all day doing it, and caught an evening train home. Stoner was arrested at Bournemouth station on his return, and now the charge was murder, for Francis Rattenbury had died that day of his wounds.

'Do you know Mrs Rattenbury had nothing to do with the affair?'

George Stoner was sitting in his cell at Bournemouth police station, and talking to the constable in charge of him. The officer got out his notebook and cautioned

Stoner, who then said: 'When I did the job I believed he was asleep. I hit him, and then came upstairs and told Mrs Rattenbury. She rushed down then. You see, I watched through the french windows and saw her kiss him goodnight, then leave the room. I waited, and crept in through the french window which was unlocked. I think he must have been asleep when I hit him. Still, it ain't much use saying anything. I don't suppose they will let her out yet. You know, there should be a doctor with her when they tell her I'm arrested, because she'll go out of her mind . . .'[10]

Next day, a smiling George Stoner tripped lightly into the dock at Bournemouth police court to be remanded in custody accused of murder. He was wearing the broad grey striped suit that Alma had bought him in London not ten days before.

The British public awaited the trial with as much relish as they anticipated the holiday atmosphere that marked the silver jubilee celebrations of King George V and Queen Mary. Countless foreign dignitaries streamed into London from scores of world capitals. On a balmy night in the middle of May the jubilee was celebrated with a court ball at Buckingham Palace, where the King and Queen spent much of the evening glaring at their son, the Prince of Wales, who would insist on dancing as many dances as he could with the jewel-encrusted American woman, Mrs Ernest Simpson. A few days later there was a sensation of a different sort when the legendary Lawrence of Arabia died in a military hospital from injuries received in a mysterious motorcycle accident. Space in the newspapers was at a premium, but this was a major murder trial at the Old Bailey, and news editors the length of Fleet Street knew that the Rattenbury case was just what was needed to blow away the post-jubilee blues. Colour-writers were despatched as well as their top Old Bailey and crime correspondents. This was the best full-dress murder trial for years, and the newspaper-reading public would have their fill.

As it turned out, the first sensation went unreported. Accounts of the committal proceedings at the police court in Bournemouth had fashioned in the public mind a picture of Alma as a beautiful, albeit foolish, woman who had determined to take the blame for the killing in order to shield her younger, and even more foolish, boy-lover. She was, it seemed, perfectly content to sacrifice her own life for the man she loved so passionately. What few people knew – could have known – was that a few days before the trial Alma's elder son, Christopher Pakenham, had visited her in Holloway. He was still only thirteen years old. That visit had caused his mother to change her mind; as Christopher left, Alma knew that she owed a greater responsibility to her children than the responsibility she felt she owed Stoner, first as his employer and then as his seducer. She sat in her cell and wrote at length to Irene Riggs:

. . . Oh Lord, and tomorrow Good Friday and I dare not think of the children. I even pretend I haven't any here. If one thought for five minutes they'd go mad . . . I have to control my mind like the devil not to think of little John . . . If I feel awfully sad, being separated in such a ghastly way from everything one loves, S's feelings must take some weighing up, but he'll be the same and not allow himself to think. Should think his remorse at what he's brought down on my head, the children's, etc., – smashed lives – would drive him a raving lunatic – a frightful responsibility to hold in one person's hands. God deliver me from such a hellish responsibility. I couldn't have courage to bear *that pain*; my own is more than enough in a hundred lifetimes as it is . . .

Darling, God bless you, bless us all and get us out of this nightmare. My love to your M and F.

My love be with you always,

Lozanne[11]

When Alma's lawyer visited her the following day she told him that for the sake of her children she would tell the whole truth. She no longer proposed to deny that Stoner had committed the murder.

On the other side of London, Stoner was confined in Brixton Gaol. His story was that he had committed the murder under the influence of cocaine. Under no circumstances was he prepared to implicate his former mistress; he was concerned not so much to establish his own innocence but to see that Alma was acquitted. When his barrister, a vastly experienced lawyer called J. D. Casswell, visited Stoner in Brixton two days before the trial he found the prisoner sullen and uncooperative. Years later, Casswell explained his dilemma in his autobiography: 'For my part I did not press him to speak or encourage him to give his personal account of what had happened; I knew he might so easily insist on telling me that he had committed the murder and that he alone was the culprit. If he had done this, my hands would have been tied; by the rules of my profession I should not have been allowed to call any evidence to prove that he was innocent and should have been restricted merely to trying to show that the evidence against him was insufficient.'[12]

Casswell had decided already not to call Stoner as a witness, and the interview at Brixton had reinforced that decision. But Casswell determined to ask the judge at the Old Bailey to order separate trials for Alma and for Stoner. A joint trial, he reasoned, in which a mature woman of the world shared the dock with a mere teenager would be riven with bias and prejudice. Separate trials were essential if justice were to be seen to be done. Casswell's strategy was given added impetus when he received from Alma's solicitors a copy of her letter to Irene Riggs. He scanned the text anxiously: 'S's feelings must take some weighing up . . .'; the implication was clear. Alma was planning to put the blame for the murder squarely on Stoner's shoulders. Alma was finally prepared to say that Stoner had indeed murdered Rattenbury and had done it alone.

Alma and Stoner both pleaded not guilty when the trial opened at the Old Bailey on 27 May 1935. Alma's barrister, Terence O'Connor KC, whispered to Casswell as the pleas were taken: 'Mrs Rattenbury is going to give evidence against your boy.'

Casswell was mortified. 'This was the first I knew,' he wrote, 'that Alma Rattenbury was going so far in her efforts to save her own neck as actually to give sworn testimony against her ex-lover.'[13] For a moment, Casswell dithered, and in his confusion almost forgot his application to the judge, Mr Justice Humphreys, to have Stoner tried separately. Indeed, one juror had already been sworn. However, the judge ordered the jury box to be emptied and Casswell rose to make his application for separate trials, submitting that Alma's letter from Holloway inculpating Stoner 'may have a very bad influence upon the minds of the jury, and it would be difficult to disabuse their minds of it'. After a brisk exchange with other counsel the judge dismissed Casswell's application. The trial of both prisoners went ahead as planned, and ran for five days.

The case for the Crown was outlined with singular restraint – one might almost say diffidence – by Mr R. P. Croom-Johnson KC. 'Ladies and gentlemen,' he told the jury, 'it looks as though Stoner, having borrowed the mallet, brought it back, naming some purpose or other, to the house, and it is the contention of the prosecution that one or other of the accused delivered a blow or blows at the head of Mr Rattenbury; and, if that is right, the prosecution suggests for your consideration that these two people, Mrs Rattenbury and Stoner, with one common object and one common design, set out to get rid of Mr

Rattenbury, who, as I suggested earlier stood in their way . . .'

Poor Irene Riggs was the first substantial witness for the prosecution. Casswell, for Stoner, tried to emphasize the dislike Miss Riggs felt for his client:

'In November of last year, Miss Riggs, that is about a month after Stoner had first been engaged as chauffeur, you and Mrs Rattenbury and Stoner went and stayed at the Randolph Hotel in Oxford?'

'Yes.'

'Did you know even then, or did you know from that day onwards, they were sleeping together?'

'Yes,' said Irene, softly, 'but they didn't at the hotel.'

'Was it not almost as soon as that trip was over that Stoner came to live in the house, the Villa Madeira?'

'Yes.'

'Did you approve of that?'

'I didn't mind him living in the house.'

'You didn't mind him being in the house, but you knew he was always going into her bedroom, did you not?'

'Yes.'

'You were not pleased, were you – perhaps naturally – having been a close friend of Mrs Rattenbury's for about four years, that suddenly this lad of seventeen should come in?'

'No.'

'You were not pleased about it, were you?'

'Not very,' Irene Riggs was obliged to admit.

The Rattenburys' old family doctor, Dr William O'Donnell, found himself in the unpleasant position of giving evidence for the prosecution. He described the anarchic scenes at the Villa Madeira on the murder night when he arrived to find Alma reeling with drink, heavily intoxicated and wildly excited. 'She was talking about poor Ratz, her husband,' he said, 'and she talked about sending him to a nursing home.'

'Had she a bottle or a glass of whisky in her hand?'

'Yes, a tumbler of whisky and soda.'

'When you got back to Manor Road at half-past three, describe what Mrs Rattenbury's condition then was.'

'She was very excited.'

'Was the gramophone playing?'

'The radiogram. She was running about in the passage when I arrived there, staggering about. I counted four officers in the house, and she was running about amongst them from one room to another.'

The picture of Alma Rattenbury that emerged on the first day of the trial was of an over-excitable, over-indulged vamp. Bored and frustrated by a torpid and miserable older husband, she had alighted on Stoner as casually as a butterfly might settle on a dandelion. Mr Croom-Johnson, who had begun to warm to his task as the day wore on, even went so far as to suggest that Alma regularly lounged around the house in the manner of some sort of high-class tart, and drew Irene Riggs' abashed attention to one of Alma's smart three-piece suits which was held aloft for the jury to see.

'You knew Mrs Rattenbury pretty well. Can you give the jury any assistance as to whether, usually, when she wore these three articles of clothing, she wore anything underneath them?'

The poor woman must have inwardly cringed with embarrassment. 'Yes,' she said, 'sometimes she wore a little woolly vest, and perhaps a brassiere as well.'

'Was that in the daytime?'

'Yes.'

'On this night when you found her in the drawing room with Mr Rattenbury late at night, as far as you could see had she got anything on underneath those garments or not?'

Irene Riggs was quite flabbergasted. 'Well,' she said with downcast gaze, 'one could not tell.'

It had not been a good day for Alma's defence team, and they left the Old Bailey in gloomy mood. But having heard the first day's evidence from her seat in the public gallery, Miss Fryn Tennyson Jesse, the fashionable novelist whose latest book *A Pin To See The Peepshow* had been based on the 1922 trial of Edith Thompson and her younger lover Freddie Bywaters, sensed that the tide would shortly turn. She was right. 'In the Rattenbury case,' she wrote later, 'the evidence – which seemed so damning on the first day – completely altered in character; what had seemed undoubted fact proved to be an airy nothing and the whole complex pattern shifted and changed, much as the pattern of sand changes when it is shaken, and, like sand, it slipped away between the fingers, leaving a residue of grains of truth very different from the pile that the prosecution had originally built up.'[14]

It was the arrival in the witness box of Alma Rattenbury herself that shook the sand in the jury's collective mind. For two and a half days they had watched her in the dock, sitting a few feet from Stoner but never glancing at him, wearing a fashionable and expensive dark blue suit and a short fur coat. Everyone in court had stolen a glance at Alma Rattenbury, and who would have disagreed with the estimation of a young woman reporter who wrote that she 'is more than a pretty woman: her face is attractive with its large perfect eyes, short nose and thick-lipped mouth. She was said to be thirty-eight. She looked much younger. She wears her dark blue coat and hat with gloves to match with a certain chic . . .'[15] She was led through her evidence-in-chief by Mr O'Connor, who referred at the outset to

Alma's two sons, Christopher Pakenham and little John Rattenbury.

'A little boy; I think he is six in June?'

'Yes.'

'Since the birth of that child, did you and Mr Rattenbury live together as man and wife?'

'No.'

'Did you occupy separate rooms?'

'Yes.'

'No marital intimacy, but were you cordial?'

'Absolutely.'

'Was your married life happy?'

'Like that,' said Alma, making a circle with her thumb and forefinger and gesturing to the court.

The questioning moved quickly to the hiring of Stoner, and Alma's affair with him. 'What attitude did your husband take,' asked Mr O'Connor, 'towards this, if he knew it?'

Alma didn't bat an eyelid. 'None whatsoever.'

'Did he know of it?'

'He must have known because he told me to live my own life quite a few years ago.'

'As I understand it,' said Mr O'Connor, glancing at his brief, 'there was no occasion on which you told him about Stoner, but your husband knew about it?'

'No,' replied Alma. 'I told him I had taken him at his word and was living my own life.'

'Oh, you told him that, did you? Can you tell me when that was?'

'No. I would say it was somewhere about Christmas that I told him.'

In a soft, well-spoken voice, Alma told of the gruelling events of the murder night, of her planned trip to Bridport, of Stoner's armed intervention during the telephone call to Mr Jenks, and of his distraught appearance in her bedroom when he confessed to having 'hurt Ratz'. She said she remembered finding her husband slumped senseless in his chair, the blood, the false teeth that had shot out when the mallet blows had fallen on the back of his head, and the whisky. 'I took one drink of whisky neat,' she explained, 'and I was sick, and then I remember pouring out another one. I can't remember drinking the next one; I tried to become insensible, to block out the picture.'

'Can you remember anything more about the events of that night?'

'No.'

'Do you remember the gramophone?'

'No.'

'Do you remember the police?'

'Absolutely not.'

'Mrs Rattenbury, did you yourself murder your husband?'

'Oh, no.'

'Did you take any part whatsoever in planning it?'

'No.'

Mr Casswell, for Stoner, rose to cross-examine. A few preliminary questions, then the moment when Alma and Stoner became lovers. 'Was it you who suggested it, Mrs Rattenbury?'

'No, I think it was mutual.'

'Mutual? Because, you see, he was in the position of a servant, was he not?'

'Yes.'

'And quite a young man?'

'Yes.'

'It was just an infatuation, was it not?'

'I think it was more than that.'

'You fell in love with him?'

'Absolutely.'

She faced not one cross-examiner but two. Now, Mr

Croom-Johnson for the Crown. He was interested in Alma's attitude to money, which he managed to establish was as vague as her attitude towards just about everything else. Alma admitted lying about an operation when she asked Rattenbury for £250 to finance her trip to London with Stoner. But she justified the request by explaining that she was overdrawn at the bank. 'You were not overdrawn to that extent, were you?' asked Mr Croom-Johnson.

'No,' Alma replied, 'but I thought then I would not have to go through the beastly business of asking again in June, so I would sort of kill two birds with one stone, as it were.'

'Did you ever tell your husband that you were buying clothes for Stoner?'

'I never told my husband I was buying clothes even for little John. Expenses were never brought up in my life with Mr Rattenbury.'

'Silk pyjamas at sixty shillings (£3) a suit?'

'That might seem absurd,' said Alma with a slight smile, 'but that is my disposition.'

'You have told us that on the Sunday night Stoner came into your bedroom and got into bed with you?'

'Yes.'

'Was that something which happened frequently?'

'Oh, always.'

'Always?' Mr Croom-Johnson pushed back his wig and paused. 'Were you fond of your little boy, John?'

'Naturally.'

'Did John sleep in the same room?'

'Yes, but in another bed at the other side of the room.'

There was much damage to be done here, and Mr Croom-Johnson knew it. 'It is not a very large room?' he asked.

'No,' said Alma, 'but little John was always asleep.'

'Are you suggesting to the members of the jury that you,

a mother fond of her little boy of six, were permitting this man to come into your bedroom with you, in the same room your little innocent child was asleep?'

'I didn't consider that was dreadful,' said Alma smartly. 'I didn't consider it an intrigue with Stoner.'

This somewhat unsavoury revelation – that Alma and Stoner were in the habit of fornicating just a few feet from Alma's sleeping child – was probably the single most damaging piece of evidence to tell against her as a woman. As Miss Tennyson Jesse remarked: 'This was to many people in court, including myself, a very shocking statement. However,' she added, 'it must be admitted in fairness that there are unfortunately thousands of families in England where the same thing goes on.'[16] Mrs Rattenbury later reportedly withdrew this statement, claiming she had been bewildered and had lost her head 'and heard myself saying it'. This seems a rather half-hearted attempt to repair the damage to her moral reputation, such as it was, in the wake of the trial. Otherwise, in the opinion of most observers, Alma put up a good show. In Miss Tennyson Jesse's view, she was an excellent witness. 'Her voice was low and rich. She gave a great impression of truthfulness, and she was astonishingly self-controlled. Only a nervous tick in the side of her face, which jerked perpetually, betrayed the tension of her mind.'[17] George Stoner, meanwhile, sat motionless in the dock. 'Throughout the long days,' said the *News of the World*, 'he sat with his elbow on the corner of the dock with eyes half closed, watching counsel and the judge as they asked questions, but with apparently no interest in the witnesses, and least of all in the woman in the dock with him.

'Only once did he show any emotion and that was when Mrs Rattenbury, in her deep musical voice, tense with anguish, fighting often for words that would not come and with her mobile mouth twitching with nervous strain, was laying bare her soul from the witness box.

'As she told intimate details of their illicit passion he fidgeted and became restless, and when, leaning over the box with hands outstretched, she barely breathed the words "I loved him", he showed the only signs of emotion he gave throughout.'[18]

George Stoner did not give evidence in his own defence. Under English law, an accused man has the right to remain silent. It is the burden of the prosecution to prove its case; no man is required to prove himself innocent. Smartly dressed in the grey suit and striped shirt and tie that Alma had bought him from Harrods, he looked every inch the English boy with his fair hair brushed neatly back and crowning his pale, open features. His parents gave evidence of his early life and upbringing; his father, a bricklayer, impressed the court with his simple dignity as he spoke touchingly of his 'rather reserved' son, telling the jury: 'One could not wish for a better boy.'

On Stoner's behalf, J. D. Casswell KC sought to shore up the boy's story that he had attacked Rattenbury while under the influence of cocaine. As Casswell put it in his closing speech to the jury, 'He does not deny that it was his hand that struck the blows. What he does deny is that his mind was in such a state at that time that he was responsible . . . Is it not clear that the taking of drugs . . . is the true answer to the question you have to decide?' The jury, however, proved highly sceptical, remembering Stoner's naïvety when asked to describe cocaine, and asserting that it was 'brown with dark specks in it'. It was obvious that the lad had never even seen cocaine, let alone taken any. Casswell, hamstrung in his defence of Stoner because of the boy's absurd story, 'did what I could, but with so preposterous a defence as that with which I was saddled, it was very difficult to make a really persuasive (closing) speech. I pinned my hopes on drumming home to the ten men and two women of the jury, that if they were so minded, they could find Stoner guilty of manslaughter instead of the ultimate crime of murder.'[19]

Mr Croom-Johnson made his closing speech for the Crown, summing up the affair as 'a story of immorality and vice'. The last word to the jury was that of Mr O'Connor on behalf of Alma Rattenbury. The listening Miss Tennyson Jesse described it as one of the greatest defence speeches ever uttered. Mr O'Connor spoke of the jury's difficult task in trying to separate from their minds the natural revulsion they felt against behaviour which nobody sought to condone or commend. 'I am not here to condone, still less to commend, her conduct. I am not here to cast one stone against that wretched boy whose position there in the dock may be due to folly and self-indulgence on her part, to which he fell a victim . . .

'I will say no more about what is past in Mrs Ratten-bury's life,' Mr O'Connor continued. 'I would only say that if you may be tempted to feel that she has sinned, that her sin has been great and has involved others who would never otherwise have been involved, that you should ask yourselves whether you or anybody of you are prepared first to cast a stone.'

Of Stoner, he was no less eloquent. 'He is still but a lad; his upbringing was simple; he had but few friends and no girlfriends. He is flung, at the age of eighteen into the vortex of illicit love . . . an unbalanced, melodramatic boy, given to violent outbursts. Consider his first associations with passionate womanhood . . . He is taken away from his work as chauffeur, stays sumptuously in a West End hotel for a week with his mistress, dressed in silk pyjamas from a West End store, and then brought back to earth and to his drudging duties.

'If you were judging of moral responsibility in this case,'

O'Connor told the jury, 'your task might be a light one, for you cannot resist nausea and disgust at the way in which this middle-aged woman has ensnared and degraded this hapless youth. But that is not your task today. If you are tempted to cast moral reproach, I would say to you with reverence: "Let him that is without sin cast the first stone." Perhaps also you may think that during that fatal night there were indications of a belated nobility on Mrs Rattenbury's part in the way in which she sought to shield her lover and in the indications of her anxiety at all hazards to take the blame.

'Too late, like Frankenstein, she had discovered that she had created a monster which she could not control.'

The whole of the fifth and final morning of the trial was taken up with Mr Justice Humphreys' censorious but otherwise admirable summing up. The jury needed less than an hour to reach their verdicts: Alma Rattenbury was not guilty of the murder; Stoner was guilty. At the fatal word Alma reeled forward, crying almost voicelessly, 'Oh no ... oh ... oh no ...' and thrust out her hands in a desperate gesture. Two wardresses bundled her down the steps from the dock, leaving George Stoner standing alone. At the very outset of the trial, Stoner had pleaded not guilty to the indictment. Now, at the end, he spoke again when asked by the court clerk if he had anything to say before the death sentence was passed. Stoner, staring at the black-capped judge in a final supreme effort of self-control, said simply: 'Nothing at all, sir.' Sentence was duly passed, the judge noting the jury's recommendation to mercy.

Stoner's head disappeared down the stairs to the cells, and Alma was led back, ashen and shaken. The judge ordered the jury to return a formal not guilty verdict on a second indictment of being an accessory to murder. A reporter called Margaret Lane described the scene in the *Daily Mail*: 'Her self-control gone, her eyes shadowed with exhaustion, and her white face smudged with tears, this woman whom the judge had described in his summing up as "a woman so lost to all decency, so entirely without any moral sense that she would stop at nothing to gain her ends" hung limp and weeping in the strong grasp of the two wardresses who supported her. On their strength only – for her own had broken utterly – was she able to leave the dock and pass, what is ironically called "a free woman", for the last time down the steps of the Old Bailey.'[20]

A scandalized crowd booed her as she was driven away. A jury had acquitted her, but she was left with nothing but an inner maelstrom of remorse, shame and despair. 'We are often told that a criminal court is not a court of morals,' Miss Tennyson Jesse wrote. 'In this trial apparently it was. Mrs Rattenbury was in some ways a vulgar and silly woman, but she was a generous, kindly, lavish creature, capable of great self-sacrifice. She was innocent of the crime of which, entirely on the strength of her own drunken maunderings, she was accused, but, nevertheless, though her life was handed back to her, it was handed back to her in such a shape that it was of no use to her. "People" – that dread judgement bar of daily life known as "people" – would always say: "Of course she told him to do it. And, anyway, she was a dreadful woman." For the world has progressed very little since Ezekiel wrote: "And I will judge thee as women that break wedlock and shed blood are judged, and I will give thee blood in fury and jealousy." Such was the judgement of society on Mrs Rattenbury, and she knew it.'[21]

The final act in the Villa Madeira tragedy took place three days later at a quiet spot on a tributary of the River Avon near Christchurch, a few miles from Bournemouth. At a turn of the river where it is crossed by the main railway line to London, known as Three Acres Bend, the broken-hearted Alma Rattenbury sat and wrote her farewell to the world. Her husband was dead; her children left fatherless; her lover locked in a condemned cell. Alone in a deserted field of buttercups, she lit a cigarette and scribbled on the back of an old envelope. It was a fine June evening.

Eight o'clock, and after so much walking I have got here. Oh, to see the swans and spring flowers, and to smell them ... It is beautiful here. What a lovely world, really. It must be easier to be hanged than to do the job oneself, especially under these circumstances of being watched all the time. Pray God nothing stops me tonight ... God bless my children and look after them ...

Then, on another scrap of paper, she wrote:

I tried this morning to throw myself under a train at Oxford Circus. Too many people about. Then a bus – still too many people about. One must be bold to do a thing like this. It is beautiful here, and I am alone. Thank God for peace at last.

She folded her bits of paper and placed them in her handbag, then rose and walked to the edge of the water. She clutched in her hand a knife she had bought that morning in London. Bending forward slightly, she thrust the blade into her breast, six times, and fell forward into the water.

Told of Alma's suicide in the condemned cell at Pentonville, George Stoner broke down and cried.

At the inquest, the coroner read extracts from more of Alma's last letters. One said: 'If only I thought it would help Stoner I would stay on, but it has been pointed out to me only too vividly that I cannot help him – and that is my death sentence.' As her solicitor told a *News of the World* reporter, her one thought from the beginning had been to protect the boy Stoner. When she realized that he had been condemned to death and she could do nothing to save him, life meant nothing more to her. 'If ever I saw into a woman's soul I saw into Mrs Rattenbury's, and I am convinced, as I was from the start, that she had no hand in the murder'[22], he said.

The last irony was still to come. Stoner lost his appeal, but was reprieved and his sentence commuted to penal servitude for life. In the event, he served only seven years. In 1942 when he was twenty-six, Stoner, who had been a model prisoner, was released and joined the Forces, taking part in the Normandy Landings. After the war, he returned to Bournemouth, married and settled down. He is still alive, living in the same house that his parents occupied at the time of the trial.

To me, and to the many journalists who have knocked at his door, George Stoner has resolutely refused to speak about the events at the Villa Madeira on that terrible Sunday night in long ago March 1935. So it is the present occupier, Mrs Antonia Landstein, who provides the haunting postscript to the story. 'Every spring,' she told me, 'on the anniversary of the murder, an elderly man walks slowly past the house, first on one side of the road, then the other. He just walks along very slowly and looks at the house. Not knowing really who he is, I cannot say for certain, but I think it is George Stoner. Every year he is drawn to the same place, and remembers.

'I feel very sorry for him. It must be a terrible thing to live with a thing like that. Poor man. His whole life was ruined, and not only *his* life.'

Mrs Landstein lights a candle on the anniversary of the murder and sits alone in the Villa Madeira with her ghosts. 'If I feel that Alma herself is somehow here, it's only in a very vague way. But when I think about it, and when I'm feeling not too well, I think about that poor woman, not as a person, but as the architect of all those tragic happenings here. Even after all these years they are almost tangible.

'And when the evening comes, many a shadow has its fear. And when the wind howls about the house, I seem to hear a sort of moaning noise, and I imagine poor Mr Rattenbury, sitting mortally injured in this very room.'

10

Carrickowl, Porthpean, Cornwall

Nearly a century separates the case of Madeleine Smith and that of Miles Giffard, hanged in 1953 for the brutal killing of his parents. The two cases come from contrasting eras and from different countries; Miss Smith plotted with the deadly stealth of the poison cup, while Giffard, in a fit of rage, wielded the bludgeon. And yet despite the general disparities, the two cases occasionally coincide. Both revolve around young misfits from a privileged background, trapped in a social milieu which most of their contemporaries would have envied, but which both Madeleine and Miles found oppressive and inhospitable.

The Smiths of Glasgow were drawn from the swelling ranks of the provincial Victorian bourgeoisie; the Giffards of Cornwall, however, were decidedly upper-class, county people. The family was descended from one Osborn de Giffard who fought with William the Conqueror. Miles's father, Charles Giffard, was a prominent solicitor in the town of St Austell, clerk to the local magistrates and under-sheriff of Cornwall. He was fifty-three, and managing partner in the old-established legal firm of Coode and Giffard. As clerk to the justices, Charles Giffard had officiated in many court cases. During the Second World War he served as a superintendent of the special constabulary for mid-Cornwall. Miles's mother was a blue-rinse Tory lady, vice-chair of the St Austell Conservative Association and president of the women's section. She worked hard for local charities and sat on several local committees.

The family home, Carrickowl, was a large but nondescript two-storey house of a dozen rooms, set 200 yards from precipitous, sea-washed cliffs overlooking Carlyon Bay. (Today it is known as Blue Waters and is occupied by a local surgeon and his family.) The Giffards employed a live-in housemaid and a full-time gardener. It was, in the words of Miles's lawyer at his trial, a charming English home. 'Everything was neat and tidy – the fishing rod near the door, the polished staircase.' In this idyllic setting, Charles and Elizabeth Giffard spent most of their evenings relaxing at the fireside, discussing the events of the day, reading, or listening to the wireless, activities invariably accompanied – in Charles Giffard's case at least – by a cut-glass tumbler of the finest whisky. Mr Giffard developed a serious drink problem following the death of his partner, Mr Coode, and his general health suffered as a result; at one stage he developed pneumonia and had to be treated in hospital. Two doctor friends told him bluntly that he was an alcoholic; with a typical show of iron resolve and self-discipline, Charles Giffard met his problem head-on, and drastically reduced his daily intake of hard liquor. 'We tried to terrify him out of his drinking habits,' one of the doctors explained later. 'Our advice was to give up alcohol one hundred per cent. He had alcoholic neuritis. He made a strong effort, and cured himself without becoming one hundred per cent teetotal.'

Sinking into the comfort of his favourite armchair at the end of a busy day and gazing into the amber glow of his nightly glass, Charles Giffard doubtless brooded over his greatest disappointment in life – his feckless son, Miles. How he must have reflected on the wasted opportunities, the missed chances that could have set the boy up for life. But Miles Giffard was an idler, the prodigal son who had wasted his substance on riotous living and who now paced moodily around the house, frittering away his days – and nights – in idleness. This was not what Charles Giffard had expected from his son in return for a loving home and an expensive education. First there had been Rugby School, where Miles had lied, cheated and generally behaved so badly that he had been expelled after only four terms. Then Blundell's, where at least the boy had done well at sport. He was absolutely mad about cricket, an adventurous, forcing batsman, and there had been a time when a sporting career had seemed a possibility. 'If only he had been more steady,' a schoolfriend was to recall, 'and had applied a little more concentration, he could easily have been a great batsman.' But Miles Giffard was not a man to go steady at anything, and although he played cricket for Cornwall as a minor county amateur, he soon wearied of the discipline and the training it demanded, and turned instead to other, unsporting pursuits: drink and women.

He was able to indulge these twin passions to excess when, on leaving school, he joined the Royal Navy. Consequently, despite his background and education, Miles never gained a commission. His naval career was spent entirely on the lower decks, and after three years' service Miles Giffard returned to civilian life. His father hoped that Miles would follow him into the legal profession, but he proved (in the words of his counsel at his trial) 'utterly hopeless' as a trainee solicitor. Now in his early twenties and with few prospects, despite the advantages of his birth, Miles Giffard was living the life of an idle waster.

In November 1951, having, in his own words, given up work altogether, he inherited a legacy of £750. On the strength of this, Miles moved to Bournemouth where he managed to spend the lot in four months. He 'scrounged around a bit', taking a job as an icecream salesman, but in June, bored and broke again, he moved back to Carrickowl. In mid-August Miles moved to London where he sponged off friends and acquaintances and took a series of dead-end jobs to supplement a monthly allowance of £15 sent from Cornwall by his disappointed father. Like other spoiled loafers of his generation who lived off their wealthy parents in this way, Miles was known as a remittance man. 'He was a quiet, pleasant boy,' a friend of the family told me, 'but quite unable to live up to the expectations of his forceful, heavy-drinking father. Charles Giffard didn't realize that Miles wasn't lazy, but mentally incapable of living up to his father's idea of his capabilities. Miles's family life, therefore, was full of tension, frustration and unhappiness.'[1] The overbearing father frequently lost his temper with his recalcitrant son, often locking him out of the house and forcing him to spend the night with neighbours.

Miles's casual attitude to money occasionally got him into trouble. During an ill-fated attempt to train as an estate agent he was caught with his fingers in the till. The firm threatened to call in the police, and only his father's offer to make good the deficiency saved Miles from prosecution. Even at home, he secretly and habitually stole money from his parents to finance his drinking and his girlfriends. For although Miles Giffard was a failure in most things, he was conspicuously successful with women. He was a charmer. His tousled, clean-cut, good looks attracted a string of girlfriends both in London and Cornwall. Like any young man in his mid-twenties, Miles was anxious to impress. But his well-mannered, if raffish, posturings in the fashionable restaurants and bars of the West End were a hollow charade. As he later admitted to the police: 'I was living from hand to mouth. I had odd bits of money from various people, and there were some cheques which were RD (returned to drawer). I was drinking very heavily.'

He was living the life of a bar-fly, flitting on the fringe of a set of young people in Knightsbridge, Kensington and Chelsea who (unlike Miles) could well afford an indolent lifestyle of expensive meals, fast cars and fashionable clothes. Miles battened on as best he could, scrounging money from the wealthy young men about town who seemed, in turn, amused then faintly irritated by his embarrassed promises of repayment 'when my father's cheque arrives'. As usual, of course, he had better luck with the young women in the set, and conducted a series of brief, ineffectual affairs. On every weekend trip home to Cornwall, he seemed to appear with a different girl. But none lasted more than a couple of weeks. This was probably just as well. Miles Giffard, dissolute, shiftless and spendthrift, would have made a thoroughly unsuitable husband for any of them.

In London, Miles had taken a furnished room in Walpole Street, Chelsea, and was drinking regularly at the White Hart pub in the King's Road. It was now early October 1952, and Miles was twenty-six. Among his more unlikely cronies at the White Hart was a Chelsea Pensioner from the nearby Royal Hospital who introduced him to a smart, middle-aged lady called Mrs Vallance and her attractive, nineteen-year-old daughter, Gabrielle. In a flash, Miles Giffard knew that he was seriously in love. He was instantly besotted both with Gabrielle's striking good looks, and the equally attractive fact that she was 'of independent means'. The couple began dating, but Miles's money soon ran out and he was forced to confess his plight to Gabrielle. At the beginning of November, Miles kissed her goodbye and set out to hitchhike home to Cornwall. There he planned to wheedle more money out of his parents. But on Tuesday 4 November, Gabrielle received a letter from Miles:

What I was afraid would happen has happened. I have had a terrible row with the old man, made worse by the fact that, as usual, he is right. Anyway, the upshot of the whole thing is that he has forbidden me to return to London, at any rate for the time being. He says he will cut me off without the proverbial penny, so there does not seem to be any alternative until I can get a job.

Darling, I shall not be able to take you to Twickenham. Who will? I hope no one. I am terribly fed up and miserable as I was especially looking forward to seeing you tomorrow, and now God and the old man (hereafter called the O M) know when I shall. Short of doing him in I see no future in the world at all. He has stopped my allowance anyway, and is giving me a pint of beer and 20 cigarettes a day and said: 'No pubs'. No doubt your mother would approve. Give her my love and tell her, when she next sees me I will be a reformed character, nominally anyway.

Gabby, my sweet, I love you terribly and it really is breaking my heart to leave you in that den of wolves there. God bless you and write to me soon and often. All my love, my precious. Yours, Miles.

The following Friday evening Gabrielle Vallance received a telephone call from Miles Giffard in Cornwall. He told her he was probably returning to London that weekend, but that he wasn't absolutely certain. He was going to borrow his father's car and would phone her again later. That call never came, but at 8 A.M. next morning, unshaven and dishevelled, Miles appeared in person on the doorstep of Gabrielle's flat in fashionable Tite Street, Chelsea. He had been driving all night, at the wheel of his father's large Triumph saloon, ERL l, which now stood parked outside at the kerb. Gabrielle thought Miles seemed unusually quiet. She gave him breakfast and he left at about 9 A.M. Shortly after midday he telephoned Gabrielle, suggesting that she and her mother meet him at the Odeon, Leicester Square at 2 P.M. The three of them spent the afternoon at the cinema watching Charlie Chaplin's *Limelight*. After the film, Mrs Vallance went home, leaving Gabrielle and Miles in the West End. They drifted into a bar near Hyde Park and drank gin. Over a meal, Miles complained of aching feet and said he wanted to go home. Gabrielle said it was rather early, and the couple spent the evening on a sort of low-key and somewhat despondent pub crawl that led eventually to the Star in Chesham Mews. Here Miles, still subdued, proposed marriage to Gabrielle, but she said she would not marry him until he had a proper job. His mumbled response was that he could not see her any more. He stared into his drink. Then he said: 'I have done something frightful.'

'What?' said Gabrielle, teasingly. 'Pinched your father's car?'

Miles suddenly got to his feet, grabbed Gabrielle's hand, and said: 'Let's go.'

Outside the pub, in the street, she tugged at his arm. 'What have you done?' she asked.

Miles Giffard stopped and turned to Gabrielle. 'I have murdered my father and my mother,' he replied.

The bodies had already been found, broken and spread-eagled on the rocky beach at the foot of the cliffs at Porthpean. Miles, having murdered both parents at Carrickowl, had loaded their bodies one by one into a wheelbarrow which he had then pushed out of the garden gate and along a track that led along the cliffs. At a spot where the track skirted the very edge of the cliffs Miles had tipped the bodies over, sending them plunging 120 feet on to the rocks below. Then he had returned to the house, cleaned up some of the blood, and started out for London in his father's car.

Miles Giffard's departure was almost interrupted by the family housemaid, Barbara Orchard, returning from a village dance with her fiancé in his car. As the couple pulled up outside Carrickowl they heard another car start up and pull away. This was at 10.15 P.M. Miss Orchard, not suspecting for a moment that anything was amiss, spent a quarter of an hour kissing her fiancé goodnight before going into the house alone and finding it empty. The lights were on, and on the kitchen floor she noticed what appeared to be a bloodstain, although it looked as if someone had tried to wash it clean. She found items of Mrs Giffard's clothing scattered in the hall and the kitchen. The young servant was nonplussed. Uneasily she telephoned the local hospital, but they had no record of treating Mr and Mrs Giffard. So Barbara Orchard went to bed. But she couldn't sleep for worrying. By 5 A.M. she had convinced herself that the worst had happened. Dressing hurriedly, she ran to her fiancé's house and raised the alarm.

The police had to wait until daylight on that grey November Saturday before the full horror of what had happened became apparent. As well as spilled blood in the kitchen, they found heavy bloodstaining in the empty garage at the side of the house. The Giffards' gardener, Harry Rowe, found that the wheelbarrow normally kept at the side of the house was missing. Someone had knocked over all his potted chrysanthemums. 'In the garage I found a lot of blood,' he testified later. 'Someone had apparently tried to brush it out, and the floor was wet and mucky.' Harry Rowe found dried mud and bloodstains in the kitchen and, like Barbara Orchard, he thought someone had tried to clean it up. A trail of blood led out of the garden gate. The gardener and a police sergeant followed the trail along the clifftop until they were overlooking the beach. Looking down in the grey November morning light, they saw Mr Giffard's body lying on the rocks below. The wheelbarrow was nearby. About a hundred yards away, they could see Mrs Giffard's body.

The county pathologist, Dr Hocking, examined the bodies where they lay. He concluded that Mr Giffard had fallen head first on to the rocks, but that he had been dead when he was thrown over the cliff. Mrs Giffard, on the other hand, had been alive at this point, but probably unconscious. Later, Dr Hocking conducted full post-mortem examinations. He found that Mr Giffard had sustained very severe head injuries before being thrown on to the rocks. At least five heavy blows had been struck with a blunt instrument. Mrs Giffard also had extensive injuries, including two broken wrists and a broken arm. There was a deep jagged cut above one eye, and both eyes were black. Her skull was shattered and the base fractured. Almost all her injuries, concluded Dr Hocking, were caused before death. He thought the wrists were fractured by Mrs Giffard falling on her hands while still conscious. At least two heavy blows had been dealt to her head.

Local detectives were appalled at the brutality of the killings, and immediately flashed a message to Scotland Yard. Miles Giffard was believed to be in London, and wanted for questioning about the murder of his parents. The Cornish police also imposed a news blackout on the case, telling the pack of crime reporters who arrived from London on the Saturday lunchtime train: 'We cannot say anything.' Despite this, the Giffard murders led the front pages of most of the Sunday newspapers on 9 November. 'For some inexplicable reason known only to themselves,' wrote the man from the *News of the World*, 'Cornwall's county constabulary threw an iron curtain over the sensational double murder . . . No one, from the chief constable down to the ordinary policeman will say a word about the crime.'

This was almost literally true. The reporters spent an exasperating evening at St Austell police station trying to solve the riddle of the official silence behind the riddle of the bodies on the beach. The pressmen knew that Miles Giffard was wanted for questioning, and that his father's large black Triumph car – with the distinctive registration ERL 1 – was missing from the garage at Carrickowl. A press appeal for information on its whereabouts would almost certainly locate the car within hours; the reporters were hungry for an angle, but as they shot questions at the officer manning the police station counter, the 'iron curtain' of silence descended once more.

'Did Mr Giffard own a Triumph car, ERL 1?'

'That was a car used by Mr Giffard,' said the officer.

'You are looking for that car?'

'No.'

'You have found the car?'

'No.'

'You know where the car is?'

'No.'

'Officer,' said the man from the *News of the World* wearily, 'we are trying to be co-operative. If the car is wanted and we publish the description, it is almost certain that it will be found by tomorrow morning.'

The beleaguered policeman did not flinch. 'That will not be necessary,' he said.

'Then you do know where it is?'

'No. I have already said it is not necessary. There is nothing more I can tell you.'

In fact, shortly before midnight, police in London had found the distinctive Triumph roadster parked in Tite Street outside Gabrielle Vallance's flat. A pile of blood-stained clothing was found stashed in the boot. Miles Giffard was arrested as he returned with Gabrielle after their desultory drinking spree in the West End. On the Sunday morning, sober but unshaven, he was interviewed at Scotland Yard by Detective Superintendent Kenneth Julian of Cornwall CID. Miles Giffard was in no mood for formalities and interrupted the detective's opening remarks. 'I know what you're referring to,' he said quietly. 'Let's clear it up with as little trouble as possible. I had a brainstorm.'

Giffard amplified this later in a formal written statement to Detective Superintendent Julian:

At the time of my first phone call (to Gabrielle Vallance) my father and mother were both out. They came back almost together in separate cars at about 7.30 P.M.

My father was doing something to my mother's car. Both cars were in the garage. God knows for what reason I hit them over the head with a piece of iron pipe. I hit him once then. He slumped to the ground unconscious. Mother had gone into the house. I went into the house after her. I found her in the kitchen. I hit her from behind.

Everything went peculiar. I got into a panic. Shortly after this I made a second phone call to Gabrielle in London about 8.15 P.M. and told her I was definitely coming to London with my father's car. I asked her if I could come round to her house for a wash and shave.

I went with the intention of getting the car and found my father coming around. I hit him again several times, then I got the car out and went in to get some clothes and my mother was coming round then. So I hit her again. She was bleeding very heavily. They both were by this time. I did not know what to do. There was blood everywhere. I got out the wheelbarrow, put my mother in it, took her out to the point and pushed her over. I then went back and did the same with my father's body. I pushed the wheelbarrow over that time.

I went back to the house and washed the place out. I went to my mother's room and took some pieces of jewellery . . . I took some money from father's coat pocket. I packed a change of clothing. My own clothes were very bloodstained. Then I got the car out and drove to London.

Later in his statement Miles Giffard described how, the morning before he was arrested, he had visited a jeweller's shop in Piccadilly where he had sold a ring and two brooches belonging to his mother for £50. He also told police what he had done with the murder weapon. Accordingly, back in the West Country, police searched a stretch of the River Otter near Honiton where they found a length of piping and a bloodstained coat and trousers.

The story of Miles Giffard's last night of freedom in London was related a few weeks later at St Austell, in the tiny magistrates' court where Charles Giffard had worked for twenty-three years as clerk. The star witness was Gabrielle Vallance, who stood in the witness box wearing a green coat and a small, tight-fitting hat. She explained how, after she met Miles in early October, he had returned to Carrickowl for more money and a change of clothes. He had hitch-hiked, getting a lift as far as Ilminster and sleeping the night in a Dutch barn surrounded by rats. Then came Miles's letter explaining that his father had forbidden him to return to London, and reporting a 'terrible row with the old man'. Gabrielle had written back in reply:

My darling Miles – I can't tell you how disappointed I am that you are not going to come back to London. I certainly will miss you, but your father is right for not letting you come back because you are very extravagant (partly my fault) . . .

Miles, darling, how awful for you not having any money in your pocket. You won't be able to take any women out. (I write that with relief.) I am very disappointed about Twickenham . . . Shall I dare go by myself?

It is a shame about Christmas. I was hoping to have a lovely time with you. I wonder if it would be possible if you came up and stayed with us. Try to if you can, otherwise I will only have John to go out with!!!

We have stopped going to the White Hart and the more expensive pubs. Darling, don't be worried. If you really want me to be good, I will try very hard. When you write again, will you write more clearly?

Well, darling, I do hope to see you again. I love you. All my love, sweetheart. Gabrielle.

In her evidence, Gabrielle explained that John, mentioned in this letter, was a public schoolboy, 'an acquaintance of mine'. He was only sixteen years old and 'more or less a joke between me and Miles'.

Miles's next letter was also read in court:

Gabrielle, my sweet, I will make an effort to get to London at the weekend as I feel sure it must be very near John's half-term. I cannot have that little perisher around. I will write to him. Things have become a little more reasonable and people are becoming a little more co-operative, including myself. So perhaps it will not be long before I see you.

Christmas sounds a good idea, but we must wait and see what happens. I was given 2s (10p) for a haircut, so I had 10 cigarettes and had the haircut on tick. Must you use smelly notepaper? Use it for John. I must give this to the gardener to post. I love you – Miles.

Gabrielle told the court how Miles had arrived at her flat early on the Saturday morning then later that evening had announced that he would not be seeing her again, and had confessed to murdering his parents.

Miles Giffard's assertion that he carried out the murders while temporarily unhinged formed the basis of the defence at his trial at Cornwall Assizes which opened at Bodmin the following February. The prosecution, however, disagreed with the brainstorm theory. Mr John Scott Henderson QC, for the Crown, claimed that Giffard had planned the murder over a period of several days. The motive was clear: Miles had made up his mind to return to London to be with Gabrielle Vallance. But having no money or means of transport he decided to kill his father and take his car. On the murder night, after telephoning Gabrielle, Giffard had run amok at Carrickowl with an iron pipe, attacking first his father in the garage and then his mother in the kitchen. Mr Scott Henderson quoted from Miles's statement to the police after his arrest: 'I can only say I had a brainstorm. I had drunk about half a bottle of whisky on the Friday afternoon; it seemed that nothing mattered except getting back to London. Gabrielle just fascinated me.'

Miles's fascination for Gabrielle did not show in court. Seated in the witness box Gabrielle sobbed as Mr Scott

Henderson read passages from their letters. A woman attendant handed her a glass of water, but Miles Giffard gazed straight ahead unflickering.

Describing their last evening together in London, Gabrielle told the jury how Miles had confessed to murdering his parents. The judge interrupted with a question that must have sealed Miles's fate in the minds of the jury. 'Did he,' asked the judge, 'use the word "murder"?'

'Yes,' said Gabrielle Vallance.

Opening the case for the defence, Mr John Maude QC said there was no doubt whatever that Miles Giffard killed his parents. The ultimate question would be: did he know what he was doing? Was he sane at the time he killed his parents, or was he labouring under a defect of reason to the extent that he did not know that what he was doing was against the law?

Mr Maude then revealed that Miles Giffard had a long history of grave mental illness. As early as 1941, a mental specialist had diagnosed him as a juvenile schizophrenic with a psychopathic personality, someone who was impossible to control. There would be evidence that Miles was a most abnormal boy at school. Turning to the jury, Mr Maude said: 'I want you to say that in all probability Miles Giffard was insane. It is true that he has done this, but he is not a brute in the ordinary way at all. The doctor who saw him twelve years ago was not surprised at this breakout and at the ghastly things that occurred.'

The first witness for the defence was Miles's childhood nurse, Mrs Nora Sanders, who said that between the ages of four and nine, Miles had suffered from dreadful nightmares. His old housemaster at Rugby, Mr George Keay, described Miles as very abnormal. He would screw up the bed sheets with his hands and bite holes in them an inch or two in diameter. He was far dirtier and more untidy than the other boys. Eventually, after four terms, Miles was

taken away from Rugby and transferred nearer home to
Blundell's School at Tiverton, Devon. Mr Peter Saunders,
who was there with Miles, described how once he flew
into a rage and threatened to cut himself with a knife. He
actually stuck the point of the knife into his leg 'and then
seemed surprised that it hurt and that it was bleeding'.

Mr Maude then called his chief expert witness, Dr Roy
Craig, the psychiatrist who had treated Miles as a boy. Dr
Craig described how he had learned that Miles had suffered
from paroxysms of fear for no apparent reason. He more
often told lies than the truth, yet the lies were purposeless.
Dr Craig said he diagnosed a rare form of schizophrenia
which attacked young people and from which there was no
recovery. The doctor had started a course of treatment but
abandoned it after two years because he found that deep
down in the mind was a condition too grave to persevere
with further. 'It wasn't safe to try to ease the underlying
difficulties any longer,' said Dr Craig. 'If an acute outburst
had been precipitated, an enormous amount of damage
may have been done.'

Questioned further, Dr Craig said he did not think that
Miles Giffard had ever been normal mentally. It had
emerged during treatment that the origin of the boy's
terrors was a sadistic nurse (not Mrs Sanders) who had
beaten him as a child and locked him in a dark cupboard
when he was two or three years old. The nurse had been
dismissed. Dr Craig revealed that 'within the last two
years' he had pointed out to Charles Giffard that his son
was deteriorating and that something should be done.

Mr Maude was anxious to impress on the court that at the
time of the killings Miles Giffard was insane. He knew that
his only hope of saving Miles from the gallows lay in
convincing the jury of that fact. He put the question baldly
to Dr Craig: 'Do you think that at the time when he killed
his parents, Miles Giffard was in a "schizophrenic episode"?'

'Yes,' replied Dr Craig emphatically. 'I do.'

Any schizophrenic patient would have a fixed idea, one that dominated all his thoughts, the doctor explained. In this case, Miles Giffard's fixed idea was to go to see Gabrielle Vallance in London. 'In my view,' he added, 'Giffard did not know at the time of the killing that what he was doing was wrong in law or morally, owing to his disease of the mind.'

Later, under cross-examination, Dr Craig admitted that at first he had been doubtful about diagnosing Miles as a schizophrenic. But he had become convinced when Charles Giffard suffered a mental breakdown himself due partly to overwork during the war. That, said Dr Craig, had provided hereditary evidence. Charles Giffard, working hard and late with a glass of whisky at his side, had suffered from alcoholic neuritis. There had also been some psychological trouble: Mr Giffard was confused and hallucinated.

The jury had now been presented with a clear and logical diagnosis of Miles Giffard's mental condition at the time of the killing. And yet they refused to accept it. Had they done so, Giffard would almost certainly have escaped the gallows and been committed to a hospital for the criminally insane. Unfortunately for Giffard, the defence overstated matters and succeeded only in confusing the jury. John Maude QC called a second eminent psychiatrist, Dr Arthur Lewis from Harley Street, to support the defence theory. He had examined Miles Giffard in prison and although he had no doubt that the young man was indeed insane (within the definition of the M'Naghten Rules[2]), the insanity was not caused by his schizophrenia but by spontaneous hypoglycaemia. At the time of the trial this was a rather new-fangled medical term to describe a low blood-sugar content, which might have impaired Miles Giffard's brain. Some of the symptoms would be confusion, irritability, sudden impulsive outbursts, impaired judgement, sudden impulsive behaviour and no appreciation of rightness or wrongness. But this evidence was disputed by the prison doctor, Dr John Matheson. He said he failed to find any evidence that Miles might have been suffering from spontaneous hypoglycaemia on the day of the killings, since Miles had admitted eating a big lunch and drinking half a bottle of whisky. 'A hypoglycaemia patient could not exert himself after an attack,' said Dr Matheson, 'without the risk of going into a coma.'

The judge, Mr Justice Oliver, interrupted. 'The moving of these two very heavy bodies over very rough ground for several hundred yards, all the cleaning up, a long drive to London – you do not think a hypoglycaemia patient could have done that?'

'I am certain he could not have done it,' said Dr Matheson.

The judge's summing up at the end of the four-day trial was strongly skewed against the defence. Referring to Giffard's behaviour in London the morning after the killings, when he sold his mother's stolen jewels for £50, he asked the jury: Was that the act of a madman, or the act of an utterly wicked man? Reviewing the murder night itself, the judge told them: 'If he sent those bodies over the cliff and hoped the sea would wash them away, or if he sent them over expecting that the injuries he had inflicted would be completely submerged in the wreck that would take place to bodies falling on to rocks 120 feet, in your view does that mean he knew he had done wrong when he did that?' It took Giffard much time and effort to dispose of the bodies and to wash out the kitchen and garage, and if he didn't make a particularly good job of it, was it to be said that he was mad for trying? What motive could he have had, asked the judge, except to conceal what he had done? 'What motive could there be for taking clean clothes except to conceal what he had done? It might be said that he took a change of clothes because he could not be presentable in his bloody ones in London. But what about throwing his bloody clothes in the river and the bloody steel in the river? Could there be any motive for that except to conceal what he had done?'

The judge's final instruction to the jury was simple. They had to decide only whether Giffard was guilty, or guilty but insane. In no case could there be an acquittal. The jury spent just thirty-five minutes deciding that Miles Giffard was guilty of murder. He was not, in their view, insane. Giffard received the sentence of death without a tremor. Pale and expressionless, he was heard to whisper 'Amen' at the same time as the judge's chaplain as the time-honoured words of the death sentence trailed away. One of the woman jurors who had complained of feeling faint during the hearing broke down in tears. Miles, in his best light-brown check suit, his dark wavy hair slightly ruffled, was escorted from the tiny dock. Young women in the public gallery craned forward to watch for any sign of emotion. But there was none.

Gabrielle Vallance was not in court to witness these final scenes. She burst into tears when told of the verdict at a nearby hotel and later drove away in a taxi accompanied by two men friends.

There was no appeal; Miles Giffard's lawyers could suggest no ground for one. Miles's fate rested with the Home Secretary, Sir David Maxwell Fyfe. A month earlier, Maxwell Fyfe had sparked considerable controversy by refusing to recommend a reprieve in the case of Derek Bentley, a nineteen-year-old dimwit convicted as an accomplice in the shooting of a policeman on a warehouse roof in Croydon. The youth who actually fired the gun, sixteen-year-old Christopher Craig, had been ordered to be detained at Her Majesty's pleasure, being two years too young to hang. Bentley, however, was sentenced to death. Although there seems little doubt that in law Bentley was indeed guilty of murder, a passionate and nationwide debate ensued as to whether he was entitled to mercy. Maxwell Fyfe could have recommended it; he did not, and his reasons remain hidden. But now, in the case of Miles Giffard, the Home Secretary had a very different set of circumstances to consider. Here was a young man from an upper-class background; Bentley, rejected for National Service as being 'mentally substandard', worked as a council dustman. Miles Giffard, ex-public schoolboy and amateur county cricketer, a man with almost every advantage given to a 20th-century Englishman, had, in the Home Secretary's view, failed to come up to scratch. Writing on the case in the mid-Sixties, journalist and lawyer Fenton Bresler summed up the official view of Miles Giffard: 'When Maxwell Fyfe sat down with the Giffard papers in front of him, he was not a sophisticated politician considering the plight of someone remote from his own experience. This was like deciding on like – the Establishment passing judgement on a member of the Establishment.

'It used to be said that law in England is a class-conscious affair. It certainly was not in the Giffard case. Maxwell Fyfe decided Miles Giffard's fate as coldly and clinically as he would that of a barrow-boy from Stepney. Perhaps – who knows? – even more coldly.

'For Giffard had "let the side down" . . .'[3]

In considering the case for recommending Miles Giffard to mercy, the Home Secretary studied all the evidence at the trial. But for all the talk of schizophrenia and spontaneous hypoglycaemia, it was Mr Scott Henderson's scathing picture of Miles Giffard as 'an idle little waster' that found an especial resonance in the mind of Sir David Maxwell Fyfe. To add to the trial transcript and the voluminous files and reports on the case that piled up on his desk, the Home Secretary soon accumulated a large file of letters, including one from Miles's uncle, General Sir

George Giffard, who had paid for his nephew's defence. Other letters of intercession followed from the great and the good, among them the Bishop of Coventry who had been Miles's headmaster at Blundell's School. But the letter that caused the most waves at the Home Office came from a member of the jury at Miles Giffard's trial. Her name was Angèle Clemence Godfrey and she was of French extraction. In her letter, Mrs Godfrey said she disagreed with the verdict of guilty because she was convinced that Miles Giffard was insane at the time of the murder. However, because of a misunderstanding, her dissent from the verdict was not communicated to the judge; being of French origin, she did not understand English court procedure.

This misunderstanding was critical, and conceivably cost Miles Giffard his life. In 1953, a judge in a murder trial required a unanimous guilty verdict before passing sentence of death. There was no such thing in those days as a majority verdict. Failure to agree a verdict would have meant a retrial, at which the defence may have been able to convince the new jury that Miles was indeed mad when he murdered his parents. This would have meant Miles being committed to an institution for the criminally insane. As it was, Mrs Godfrey's muddle meant the unanimous guilty verdict stood. The jury had found Miles Giffard guilty of murder, and there was only one course open to the judge. In the absence of an appeal, only a recommendation to mercy from the Home Secretary could save Miles Giffard from execution. In the event, having considered Mrs Godfrey's letter, the Home Secretary remained unmoved. And on Saturday 22 February 1953, Sir David Maxwell Fyfe announced that there would be no recommendation for a reprieve for Miles Giffard. The Sunday papers, meanwhile, had been digging into Miles's past, and the *News of the World* regaled its readers with 'playboy Giffard's fantastic story':

Throughout the trial there was much publicity for 19 year old
Gabrielle Vallance, for whom Giffard professed love and who
tried to reform him from his irregular ways in the short while
they knew each other.

Miss Vallance's story was told fully in court, and my inquiries
disclosed that many other girls and women admired – and loved
– Miles Giffard at one time or another. Some, like Miss Vallance,
were quiet and respectable. Others did not have such good
reputations.

Giffard spent lavishly, as he could well do when using other
people's money. It was common to see him at a well-known club
in the West Country drinking with a heavily-made up blonde, or
out for an evening's dancing with an irresponsible young wife of
some other man.

Those girls did not stay long. They usually vanished when the
Giffard funds ran out temporarily.

'Miles seemed to enjoy cutting the figure of a rake,' said a
friend, 'though the unpleasant boasting which usually accompan-
ies such a personality was missing in his case.'

One woman in Giffard's life nearly had her own ruined. She
was a beautiful former showgirl, now married. They met at a
dance, and soon he was pestering her to go away with him.

Eventually she agreed and they toured England together. In the
end she realized her mistake and her husband took her back.

Giffard knew only too well that he had the power to interest
women without undue effort and he was unscrupulous in his
conquests.

They were all the same to Miles – married, experienced women,
girls just out of school, daughters of the well-to-do, waitresses.

It was a life that had to end in disaster, but no one foresaw the
tragedy which horrified the country. Little did Mr and Mrs
Giffard know that behind their son's warped personality was a
dark trait which eventually would lead him to wipe out everything
he and his family ever stood or hoped for.

The tragedy at Carrickowl had its inevitable consequence
when Miles William Giffard walked to the gallows at
Bristol Gaol on 25 February 1953.

Why did he do it?

Miles Giffard may or may not have been clinically mad,

but he was certainly a reckless chancer. He seems to have relished dicing with authority, be it in the shape of his housemaster at Rugby, his officers in the Royal Navy, or especially his domineering and volatile father. He must have realized how much resentment his father felt at having a son turn out so badly: no amount of sporting achievement would compensate for the disgrace Miles had brought to Carrickowl in his years of trying to buck the system. But perhaps not. Miles Giffard was a vain and self-centred young man, who lived only to please himself. He knew he was a success with women. He also knew he lacked the money, the means, the trappings of success, to keep even one woman interested for very long. He was trapped by his own inertia. And when, at last, he managed to engage Gabrielle Vallance, a girl who seemed to promise some sort of future, Miles knew the game was up. His only recourse was again to beg money from his father, whose wholly reasonable response was to forbid Miles to return to London without a proper job. At twenty-six, Miles's humiliation at being imprisoned in his provincial home by provincial parents must have been the last straw. Perhaps, returning to Carrickowl at the end of an exhausting week, Charles Giffard, the Victorian martinet, gruffly taunted his son as they confronted each other in the garage. Whatever was said, something seems to have unhinged itself in Miles's troubled, tortured and whisky-befuddled mind. Then, as he explained, everything went peculiar . . .

A few days after the execution, Miles's anguished uncle, General Sir George Giffard, wrote to *The Times*:

The accused man had a long history of abnormality and mental illness from the age of four. As this was given fully in evidence at his trial I will not mention details beyond emphasizing that the distinguished mental specialist (Dr Craig) who was called in to examine him at the age of 15, and subsequently treated him for two years, warned his parents then of the possibility of mental breakdown in the future ... Very little weight was given at the trial to the long history of abnormality and mental disease, and the attention of the court was focused on the point whether his behaviour on the night of the crime did or did not come within the M'Naghten Rules ... [4]

Miles Giffard was clearly guilty of two monstrous murders (although in fact he was tried on only one count, that of murdering his father). But should he have hanged? There is no evidence that the killings were carefully plotted or premeditated; Miles's remark about 'doing the old man in' seems as vague and as empty as the small talk he enjoyed in the plush, softly lit clubroom bars of post-war London. He stood to gain his freedom and possibly even the girl he thought he loved, but to lose almost everything else. He hated his father, it is true, but adored his mother. In the boiling, emotional whirlpool of that terrible night at Carrickowl, Miles Giffard's temper just snapped, and he was powerless to help himself. Seized by a brainstorm ('God knows for what reason'), he went crazy and hacked his parents down in a frenzy. Having left the bodies on the beach at the foot of nearby cliffs, he then climbed into his father's instantly recognizable car and drove straight to London, to the home of his girlfriend, where he was picked up in less than twenty-four hours. Some plot. Some premeditation. Quite why the jury at Bodmin rejected the defence theory that Miles was a schizophrenic, a victim of a childhood condition too deep down in the mind to interfere with, is hard to credit. For half an hour, in a drink-inflamed rage, a young man went on a murderous rampage, destroying the only two people in the world who represented and embodied his future security. Far from covering his tracks, he drove directly to an address in London where he was known. One can only agree with his counsel, John Maude QC, when he addressed the jury towards the end of the trial. 'He was motoring himself straight to the gallows, and there was no hope in it whatsoever.'

Notes

7 BLYTHSWOOD SQUARE, GLASGOW

1 Henry Blyth's description in *Madeleine Smith* (Duckworth, 1975).

2 Interview with author.

3 The letters of both Madeleine and Emile were quoted verbatim at the trial, and are reproduced with the original (idiosyncratic) spelling, punctuation, syntax and usage. See *The Trial of Madeleine Smith* by F. Tennyson Jesse (Hodge, 1927).

4 Christina Haggart.

5 W. Somerset Maugham in *A Writer's Notebook* (Heinemann, 1919).

2 DALTON SQUARE, LANCASTER

1 Conversation with author.

2 Ruxton's trial evidence.

3 Conversation with author.

4 These extracts are from Ruxton's statement dated 13 October at Lancaster police station.

5 According to Birkett's biographer, H. Montgomery Hyde, this 'trivial token of gratitude' was a set of silver fish knives and forks with mother-of-pearl handles. Birkett, however, felt unable to accept the bequest.

6 Quoted in *Norman Birkett* by H. Montgomery Hyde (Hamish Hamilton, 1964).

7 Letter in the possession of Captain Henry Vann.

8 Information from Captain Vann.

9 Conversation with author.

THE HOMESTEAD, 339 DEVONSHIRE ROAD, BLACKPOOL
1 *Daily Mail*, 4 September 1953.
2 *Manchester Guardian*, 19 September 1953.

MAYFIELD, HAY-ON-WYE
1 Conversation with author.
2 See *Exhumation of a Murder* by Robin Odell (Harrap, 1975).

THE PRIORY, BALHAM
1 Conversation with author.
2 Heinemann, 1957.
3 Jarrolds, 1956.

PROVIDENCE HOUSE, PEASENHALL, SUFFOLK
1 Another two children had died in infancy.
2 In *Trial of William Gardiner* (Hodge, 1934).
3 This person's identity was never explained.
4 Later Sir Ernest Wild, Recorder of London.
5 It transpired that one dissenting juror held out for Gardiner's guilt. The eleven others had voted for an acquittal. Curiously, this was an exact reversal of the jury's vote at Gardiner's earlier trial.

63 TOLLINGTON PARK, NORTH LONDON
1 Filson Young in *The Trial of the Seddons* (Hodge, 1925).
2 Martin Fido, *Murder Guide to London* (Weidenfeld and Nicolson, 1986).
3 *The Life of Sir Edward Marshall Hall*, by Edward Marjoribanks (Gollancz, 1929).
4 Filson Young, op. cit.

TRENHORNE HOUSE, LEWANNICK, CORNWALL
1 *Mostly Murder* by Sir Sydney Smith (Harrap, 1959).

VILLA MADEIRA, 5 MANOR ROAD,
BOURNEMOUTH

1 *The Trial of Alma Victoria Rattenbury and George Percy Stoner*, edited by F. Tennyson Jesse (Hodge, 1935).

2 Later Mawson and Hudson.

3 Pronounced 'Eye-a-chineel'.

4 Untrue. The boy's claim to the title was too remote.

5 Quoted in *Tragedy in Three Voices* by the Rt. Hon. Sir Michael Havers QC, Peter Shankland and Anthony Barrett (Kimber, 1980).

6 In *Tess of the d'Urbervilles*, in which Bournemouth becomes Sandbourne.

7 In *The English Companion* (Pavilion/Michael Joseph, 1984).

8 Jesse, op. cit.

9 Ibid.

10 Quoted in Havers, op. cit.

11 Ibid.

12 *A Lance for Liberty* by J. D. Casswell QC (Harrap, 1961).

13 Ibid.

14 Jesse, op. cit.

15 *Daily Mirror*, 28 May 1935.

16 Jesse, op. cit.

17 Jesse, op. cit.

18 *News of the World*, 2 June 1935.

19 Casswell, op. cit.

20 *Daily Mail*, 1 June 1935.

21 Jesse, op. cit.

22 *News of the World*, 9 June 1935.

CARRICKOWL, PORTHPEAN, CORNWALL

1 Letter to author.

2 These govern the law of insanity. The main rule is that, in order to constitute a defence, the accused must prove

that at the time of the crime he was labouring under such a defect of reason, from disease of the mind, as not to know the nature and quality of the act he was doing, or, if he did know it, as not to know it was illegal. Insanity may be a complete defence to a criminal charge if it satisfies the legal tests laid down in the M'Naghten Rules. They were drawn up by a panel of judges in 1843 in the case of a defendant named M'Naghten. He was acquitted.

3 *Reprieve* by Fenton Bresler (Harrap, 1965).
4 *The Times*, 7 March 1953.

Index

(Street numbers are listed as if they were spelt out in full)

True crime – now available in paperback from Grafton Books

Professor Keith Simpson
Forty Years of Murder (illustrated)   £2.95 ☐

Vincent Teresa
My Life in the Mafia   £2.50 ☐

Robert Jackson
Francis Camps   £1.95 ☐

John Camp
100 Years of Medical Murder (illustrated)   £2.50 ☐

Colin Wilson
A Criminal History of Mankind   £3.95 ☐

Stephen Knight
Jack the Ripper: The Final Solution (illustrated)   £2.95 ☐
The Killing of Justice Godfrey (illustrated)   £2.95 ☐

Peter Maas
The Valachi Papers   £2.50 ☐

John Pearson
The Profession of Violence (illustrated)   £2.95 ☐

Sir Sydney Smith
Mostly Murder (illustrated)   £2.95 ☐

Stewart Tendler and David May
The Brotherhood of Eternal Love (illustrated)   £2.50 ☐

Roger Wilkes
Wallace: The Final Verdict (illustrated)   £2.50 ☐

To order direct from the publisher just tick the titles you want
and fill in the order form.   GF2581

Crime fiction – now available in paperback from Grafton Books

To order direct from the publisher just tick the titles you want and fill in the order form.

All these books are available at your local bookshop or newsagent, or can be ordered direct from the publisher.

To order direct from the publishers just tick the titles you want and fill in the form below.

Name _____

Address _____

_____

Send to:
Grafton Cash Sales
PO Box 11, Falmouth, Cornwall TR10 9EN.

Please enclose remittance to the value of the cover price plus:

UK 60p for the first book, 25p for the second book plus 15p per copy for each additional book ordered to a maximum charge of £1.90.

BFPO 60p for the first book, 25p for the second book plus 15p per copy for the next 7 books, thereafter 9p per book.

Overseas including Eire £1.25 for the first book, 75p for second book and 28p for each additional book.

_____

Grafton Books reserve the right to show new retail prices on covers, which may differ from those previously advertised in the text or elsewhere.